AF531704

Internet Governance

Internet Governance

An Introduction

Edited by

Ravi Kumar Jain Bandamutha

2010

Icfai Books
The Icfai University Press

INTERNET GOVERNANCE: AN INTRODUCTION

Editors: Ravi Kumar Jain Bandamutha

First Edition: 2010
Printed in India

Published by

The Icfai University Press
52, Nagarjuna Hills, Punjagutta
Hyderabad, India – 500 082
Phone: (+91) (040) 23430–368, 369, 370, 372, 373, 374
Fax: (+91) (040) 23352521, 23435386
E-mail: info@icfaibooks.com, icfaibooks@icfai.org, ssd@icfai.org

ISBN: 9788131407271

Editorial Team: Vijay G and Susama Mishra
Quality Support: V Sandhya Srikanth and S Sirisha

Contents

Overview

Internet governance is the development and application by Governments, the private sector and the civil society, in their respective roles, of shared principles, norms, rules, decision making procedures, and programmes that shape the evolution and use of the Internet (WGIG, 2005).

The idea of Internet started in the year 1969, as part of a US military research project. Since then, it has grown by leaps and bounds to eventually evolve into the world's communication nervous system, an inexhaustible library, a super-efficient vehicle of commerce and an engine of economic growth. As its importance has gained momentum, so too have the issues related to its governance become a debatable topic.

Internet governance consists of a wide range of issues with different relevance to social, economical, technological and political developments. These issues are interrelated and cut across sectoral, political, and geographical boundaries. The issue of who governs the

Internet is the prime concern among the developing countries. These countries are thwarting the attempts of US to unilaterally control the Internet. They fear that, if a country unilaterally controls the Internet, any country can be kicked off from being connected to the Internet, for instance, by simply manipulating a country's domain code, which is under the control of some private agencies in the US. A whole country can be deprived of access to specific resources on the Internet.

Moreover, the relevance of public policy of individual countries interfering in the operations of Internet is debatable. For example, countries like China, have banned foreign content, restricting the people of china from accessing certain content or blocking those websites that provide the banned content, on the Internet. These interferences in the Internet activities are often justified either in the name of protecting cultural diversity or ensuring the compliance of local laws or preventing restrictive trade practice by foreign companies and myriad such activities.

Similarly, the legal quandary to ensure user privacy on the one hand and handle the growing anti social elements and unlawful acts exploiting the anonymity provided by the Internet, on the other, is a major issue in the Internet governance. In the absence of a global legal framework coupled with the incompatibility of local laws of different countries, addressing these issues becomes more complex. This poses a risk of the Internet getting fragmented and ultimately falling apart. The significance of Internet Governance lies in controlling legal issues and social consequences resulting from Internet frauds, information theft, harassment, illegal transactions, theft of resources, hacking, copyright infringement etc.

Today, a host of issues related to the Internet Governance are hotly debated among the leaders from different countries at various international forums, regarding what they want and what they do not want on the Internet, who should control it, and how it has to be governed and so on. Internet Governance revolves around the control and supervision of this global resource and its logical and physical infrastructure – definition of protocols, control of root servers, and domain name resources etc. It primarily refers to all policies and regulations that influence the way the Internet is structured, the way it works and the way it is used.

This book "**Internet Governance: An Introduction**" is an anthology of several articles discussing the concept, evolution and foundation of network governance and Internet Governance. Various aspects like human rights, privacy, law, and technology have been discussed. Further, various perspectives like, business, governance practices, and technologies are presented. It also highlights the framework of Internet Governance developed to deal with the policy and privacy issue and its impact on different countries. The book is divided into three sections—Introduction, Principles and Models, Country Perspectives.

Section I: Introduction

The advent of WWW in early 1990s marked a significant surge in the gamut of activities and the range of participants on the Internet, subsequently increasing the dependence of people on the Internet for several personal, commercial and community activities. This raised a concern as to 'who controlled the Internet' and whether there was any body or department that governed the activities on the Internet. Given the global nature of the Internet, no single nation or department should dominate the Internet. This is a major challenge not only for technology but also political, social and economical concerns. The first article titled "**Internet Governance: A Rising Concern**" by *Ravi Kumar Jain Bandamutha,* introduces the concept of 'Internet Governance' and discusses the importance of its need from a common man's (Internet user's) perspective.

The next paper titled "**Internet Governance**" is the introductory chapter (Chapter-1) of the book titled "Internet Governance: Issues, Actors and Divides" by *Eduardo Gelbstein* and *Jovan Kurbalija,* begins with a brief note on what Internet Governance means and how it evolved. The major focus is on the Internet Governance Toolkit. The authors elaborate on several components of the toolkit—Patterns and Approaches, Guiding Principles, and Analogies. The article further provides details of various options under each head. Finally, the paper provides a classification of Internet governance issues under the following heads—Infrastructure and standardization, legal, economic, development and Socio-cultural.

Internet governance is considered to be the development and application by Governments, the private sector and the civil society, in their respective roles, of shared principles, norms, rules, decision-making procedures, and programmes that shape the evolution and use of the Internet. The third article titled "**Internet Governance: Theory and First Principles**" by *Johannes M Bauer*, starts with a brief review on the notion of governance and answers the fundamental question whether the Internet should be governed. Later, it explores the conceptual and normative foundations that could help embed the multiple dialogues in an overarching framework. The paper builds on the literature on the governance of large technical systems, the literature on policy design in dynamic environment, and more recent attempts to bridge these strands of thought in the theory of complex adaptive systems. The author explores alternative approaches to Internet governance—Spontaneous self governance, Forms of self and co-regulation, the theory of distributed governance and public interest government intervention—and explains their comparative advantages and disadvantages.

The more complex a field is, the greater is the need for its classification for conceptual mapping. Internet governance is a very complex field with its multidisciplinary, multinational aspects. The next paper titled "**The Taxonomy of Internet Governance**" by *Jovan Kurbalija*, provides Diplo's taxonomy of Internet Governance under five baskets—Infrastructure, Legal, Economic, Development, and Socio-cultural. In addition, all the relevant issues associated with each basket are discussed in detail. A comparative analysis with previous taxonomy is also provided.

The fifth article titled "**Internet Governance: A Regulative Idea in Flux**" by *Jeanette Hofmann,* presents the Internet Governance as an open-ended collective process of searching, that aims to fill the global regulatory void both conceptually and institutionally in a legitimate way in a phased manner. The author highlights that the major challenge for having a suitable Internet governance is to have a binding and legitimate regulatory capacity for a dynamically evolving infrastructure, amidst intensified conditions of transnationalism, partial deterritorialization and decentralization. The author comments that, so far, the attempts to establish a stable governance arrangement have failed; however, there are certain phased transformations of governance structure that can be observed. Three distinct phases in which Internet Governance has evolved, that are characterized by their own specific spheres of activity, constellations of actors, policy agendas, and perceived problems are discussed.

Section II: Principles and Models

The Global Knowledge Partnership (GKP) Executive Committee says that for the initial stage of any negotiations on Internet, Governance requires a mapping of the field, based on the following questions: What? (issues), Who? (actors), Where? (fora), and How? (methods). The sixth article "**Advocacy Position for Internet Governance**", prepared by *Diplo Foundation* advocates some principles that should be actively advanced and well articulated, as appropriate, in relevant fora for the discussion of Internet governance. It also suggests some working guidelines that should be used in Global Knowledge Partnership (GKP) advocacy on Internet Governance. It further advocates Training and Research for development aspects of Internet Governance, which will help create a better understanding of the role of developing countries in the Internet Governance Process.

Human rights, like 'privacy' and 'freedom of expression' etc are fundamental aspects of Internet governance. Irrespective of the model that is adopted for Internet governance it should address the human rights issues to gain acceptability. The next paper titled "**WSIS, Internet Governance and Human Rights – Background Material**" by *Johan Hellström,* enumerates WGIG's (Working Group on Internet Governance) four Internet Governance models. It highlights some of the Internet governance violations, for example, Myanmar's "cut-the-wire" policy, and China's great firewall ("Golden Shield") of censorship. It includes the two documents adopted in Geneva: the Declaration of Principles and Plan of Action.

The eighth article titled "**Community Node-Based User Governance (CNBUG): Applying Craigslist's Techniques to Decentralized Internet Governance**" by *Alice Goldmann,* says that, there are three models for governing the Internet, namely, Benevolent Dictatorship Model, Democracy Model, and Peer Production Model. Both Benevolent and Dictatorship are centralized models whereas Peer production is a decentralized one. The paper highlights the drawbacks of the present Peer Production Model and proposes a "Community Node-Based User Governance (CNBUG)", that maintains the decentralized aspects of Peer Production, while enhancing it with the administrative aspects of Craigslist.org, a community information and classifieds Website. The author explains the three principal components of CNBUG that establish its effectiveness. This paper also presents a detailed comparison between CNBUD and other three models.

The next paper titled "**Addressing the Issues of Internet Governance for Development: A Framework for Setting an Agenda for Effective Coordination**" by *William H Dutton,* says that, for the first few decades after the emergence of the Internet, its governance was dominated by a few technical expert groups (IETF and ISOC) and the US department of defense. This period saw the emergence of flexible, decentralized and pluralistic Governance arrangements. The idea that the Internet governance has to address not only technical issues but also several social, political, commercial and governmental issues, has paved the way for the emergence of Multistakeholders' model. This paper elicits that the Internet Governance Forum (IGF) provides a 'Light Touch' framework that maintains the coherence of Internet governance with multiple stakeholders without allowing the unwanted fragmentation of the Internet governance mosaic. The role and major activities of IGF that ensure that a balance of interest and effort is maintained across the Internet governance spectrum are discussed. The paper outlines a framework for helping to classify Internet Governance (IG) issues to assist, identify and prioritize issues on the global Internet governance agenda that could help promote development.

Section III: Country Perspectives

Article ten "**Internet Governance, National Interest and International Relations**" by *Kenneth Neil Cukier,* says that, Internet is a global resource, whose control and allocation is a matter of political power; instead of doing away with geopolitics, the Net creates new areas of national interest and foreign policy concerns. The article explains the Internet governance as 'infrastructure coordination' activity taking care of Root servers, protocols, IP Numbers, names etc. The author elaborates on the national interests related to the Internet control, with an emphasis on US interests. The article notes how these interests map to specific ICANN issues, which are concerns of international relations—national sovereignty over information infrastructure, control over shared resources, influence over policy process and substance, and access to content and its restriction. In addition, it tries to explain why ICANN matters not just for students of politics and international affairs, but also for ordinary individuals, companies and other stakeholders. It concludes by analyzing current tensions concerning the Internet's institutionalization.

The next article titled "**Internet Governance Priorities and Practices: India**" compiled by *Dieter Zinnbauer,* is a report by UNDP, that highlights some of the most important findings and insights regarding Internet Governance in India. It emphasizes the persistent importance of basic infrastructure issues such as access, affordability and speed of Internet in India. It also deals with issues related to local content and local language software, which are pressing concerns for the Internet community in India. Internet community in India regards cyber attacks, Spams, and Viruses as the most pressing issues for

Internet Governance. India has made considerable progress in establishing more open policies. For example, ISPs can obtain licenses for international gateways. Compared to China and Pakistan, India has taken encouraging pioneering steps to create an enabling environment for new wireless technologies by de-licensing access to the Wi-fi spectrum.

Given the global, decentralized and borderless nature of the Internet, it is not possible for individual governments (national governments) to regulate effectively or address the problem satisfactorily. The next paper titled "**Internet Governance: Towards the Modernisation of Policy Making Process in Turkey**" by *Yaman Akdeniz,* highlights the need for national governments to act proactively and fine-tune their policies and procedures to effectively address Internet related issues. The author identifies various possible modes and models appropriate for Internet governance in Turkey. The article proposes a multi-layered approach to Internet governance for not only national development but also in the light of supernational (European Union), and international (Council of Europe, United Nations, OECD, G8) developments, which will have an impact upon the formulation of policies at the national level. It argues that the modernization of the Turkish policy making process in short-term is needed for good Internet Governance. It highlights self-regulation and co-regulation and the role of other stakeholders such as industry, the NGOs working in the field of Internet Governance, and the society as a whole. At the end of the paper, the author suggests some recommendations for Internet Regulation in Turkey.

The final article titled "**Voices from Asia-Pacific: Internet Governance for Sustainable Human Development**" is based on UNDP report on the Internet government and sustainable human development—for Asia-Pacific (A-P) region, and is written by *Akash Kapur* and *Christine Apikul.* It starts with a brief note on who makes decisions in the cyber space and their implications for sustainable human development. The emerging priorities and concerns from Asia-

Pacific consist of: access costs, voice over Internet protocol, wireless networks, root servers, country-code top-level domains, internationalization domain names, IP address management, technical standards, content pollution, and cyber crime. It also presents the six key recommendation and priorities produced by the Open Regional Dialogue on Internet Governance (ORDIG) for Internet Governance in the Asia-Pacific region.

They include the need for subsidiary governments to have a role, multistakeholder participation, preserving cultural diversity, capacity building, and supplementing law with other tools.

The ever increasing adoption of the Internet as a platform for business and economic activities, as a communication and information-sharing platform has enhanced dependence on the Internet not only at business and individual levels but at national levels also. Availability, accessibility and affordability of the Internet to the public are going to be the key factors for the economic growth of a country and its global competitive ability in this digital age. Therefore, the issue of Internet Governance has become predominant.

It is hoped that the contents of this book will provide a clear understanding of the need and the importance of Internet governance.

SECTION I

INTRODUCTION

1

Internet Governance: A Rising Concern

Ravi Kumar Jain Bandamutha

This paper focuses on the increasing role of the Internet in human endeavors and also emphasizes on the need for governing it. It discusses the concept and definition of the Internet governance, presenting a different perspective of this much-debated international phenomenon.

Introduction

Today the Internet, as a network of the networked computers, has emerged as a widely used global medium for communication, information sharing, business activities, community building actvities and so on. Nearly one fifth of the world population is connected[1] to this digital information super highway consumating personal and professional activties every day. A whole new digital economy is thriving on the Internet with millions of people transacting economic actvities worth billions of dollars. The Internet has enabled internationlisation of businesses by de-territorialisation of geographical boundaries, making the whole world as a global digital village. The Internet is influencing the human life in all spheres and at all levels.

The Internet acts as a medium of communication and community building at personal level (e-mails, IMs, Blogs, communities etc), and at professional level it facilitates collaborative work and information sharing (Wikis, virtual meetings etc). In organisational spheres, the Internet serves as a new channel for buying and selling actvities, facilitates opening up of additional channels for customer service and contact point, marketing and advertising, collaboration with trading partners, interfacing with regulatory agencies and so on. The new age business concepts like integrated production planning, zero inventory models, SCM, CRM, PRM, collaborative commerce etc., can be adopted by businesses effectively at an affordable cost only by using the Internet as a platform. Even small businesses from remote places can have access to new markets, reach new customers at an affordable cost on the Internet, have a global presence owing to the Internet, which otherwise may not be possible.

At government level, the Internet enables the conduct of governance activities and delivering of public services (e.g., e-governance initiatives by governments in several countries). More and more countries, developing and under-developed, have realised that Internet is the only medium that can allow them (and their people) to surf on the high tides of ongoing globalisation and contribute to their economic growth.

The entire gamut of activities discussed above, and many more evolving, are made possible on the Internet with the help of huge logical and physical infrastructure that facilitate the very existence and functioning of the Internet. Several tools and technologies, technical protocols, communication and network standards, etc., form the logical infrastructure of the Internet; while physical network connection, telecommunication networks, Internet service providers, etc., form the physical infrastructure of the Internet.

This logical and physical infrastructures need to be maintained, managed and controlled for the efficient functioning of the Internet and for the harmonious existence of the mankind in the virtual world of the Internet. As more and more people from different countries across the globe are patronising the Internet, conducting various economic, social, political and personal activities, their dependence on this global medium for their personal, professional and economic properity and well-being is increasing phenomenally. With such an involvement of the Internet in human endeavors, it comes naturally to our minds that who owns the Internet; in a sense, who controls the Internet, or in other words who governs the Internet; how it is governed; and who are the major stake holders; what are the major aspects of the Internet governance; and so on.

These are no trivial questions. These are fundamental questions around which the very existence of the Internet as a global medium depends. However, these questions are not left unattended; in fact a lot of issues related to it are widely debated under the banner of the "Internet governance" at various international forums involving the representatives of various stake holders. Further, the international community has contemplated, discussed, developed and evolved various frameworks and models related to the Internet governance over the last few years. This paper looks at the aspect of the Internet governance from a common man's perspective.

Before we look at what the Internet governance is, let us dwell on the major technical strides taken by different agencies and organisations that were instrumental in the evolution story of the Internet.

The Internet Story

To understand how the Internet is run today, it is necessary to know a little of how it has evolved. From a network of four interconnected computer nodes in a laboratory as a part of a defence project in the US, to evolve as a global information superhighway interconnecting millions of computers spread across the globe, and hundreds of thousands of computers connecting to it every day—the evolution of the Internet is one exciting story of a series of technical innovations undertaken by various research agencies and government organisations.

The first network of computers, called ARPANET (Advanced Research Project Agency NETwork) was developed by a team of researchers in the year 1969 as a part of a research project under the aegis of the Department of Defence of the United States of America. In the later years, ARPANET connected University research laboratories, and by 1975, it became a major computer network spreading beyond the US to Norway and London. By then ARPANET has grown out of its label as "research project" to become an utility to share computer files across geographically dispersed locations. Therefore, the control of ARPANET was transferred to the US Defense Communication Agency (now US Defense Information Systems Agency, *http://www.disa.mil/main/whca.html*).

During this evolution, a lot of technical decisions were taken to scale up the network capabilities, tweak the protocols to accommodate new nodes into the original ARPANET. Such decision and other methods of working were documented as a series of RFCs (Request For Comments)[2] memos. Even today any new changes in the standards or protocols or any other technical aspect related to the Internet are documented as RFCs.

During the same period, another networking standard, namely, X.25 message handling system has evolved as a dominant technology in Europe and other countries outside the USA. Using this technology an "International Packet Switching Service" was created with the collaboration of UK's General postoffice, USA's Western Union International and Tymnet[3] in 1978 and that was further extended to Canada, Hong Kong, Australia to evolve as a worldwide networking infrastructure connecting a variety of online databases and mainframe systems. *(http://www.answers.com/topic/international-packet-switched-service)*

Another interesting development in the computer networking world happened with the advent of UUCP, Unix to Unix Copy Program (Unix systems were dominant in those days) during 79 and 84. UUCP used X.25 links, ARPANET connections and leased lines to connect host computers. UUCP facilitated mail transfer, discussion boards and Usenet news among computer users. This later evolved into FTP, SMTP and NNTP, which form the critical components of the today's Internet. *(http://www.webopedia.com/TERM/U/UUCP.html)*

All the above mentioned networked systems used different protocols, different communication and network standards serving different purposes. Possible synergies were envisaged among these diverse networks and hence a new set of protocols, called "Internet Protocol (IP) suite", were developed with the initiative of ARPA in 1977. This protocol suite was intended to make transparent the differences between different underlying networks to enable to run diverse applications over a common network. Later in 1983, Domain Naming System (DNS) was invented to identify every computer on the ARPA Internet (by this time defence systems were separated from ARPANET) computers by their names and IP addresses, and ARPANET has adopted IP suite replacing their Network Control Program (NCP).

Another technical milestone in the field of computer networking was the creation of NSFNET, by the US National Science Foundation (NSF) in the year 1986, that connected supercomputing centers for the academic research purpose. NSFNET used TCP/IP suite of protocols. Later, it was integrated with the ARPA's Internet to form a bigger network of networks extending the connectivity to academic institutions and government research agencies in UK, Japan, Australia and several other countries. *(http://www.nsf.gov/about/history/nsf0050/internet/launch.htm)*

Eventually, in the year 1991, all the above mentioned networks culminated into a major network of networks, what we today know as the Internet, with no restriction on its commercial usage. ARPANET was scrapped in 1990, and NSFNET has thrown open its part of the Internet for commercial use, thus encouraging commercial network providers to plug in and extend the Internet.

Controversies

The position of the US Department of Commerce as the controller of the Internet gradually attracted criticism from those who felt that its control should reflect its international nature. A hands-off approach by the DoC helped contain this criticism.

When the IANA functions were handed to a new US non-profit Corporation called ICANN, controversy increased. ICANN's decision-making process was criticised by some observers as being secretive and unaccountable. When the directors' posts which had previously been filled by the "at-large" community of Internet users were abolished, some feared the worst. ICANN stated that they were merely streamlining decision-making processes, and developing a structure suitable for the modern Internet.

Other areas of controversy included the creation and control of generic top-level domains (.com, .org, and possible new ones, such as .biz or .xxx), the control of country-code domains, recent proposals for a large increase in ICANN's budget and responsibilities, and a proposed "domain tax" to pay for this.

There were also suggestions that individual governments should have more control, or that the International Telecommunication Union or the United Nations should have a role in Internet governance.

Defenders of the current system pointed out that it has served the Internet well.

Source: http://en.wikipedia.org/wiki/Internet_Governance

Since then, the world is witnessing an unprecedented growth in the size and scale of the Internet. Today, almost the entire physical network infrastructure is owned and provided by private parties located in several countries. However, the traffic on the Internet moves in accordance with the standards and protocols established by the standards making bodies, which are predominently the private and government agencies of specific countries that were instrumental in the emergence of the Internet since its early days.

Now that the Internet has become an all pervasive global platform, the active involvement by a handful of agencies from a few countries in policy making and standards devicing for the Internet is looked upon as their dominance on this supposedly global medium raising serious controversies regarding the Internet governance in the recent times.

Internet Governance: How do we Read this?

The term Internet Governance needs to be properly read in terms of its meaning and scope. Often the term "Governance" leads to ambiguity, as people tend to equate it with "Government". However, there is a difference between government and governance, especially while dealing with international phenomena. A government refers to a supervisory body that has the authority to administer and control activities of a group of people, an organization, a state or a country by way of making laws in a civil, corporate, religious or academic frameworks.

On the contrary "Governance" refers to a set of rules, procedures and practices through which organizations operate. Governance can be extended to the entire society at national and international levels. While the concept of "government" is restricted to a state or a country, "Governance" is wider in scope and transcends national/state boundaries.

It should be, therefore, understood that whenever the term "Internet governance" is used, it refers to a set of procedures and practices that are used or envisaged to maintain health and harmony in operating the Internet. This leads to a fairly simple definition of "Internet governance." Internet governance can be defined as: *Collective action, by governments and/or the private sector operators of TCP/IP networks and end-users to establish rules and procedures to enforce public policies and resolve disputes that involve multiple jurisdictions.*[4]

Definition

A report of the Working Group on Internet Governance (WGIG), published in June 2005, provides this working definition of Internet governance:

> *Internet governance is the development and application by Governments, the private sector and civil society, in their respective roles, of shared principles, norms, rules, decision-making procedures, and programmes that shape the evolution and use of the Internet.*

One way to conceptualize the term "Internet Governance" is with reference to the layers of governance. According to Yochai Benkler, there are three layers for Internet Governance—Content layer, Logical layer, and Infrastructure layer.

Content layer pertains to the content/information on the Internet. Governance at this layer addresses issues like content pollution, information theft, cyber crimes and IPRs etc. Logical layer is concerned with the standards and protocols, on which the networks function, domain names and IP allocation and resources management. At Infrastructure layer, the governance addresses the issues related

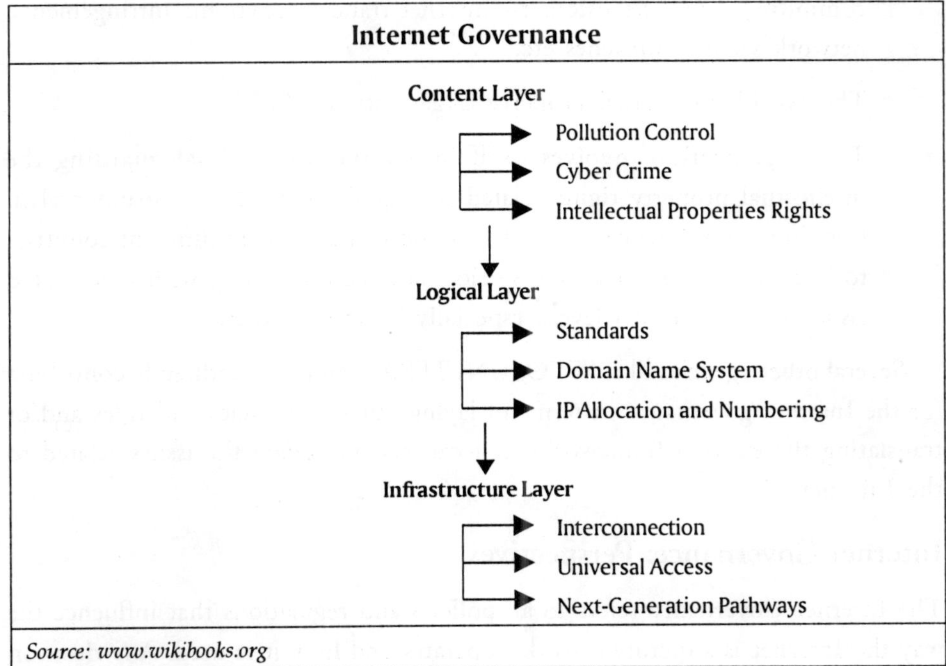

Source: www.wikibooks.org

to the management of the physical infrastructure—Internetworking, universal access and so on.

The ambiguity of the term "Internet Governance" can also be attributed to the fact that there is no single authority to govern all the aspects of the Internet. Instead, there are bodies, institutions and organisations that have some form of authority on various aspects related to the Internet in a variety of ways and at multiple levels. Some of those bodies/institutions/organisations are:

- The Internet Corporation for Assigned Names and Numbers (ICANN)

  ICANN maintains the global supply of domain names and set regulations (technical and economical) for the global domain name supply industry. It also sets policy for domain name disputes, allocation and assignment of specific and top level domains (.com, .net, .edu, and two letter country domains like .uk, .in, and .ca) and several other issues related to domain names.

- The Council of Europe's Draft Convention on Cybercrime.

  This international body deals with cyber crimes or criminal offenses committed using the Internet—Internet frauds, copyrights infringements, network security breaches etc.

- The World Intellectual Property Organisation (WIPO)

  This organization involves itself in maintaining and safeguarding the intellectual property rights related to digital media. It is instrumental in bridging the differences in copyright and related laws in different countries to bring out an international version suitable for dealing with IPR related issues at international levels, especially on the Internet.

Several other agencies like, WTO, UNCITRAL, and ITU indirectly contribute for the Internet governance in terms of laying out new policies and rules and/or translating the existing frameworks that can accommodate the issues related to the Internet.

Internet Governance: Perspectives

The Internet Governance refers to all policies and regulations that influence the way the Internet is structured, works, operates and how it is used. Any decision regarding these policies can influence the costs for access and content, speed, reliability and privacy of the users. Moreover, Internet governance consists of wide range of issues with different relevance for development. These issues are interrelated and cut across sectoral, political, and geographical boundaries. The importance of Internet Governance varies from an individual perspective to business organisation perspective to a national perspective.

Referring to the above discussed layered definition of the Internet governance, we can say that the first layer deals with more direct and visible aspect of the Internet, while the other two layers deal with the not so visible aspects (transparent to the user) of it. As a common user of the Internet, one may be really keen to understand whether their rights are sufficiently protected, and can the users have a redressal after being victimized by the criminals on the Internet. Are there any rules to address these issues?

At individual level, the users are more concerned about cost involved in accessing the Internet, whether the Internet content and services are available in their native language or not, whether the Internet they are using is secure and reliable, whether they are getting the technical advice on how to access the Internet, whether any of their acts on the Internet in their country are likely to put them legally liable in other countries, is their privacy sufficiently protected, do they have any say in the Internet activities directly affecting their economic, social and emotional value on the Internet? Are they sufficiently represented?

The above-mentioned aspects signify the user's concern of what Internet governance should address in order to ensure universal access at affordable cost, sufficient protection against IPR and related infringements and the user's privacy. In addressing these issues thrust is put on whether their concerns are properly represented by appropriate and competent authorities or they are at the mercy of foreign hands. Thus, at individual level Internet governance is something that will address all the issues that limit their freedom and security in using the Internet rather than dwelling on what new standards or protocols that are introduced on the Internet and by whom or whether ICANN has incorporated certain technical upgradations or not.

However, for business organisations the take on the Internet governance will be different as their concerns are different from that of the individuals. From the business perspective the Internet governance is a mechanism that ensures stability, consistency and continuity of the Internet and makes strides to improve it continuously making it a better platform and a level playing field for conducting business. Even they may not expect local (state or national) governments to interfere in regulating the Internet (speech, content and cross-border information flow). It may be preferred that the Internet remains in a self-regulatory regime. Business organizations will be more concerned about IPR protection, fraud protection, domain name allocation and disputes resolution, payment protection etc., and shall look at the Internet governance as a comprehensive and inclusive measure to provide a congenial, safe and unbiased environment to conduct business.

While individuals and businesses essentially look at the Internet governance as a means to streamline the operation on the Internet and protect the Internet as a global medium, the government may be interested in the issues like control and ownership of the Internet. The international nature of the Internet should be reflected in its controlling activities like the representation of various stakeholders in developing and implementing new protocols, devising new data communication and networking standards and allocation of domain names and similar activities that decide future direction of the Internet development.

For instance, changes in networking standards and data access protocols may require substantial investments in upgrading the physical infrastructure to access the Internet, thereby hampering the accessibility and affordability to poor countries. Similarly, if any country is allowed to have unilateral control over agencies like ICANN, then all other stakeholders will be at the mercy of this country as there is every possibility that every other country can be simply kicked off from the Internet by simply deleting that country's domain name (they are disconnected from the world). This will have catastrophic effect on the economy of the victimized country, if its economy is significantly dependent on the Internet activities.

In short, too much of private control at strategic level will also pose high risk of restrictive practice, or worse, hijacks during political unrest or trade competition among various countries.

Similarly, public policy of each country will be oriented towards their cultural diversity, lore and languages and hence it should be reflected in the Internet also.

Several activities and the content on the Internet may not be consistent with the regional laws, cultural practices and public policy of some countries and hence need to be customized accordingly. This is possible only when equitable participation is allowed in structuring the Internet with more freedom being given to local governments to decide on various public policy issues that the Internet is likely to effect. Therefore, from government's perspectives, Internet governance concerns are more regarding equitable participation and controlling stakes in conducting the Internet as a truly international platform.

Conclusion

The ever-increasing adoption of the Internet across the globe and the growing dependence of individuals, business organisations and governments on the Internet has lend the concept of its governance more importance in the recent times. A lot of strides are being made by the International bodies and national governments of few countries to address issues related to the Internet government. However, for a common user of the Internet this topic still remains a subject of confusion. This paper emphasizes that the Internet being a global medium, it is very important that its international nature should be reflected in the way it is conducted, controlled and governed.

(Ravi Kumar Jain Bandamutha is Consulting Editor at Icfai Books, a division of the Icfai University Press. He can be reached at rkjain@icfai.org).

Endnotes

1 *http://www.internetworldstats.com/emarketing.htm.*

2 According to Wikipedia, RFC are a series of memoranda encompassing new research, innovations, and methodologies applicable to Internet technologies in internetworking and computer network engineering parlance. Through the Internet Society, engineers and computer scientists may publish discussion papers in the form of an RFC memorandum, either for peer review or simply to convey new concepts, information, or (occasionally) engineering humor. The Internet Engineering Task Force (IETF) adopts some of the proposals published in RFCs as Internet standards. *http://en.wikipedia.org/wiki/Request_for_Comments*

3 Tymnet was an international data communications network headquartered in San Jose, California that utilized virtual call packet switched technology and used X.25, SNA/SDLC,

ASCII and BSC interfaces to connect host computers (servers) at thousands of large companies, educational institutions, and government agencies.

4 *http://www.circleid.com/backgrounders/view/Internet%20Governance/*

References

1. Michael R Nelson, "Let the Internet Be the Internet", *http://www.issues.org/22.3/p_nelson.html*
2. Ayesha Hassan, "Internet Governance: Strengths and Weaknesses from a Business Perspective", *http://www.wgig.org/docs/book/Ayesha_Hassan%20.pdf*
3. Syracuse University, Milton Mueller, John Mathiason, Lee W.McKnight, "Making Sense of 'Internet Governance' Defining Principles and Norms in a Policy Context", *http://dcc.syr.edu/miscarticles/SU-IGP-rev2.pdf*
4. *http://en.wikipedia.org/wiki/Internet_Governance*
5. *http://www.answers.com/topic/international-packet-switched-service*
6. *http://www.nsf.gov/about/history/nsf0050/internet/launch.htm*

2

Internet Governance*

Eduardo Gelbstein and Jovan Kurbalija

Internet Governance is not a simple subject. Although, it deals with a major symbol of the DIGITAL world, it cannot be handled with a digital-binary logic of true/false and good/bad. Instead, the subject's many subtleties and shades of meaning and perception require an ANALOG approach, covering a continuum of options and compromises.

Therefore, this article will not attempt to provide definitive statements on Internet Governance issues, rather, its aim is to propose a practical framework for the analysis, discussion and resolution of the key problems in this field.

Introduction

In only a few years, the Internet has revolutionised trade, health, education, and, indeed, the very fabric of human communication and exchange. Moreover, its potential is far greater than what we have seen in the relatively short time since its creation. In managing, promoting, and protecting its presence in our lives, we need to be no less creative than those who invented it. Clearly, there is

* This article is the Introductory chapter (Chapter 1) of the book titled "Internet Governance–issues, Actors and Divides"

a need for governance, but that does not necessarily mean that it has to be done in the traditional way, for something that is so very different.

– Kofi Annan – Global Forum on Internet Governance (New York, 24 March 2004)

The Internet has, in a relatively short time, become an essential instrument for today's society. As of early 2005, the Internet is thought to include:

- an estimated 750 million users worldwide;
- an estimated electronic commerce turnover of US$1 billion, which is projected to rise rapidly;
- a major social impact on education, health, government and other areas of activity;
- cybercrime, such as fraud, gambling, pornography and ID theft;
- misuse and abuse in the form of malicious code and spam.

The growing awareness of the social, economic, and political impact of the Internet on society has brought the question of Internet Governance into sharper focus. The process of addressing legal issues and the social consequences of technological developments invariably lags behind technological innovation. This applies to the Internet, too.

In the case of the Internet, governance is needed among other things, to:

- prevent or, at least minimise, the risk of the fragmentation of the Internet;
- maintain compatibility and interoperability;
- safeguard the rights and define the responsibilities of the various players;
- protect end users from misuses and abuse;
- encourage further development.

We are currently in the early phase of international negotiations on Internet Governance, which is characterised by the need to establish and agree on a basic framework and to select appropriate instruments for the discussion of the many arising issues. Who are the actors likely to influence the Internet's future development? What will their policies be with regard to connectivity, commerce, content, funding, security, and other issues central to our emerging Information Society? These are some of the key questions that need to be addressed within the framework of Internet Governance.

The Evolution of Internet Governance

One of the fascinating aspects of the Internet during its development and early growth was its unique governance. The Internet started as a government project. In the late 1960s, the US government sponsored the development of the Defense Advanced Research Projects Agency (DARPANet), a resilient communication facility designed to survive a nuclear attack.

By the 1980s, a wider international community was using the facilities of this network, which by this time was referred to as the Internet. In 1986, the Internet Engineering Task Force (IETF) was established. The IETF managed the further development of the Internet through a cooperative, consensus-based, decision-making process, involving a wide variety of individuals. There was no central government, no central planning, and no grand design.

At this point, life was relatively simple. However, in 1994, the US National Science Foundation decided to involve the private sector by subcontracting the management of the Domain Name System (DNS) to Network Solutions Inc (NSI). This was not well received by the Internet community and a "DNS War" started.

This "DNS War" brought other players into the picture: the business sector, international organisations, and nation states. It ended in 1998 with the establishment of a new organisation, the Internet Company for Assigned Names and Numbers (ICANN).

Since 1998 and the establishment of ICANN, debate on Internet Governance has been characterised by the more intensive involvement of national governments, mainly through the UN framework.

International Negotiations on Internet Governance

The World Summit on the Information Society (WSIS), held in Geneva in December 2003, officially placed the question of Internet Governance on diplomatic agendas. The Declaration of Principles and Action Plan adopted at WSIS proposed a number of actions in the field of Internet Governance, including the establishment of a Working Group.

Below is an excerpt on Internet Governance from the WSIS Declaration of Principles:

50. International Internet Governance issues should be addressed in a coordinated manner. We ask the Secretary General of the United Nations to set up a working group on Internet Governance, in an open and inclusive process that ensures a mechanism for the full and active participation of governments, the private sector, and civil society from both developing and developed countries, involving relevant inter-governmental and international organisations and forums, to investigate and make proposals for action, as appropriate, on the governance of Internet by 2005.

Following is an excerpt on Internet Governance from the WSIS Action Plan:

13. b) We ask the Secretary General of the United Nations to set up a working group on Internet Governance, in an open and inclusive process that ensures a mechanism for the full and active participation of governments, the private sector, and civil society from both developing and developed countries, involving relevant intergovernmental and international organisations and forums, to investigate and make proposals for action, as appropriate, on the governance of Internet by 2005. The group should, *inter alia:*

i. develop a working definition of Internet Governance;

ii. identify the public policy issues that are relevant to Internet Governance;

iii. develop a common understanding of the respective roles and responsibilities of governments, existing inter-governmental and international organisations and other forums, as well as the private sector and civil society from both developing and developed countries;

iv. prepare a report on the results of this activity to be presented for consideration and appropriate action for the second phase of WSIS in Tunis in 2005.

WSIS and WGIG most likely comprise the first phase of the Internet Governance process, which should result in clarifying Internet Governance issues, setting the agenda, as well as introducing procedures and mechanisms.

The Multilateral Negotiation Process and Internet Governance	
Negotiation Phase	**WSIS Activity**
Pre-negotiation	From 1998 until the WSIS Summit in Geneva (2003).
Agenda-setting and Issue Clarification	Started in December 2003 at the WSIS Summit in Geneva with the decision to establish the Working Group on Internet Governance (WGIG); to be concluded in Tunis.
The Search for Formulas	After Tunis 2005.
Negotiation on details	
Agreement	
Implementation	

What Does Internet Governance Mean?

At the Global Forum on Internet Governance, held at the United Nations in New York on 24-25 March 2004, several speakers told various versions of the story of the blind men and the elephant.

The moral of the poem makes it clear that a discussion of the meaning of "Internet Governance" is not merely linguistic pedantry. Different perceptions of the meaning of this term trigger different policy approaches and expectations.

Telecommunication specialists see Internet Governance through the prism of the development of the technical infrastructure. Computer specialists focus on the development of various standards and applications, such as XML or Java. Communication specialists stress the facilitation of communication. Human rights activists view Internet Governance from the perspective of the

> It was six men of Indostan To learning much inclined, Who went to see the Elephant (Though all of them were blind),
>
> ....
>
> And so these men of Indostan Disputed loud and long, Each in his own opinion Exceeding stiff and strong, Though each was partly in the right, And all were in the wrong!
>
> Excerpt from the poem "The Blind Men and the Elephant" written by American poet John Godfrey Saxe (1816-1887);

freedom of expression, privacy, and other basic human rights. Lawyers concentrate on jurisdiction and dispute resolution. Politicians worldwide usually focus on media and issues that play well with their electorates, such as techno-optimism (more computers = more education) and threats (Internet security, protection of children). Diplomats are mainly concerned with the process and protection of national interests. The list of potentially conflicting professional perspectives on Internet Governance goes on.

Each of the terms "Internet" and "governance" is the subject of controversial interpretation. Some authors argue that the first part, "Internet," does not cover all of the existing aspects of global ICT developments. Two other terms: "Information Society" and "Information and Communications Technology" are usually put forward as more comprehensive. They include areas that are beyond the Internet domain, such as mobile telephony.

The argument for the use of the term "Internet," however, is enhanced by the rapid transition of global communication towards the use of TCP/IP as the main communications technical standard. The already ubiquitous Internet continues to expand at a rapid rate, not only in terms of the number of users but also in terms of the services that it offers, notably Voice over Internet Protocol (VoIP), which may displace conventional telephony.

The second part of the term, "governance," has been the cause of controversy in recent debates, especially during WSIS. Misunderstanding primarily stems from the use of the term governance as a synonym for government. When the term "Internet Governance" was introduced in the WSIS process, many, especially developing countries linked it to the concept of government. One of the consequences of such an approach was the belief that Internet Governance issues should be addressed at the inter-governmental level with the limited participation of other, mainly non-state actors.

What were the main reasons for this terminological confusion? Is it obvious that "governance" does not mean "government"? Not necessarily. The term "good governance" has been used by the World Bank to promote the reform of states by introducing more transparency, reducing corruption, and increasing the efficiency of administration. In this context, the term "governance" was directly related to core government functions.

Another potential source of confusion is the translation of the term "governance" into other languages. In Spanish, the term refers mainly to public activities or government (gestión pública, gestión del sector públic and función de gobiern). The reference to public activities/government is also noticeable in French (gestión des affaires publiques, efficacité de l'administration, qualité de l'administration and mode de gouvernement). Portuguese follows a similar pattern by referring to the public sector and government (gestão pública and administração pública). This discrepancy in the interpretation of the term "governance" might provide a linguistic explanation for why many delegations at WSIS linked the question of Internet Governance to the public sector, and centred their deliberations on the need for government intervention.

Internet Governance Toolkit

An Internet Governance regime is in the very early stages of development. Experience from other international regimes (e.g., environment, air transport, arms control) has shown that such regimes tend to develop a common frame of reference, values, perception of cause-and-effect relationships, modes of reasoning, terminology, vocabulary, jargon, and abbreviations.

In many cases, the common framework is influenced by the specific professional culture (the patterns of knowledge and behaviour shared by members of the same profession). The establishment of a common framework usually helps in facilitating better communication and understanding. However, it is sometimes also used to protect one's "turf" and prevent outside influence. To quote the American linguist, Jeffrey Mirel, "All professional language is turf language."

Any Internet Governance regime will be complex as it will need to involve many issues, actors, mechanisms, procedures, and instruments.

There are at least five dimensions to Internet issues: Infrastructure, Legal, Economic, Development, and Socio-cultural. Each one is discussed in the chapters that follow. Many actor, in the private and public sector play roles in each of

these dimensions. Most of them (root operators, ISPs, trademark lawyers, development specialists, civil society activists, etc.) have very specific and well developed professional cultures.

Each combination of issues and actors has its purpose, objectives, terminology, and spheres of collaboration and influence. It seems that many, if not most, of these combinations are currently working in relative isolation from the rest. Add to this, the multiplicity of working languages reflecting the global nature of the problems, and the challenge of bringing these elements together into a coherent governance architecture will become clear, but with goodwill from all sides, no doubt it will be manageable.

The following illustration inspired by the Dutch artist M C Escher, demonstrates some of the paradoxical perspectives associated with Internet Governance.

The complexity of implementing Internet Governance shows that linear, mono-causal and "either/or" thinking is not suited to addressing Internet Governance issues. Therefore there is a need for new cognitive tools that cater for this complexity and introduce common approaches and guiding principles.

The main purpose of such an Internet Governance Toolkit would be to:

- organise the tools currently used in the Internet Governance debate;
- create additional cognitive tools;
- facilitate the inclusive nature of the Internet Governance process by providing interested parties with the tools to understand the issues, positions, and developments.

The Internet Governance Toolkit consists of:

- patterns and approaches;
- guiding principles;
- analogies.

Like the process of Internet Governance, the toolkit is in flux. Approaches, patterns, guiding principles, and analogies emerge and disappear depending on their current relevance in the negotiation process.

Approaches and Patterns

Internet Governance as a whole as well as specific Internet Governance issues have been a part of policy discussions and academic exchanges for some time. A number of approaches and patterns have gradually emerged, representing points where differences in negotiation positions as well as in professional and national cultures can be identified. Identifying common approaches and patterns may reduce the complexity of negotiations and help to create a common system of references.

Narrow vs. Broad Approach

"Narrow vs. broad" Internet Governance has been one of the main issues so far, reflecting the different approaches and interests in the Internet Governance process. The "narrow" approach focusses on the Internet infrastructure (Domain Name System, IP numbers, and root servers) and on ICANN's position as the key actor in this field.

According to the "broad" approach, Internet Governance negotiations should go beyond infrastructural issues and address other legal, economic, developmental, and socio-cultural issues. Distinguishing between these two approaches is particularly important in the early agenda-setting phase of Internet negotiations.

The broad approach is implicitly supported by the WSIS Declaration, which gave the WGIG the mandate "to identify the public policy issues that are relevant to Internet Governance." This approach is generally supported by the policy and academic discussion following the WSIS Summit in Geneva.

The current debate has moved from the either/or stage towards identifying priorities and an appropriate balance between the "narrow" approach (ICANN-related issues) and the "broad" approach (other Internet Governance aspects).

Technical vs. Policy Aspects

A significant challenge of the Internet Governance process will be the integration of technical and policy aspects, as it is difficult to draw a clear distinction between them. Technical solutions are not neutral. Ultimately, each technical solution/option promotes certain interests, empowers certain groups, and, to a certain extent, impacts social, political, and economic life.

In some cases, an initial policy goal for a technical solution changed. For example, the Internet architecture of end-to-end networking and packet switching was designed with the policy goal to create a robust network that could survive a nuclear attack. The same architecture later became the basis for the development of creativity and freedom of expression on the Internet.

Other technical solutions, such as electronic means for the protection of copyright, are intentionally created in order to replace or enforce certain policies (in this case stricter copyright protection).

In the case of the Internet, for a long time both technical and policy aspects were governed by just one social group—the early Internet community. With the growth of the Internet and the emergence of new stakeholders in the 1990s, mainly the business sector and governments, that unity of technology and policy was broken. The reform of Internet Governance, including the creation of ICANN, was an attempt to re-establish the lost balance. This issue remains open, and most likely, will be one of the potentially controversial topics at WSIS/WGIG.

"Old-Real" vs "New-Cyber" Approach

There are two approaches to almost every Internet Governance issue. The "old-real" approach—or "new wine in old bottles"—argues that the Internet does not introduce anything new to the field of governance. The Internet is just another new device from the governance perspective, no different to its predecessors: the telegraph, the telephone, or radio.

For example, in legal discussions, this approach argues that existing laws can be applied to the Internet with only minor adjustments. As long as it involves communication between people, the Internet is no different from the telephone or the telegraph, and it can be regulated like other telecommunication devices. In the economic field, this approach argues that there is no difference between regular and "e" commerce. Consequently, there is no need for special legal treatment of "e-commerce." The "real" approach is also against e-tax moratoriums.

The "new-cyber" approach—or "new wine in new bottles"—argues that the Internet is a fundamentally different device from all previous ones. Thus, it requires fundamentally different governance. This approach was particularly popular in the early days of the Internet. There were even hopes that the innovative early method of governing the Internet—"rough consensus and running code"—might become the model for regulating other areas of human activities. The main premise of the "cyber" approach is that the Internet de-linked our social and political reality from the world of sovereign states. Cyberspace is different from real space and it requires a different form of governance.

Internet Governance Paradigm "Old-Real" vs. "New-Cyber"

The influence of this approach was noticeable in the process of the creation of ICANN, which, for example, minimised the influence of "real" world governments. The "cyber" approach was softened by ICANN's reform in 2002, which strengthened the role of governments and brought ICANN closer to political reality.

In the legal field, the "cyber" school of thought argues that existing laws on jurisdiction, cybercrime, and contracts cannot be applied to the Internet and that new laws must be created.

Given the continuous interplay between these two approaches, the "old-real" versus "new-cyber" dilemma is likely to continue and strongly influence Internet Governance negotiations.

Decentralised vs. Centralised Structure of Internet Governance

Internet Governance is a multi-faceted phenomenon involving a wide range of government mechanisms and forums, including international organisations, national governments, as well as professional and private bodies.

According to the decentralised view, the current governance structure reflects the very nature of the Internet: a network of networks. Such a complex setup cannot be put under a single governance umbrella, such as an international organisation. Another argument is that the lack of centralised governance is one of the major factors allowing for fast Internet growth. This view is mainly supported by the Internet's technical community and developed countries.

The centralised approach, on the other hand, is partly based on the practical difficulty of countries with limited human and financial resources to follow Internet Governance discussions in a highly decentralised and multi-institutional setting. Such countries find it difficult to attend meetings in the main diplomatic centres (Geneva, New York), let alone to follow the activities of other institutions, such as ICANN, W3C, and IETF. These, mainly developing countries argue for a "one-stop shop," preferably within the framework of an international organisation.

Internet and the Public Good

Most of the technical infrastructure through which Internet traffic is channelled are owned by private and state companies, typically telecommunication operators. This is analogous to a shipping company transporting containers. However, shipping lanes are open and regulated by the Law of the Seas, which states that the open seas are *res communis omnium,* while the network backbones over which data is transported are owned by telecommunication companies. This raises a number of questions:

- What are the property rights on Internet backbones?
- Can private companies be requested to manage their private property—Internet backbones—in the public interest?
- Can the Internet, or parts of it, be considered a global public good?
- Could the old Roman concept of *res communis omnium* be applied to the Internet, as in the case of some parts of the Law of the Sea?

The main challenge in this public versus private dilemma will be, on the one hand, to provide the private sector with a proper commercial environment, but, on the other hand, to ensure further development of the Internet as a public resource, consisting of knowledge and information commons.

Geography and the Internet

One of the early assumptions regarding the Internet was that it overcame national borders and eroded the principle of sovereignty. In his famous *"Declaration of the Independence of Cyberspace,"* John Perry Barlow sent the following message to all governments: *"You are not welcome among us. You have no sovereignty where we gather. You have no moral right to rule us nor do you possess any methods of enforcement we have true reason to fear. Cyberspace does not lie within your borders."*

This declaration is an example of the predominant techno-optimism typical of the mid-90s. Since Barlow's declaration, there have been many developments, including more sophisticated geo-location software. Today, it is still difficult to identify exactly who is behind the screen but it is fairly straightforward to identify through which Internet service provider (ISP) the Internet was accessed. In addition, the latest national laws worldwide require ISPs to identify their users and, if requested, to provide necessary information about them to authorities.

The more the Internet is anchored in geography, the less unique its governance will be. For example, with the possibility to geographically locate Internet users and transactions, the complex question of jurisdiction on the Internet can be solved more easily through existing laws.

"Walk the Talk" Approach

The "walk the talk" approach promotes the use of online tools for negotiating on the issues of the online world. The Internet Governance negotiation process presents a considerable challenge in multilateral diplomacy, which calls for both the use of well-proven and efficient negotiating techniques and the introduction of new innovative approaches. One of the main innovative techniques could be the use of online tools for negotiations.

Internet-based negotiations should facilitate the participation of a broader group of stakeholders, especially those who cannot afford to participate in traditional diplomatic conferences. One priority will be to assist developing countries to participate meaningfully in the Internet Governance process.

Guiding Principles

Guiding principles represent certain values and interests that should be promoted through the emerging Internet Governance regime. Some of those principles have been adopted by the WSIS, such as transparency and inclusiveness. Other principles have been introduced, mainly tacitly, through discussions on Internet Governance.

"Don't Re-Invent the Wheel"

Any initiative in the field of Internet Governance should start from existing regulations, which can be divided into three broad groups:

a) those invented for the Internet (e.g., ICANN);

b) those that require considerable adjustment in order to address Internet-related issues (e.g., trademark protection, e-taxation);

c) those that can be applied to the Internet without significant adjustments (e.g., protection of freedom of expression).

The use of existing rules would significantly increase legal stability and reduce the complexity of the development of the Internet Governance regime.

"If It Ain't Broke, Don't Fix It!"

Internet Governance must maintain the current functionality and robustness of the Internet, yet remain flexible enough to adopt changes leading towards increased functionality and higher legitimacy. General consensus recognises that the stability and functionality of the Internet should be one of the guiding principles of Internet Governance. The stability of the Internet should be preserved through the early Internet approach of "running code," which involves the gradual introduction of well-tested changes in the technical infrastructure.

However, some actors are concerned that the use of the slogan "If it ain't broke, don't fix it" will provide blanket immunity from any changes in the current Internet Governance, including changes not necessarily related to technical infrastructure. One solution is to use this as a criterion for the evaluation of specified Internet Governance-related decisions (e.g., introduction of new protocols and changes in decision-making mechanisms).

Internet Governance and Development

The current debate on Internet Governance highlights the high development relevance of the following Internet Governance issues: interconnection charges, distribution of IP numbers, investment, protection of intellectual property, and promotion of e-commerce. The Internet Governance process should be guided by overall WSIS development objectives and the UN Millennium Goals.

Promotion of a Holistic Approach and Prioritisation

A holistic approach should facilitate addressing not only the technical but also the legal, social, economic, and developmental aspects of Internet development. This approach should also take into consideration the increasing convergence of digital technologies, including the migration of telecommunication services towards Internet protocols.

While maintaining a holistic approach to Internet Governance negotiations, stakeholders should identify priority issues depending on their particular interests. Neither developing nor developed countries are homogenous groups. Among developing countries there are considerable differences in priorities, level of

"Not seeing the wood for the trees"

development, and IT-readiness (e.g., between ICT advanced countries such as India, China, and Brazil, and some least-developed countries in sub-Saharan Africa).

A holistic approach and prioritisation of the Internet Governance agenda should help stakeholders from both developed and developing countries to focus on a particular set of issues. This should lead towards more substantive and possibly, less politicised negotiations. The stakeholders would group around issues rather than around the traditional highly politicised division-lines (e.g., developed-developing countries, governments-civil society).

Make Tacit Technical Solutions Explicit Policy Principles

It is a common view that certain social values, such as free communication are facilitated by the way the Internet is designed technically (the "end to end" principle). However, this is not necessarily correct. The latest developments in the Internet, such as the use of firewall technologies for restricting the flow of information, prove that technology can be used in many seemingly contradictory ways. Principles such as free communication should be clearly stated at the policy level, not tacitly presumed at the technical level.

The Principle of Technological Neutrality

This principle is closely linked with the previous one. According to technological neutrality, policy should not depend on specific technological or technical devices. For example, regulations for the protection of privacy should specify what should

ICANN's Guiding Principles

The USA White Paper on Internet Governance (1998) specifies the following guiding principles for the establishment of ICANN:

- *Stability;* the functioning of the Internet should not be disrupted, especially in the operation of its key structures, including "root domains";
- *Competition;* it is important to encourage creativity and flexibility, which will help in the further development of the Internet;
- *Decision-making;* the new system should accommodate some of the Internet's early rules and principles, including grassroots-style organisation, openness, etc.;
- *Representation;* the new framework should accommodate the main stakeholders: both geographical (different countries) and professional (different professional communities).

be protected (e.g., personal data, health records), not how it should be protected (e.g., access to databases, crypto-protection).

Technological neutrality provides many governance advantages. First, it de-links governance from any particular technology and makes it ready for future technological developments. Second, technological neutrality is the most appropriate regulatory principle for the future convergence of the main technologies (telecommunication, media, Internet, etc.).

The European Union has introduced technological neutrality as one of the cornerstones of its telecommunications policy. While technological neutrality is clearly an appropriate principle, one can envisage many difficulties in the transition from existing telecommunication regulations to new ones. This is already obvious in areas such as Voice over IP.

Risk of Running Society through Programmers' Code

One key aspect of the relationship between technology and policy was identified by Lawrence Lessing, who observed that with its growing reliance on the Internet, modern society may end up being regulated by software code instead of laws. Some legislative functions of parliament and government could *de facto* be taken over by computer programmers and technical developers. Through a combination of software and technical solutions they would be able to influence life in increasingly Internet-based societies. Should the running of society through code instead of laws ever happen, it would substantially challenge the very basis of the political and legal organisation of modern society.

Analogies

Though analogy is often misleading, it is the least misleading thing we have.

– Samuel Butler.

Analogy helps us to understand new developments in terms of what is already known. Drawing parallels between past and current examples, despite its risks, is a key mental process in law and politics. Most legal cases concerning the Internet are solved through analogies.

The use of analogies in Internet Governance has a few important limitations. First, the Internet is a broad term, which encompasses a variety of services, including e-mail (see analogy to telephony), web (see analogy to broadcasting services—television), and databases (see analogy to library). An analogy to any particular system may over-simplify the understanding of the Internet.

Second, with the increasing convergence of various telecommunication and media services, the traditional differences between them are blurring. For example, with the introduction of Voice over IP it is increasingly difficult to make a clear distinction between the Internet and telephony.

In spite of these limiting factors, analogies are still powerful and the main cognitive tool for solving legal cases and developing an Internet Governance regime. Some of the most frequently used analogies are discussed below.

Internet – Telephony

Similarities: In the early Internet days this analogy was influenced by the fact that the telephone was used for dial-up access. In addition, a functional analogy holds between the telephone and the Internet (e-mail and chat), both being means for direct and personal communication.

A more recent analogy between the telephone and the Internet focuses on the possible use of the telephony numbering system as a solution for the organisation of the domain name system.

Differences: The Internet uses packets instead of circuits (like the telephone). Unlike telephony, the Internet cannot guarantee services; it can only guarantee a "best effort." The analogy highlights only one aspect of the Internet: communication via e-mail or through chatting. Other major Internet applications, such as the World Wide Web, interactive services, etc. do not share common elements with telephony.

Used by: Those who oppose the regulation ,of Internet content (mainly in the United States). If the Internet is analogous to the telephone, the content of communication cannot be controlled.

This analogy is also used by those who argue that the Internet should be governed like other communication systems (e.g., telephony, post), by national authorities with a coordinating role of international organisations, such as the ITU.

Internet – Mail/Post

Similarities: There is an analogy in function, namely, the delivery of messages. The name itself "e-mail," highlights this similarity.

Differences: This analogy covers only one Internet service—e-mail. Moreover, the postal service has a much more elaborate intermediary structure between the sender and recipient of mail than the e-mail system, where the active intermediary function is performed by the ISPs or an e-mail service provider like Yahoo! or Hotmail.

Used by: The Universal Postal Convention draws this analogy between mail and e-mail: "electronic mail is a postal service which uses telecommunications for transmitting." This analogy can have consequences concerning the delivery of official documents, for instance: receiving a court decision via e-mail would be considered an official delivery.

The families of US soldiers who died in Iraq have also attempted to make use of the analogy between mail (letters) and e-mail in order to gain access to their loved ones' private e-mail and blogs, arguing that they should be allowed to inherit e-mail and blogs as they would letters and diaries.

ISPs have found it difficult to deal with this highly emotional problem. Instead of going along with the analogy between letters and e-mail, most ISPs have denied access based on the privacy agreement they had signed with their users.

Internet – Television

Similarities: The initial analogy was related to the physical similarity between computers and television screens. A more sophisticated analogy draws on the use of both media—web and TV—for broadcasting.

Differences: As with telephony, the Internet is a broader concept than television. Aside from the similarity between a computer screen and a TV screen, there are major structural differences between them. Television is a one-to-many medium for broadcasting to viewers, while the Internet facilitates many different types of communication (one-to-one, one-to-many, many-to-many).

Used by: This analogy is used by those who wish to introduce stricter content control to the Internet. In their view, due to its power as a mass media tool similar to television, the Internet should be strictly controlled.

The US government attempted to use this analogy in the seminal "Reno vs. ACLU" Case. This case was prompted by the Communication Decency Act passed by Congress, which stipulates strict content control in order to prevent children from being exposed to pornographic materials via the Internet. The court refused to recognise the television analogy.

Internet – Library

Similarities: The Internet is sometimes seen as a vast repository of information and the term "library" is often used to describe it—"huge digital library," "cyber-library," "Alexandrian Library of the 21st Century," etc.

Differences: The storage of information and data is only one aspect of the Internet, and there are considerable differences between libraries and the Internet:

a) traditional libraries aim to serve individuals living in a particular place (city, country, etc.), while the Internet is global;

b) books, articles, and journals are published using procedures to ensure quality (editors). The Internet does not have editors;

c) libraries are organised according to specific classification schemes, allowing users to locate the books in their collections. Apart from a few directories such as Yahoo! and Google, which cover only a small part of the information available throughout the Internet, no such classification scheme exists for the Internet;

d) apart from keyword descriptions, the contents of a library (text in books and articles) are not accessible until the user borrows a particular book. The content of the Internet is immediately accessible via search engines.

Used by: Various projects that aim to create a comprehensive system of information and knowledge on particular issues (portals, databases, etc.).

Internet – VCR, Photocopier

Similarities: This analogy is used in cases involving the reproduction of copyright-protected materials. The Internet can be used in the process of reproducing and disseminating various materials.

Differences: The computer has a much broader function than the copying of materials, although copying itself is much simpler on the Internet than with a VCR or photocopier.

Used by: This analogy was used in the context of the US "Digital Millennium Copyright Act" (DMCA), which penalises institutions that contribute to the infringement of copyrights (developing software for breaking copyright protection, etc.). The counterargument in such cases was that software developers, like VCR and photocopy machine manufacturers, cannot predict whether their products will be used illegally. This analogy was used in cases against the developers of Napster-style software for peer-to-peer sharing of files, such as Grokster and StreamCast.

Internet – Highway

Similarities: This analogy is linked to American culture and the importance it places on highways and railroads, thereby revealing the national fascination with discovery and new frontiers.

Differences: Aside from the transportation aspect of the Internet, there are no other similarities between the Internet and highways. The Internet moves intangible materials (data), while highways facilitate the transportation of goods and people.

Used by: The highway analogy was used extensively in the mid-90s, after Al Gore introduced the term "information superhighway." The term "highway" was also used by the German government in order to justify the introduction of a stricter Internet content control law in June 1997:

"It's a liberal law that has nothing to do with censorship but clearly sets the conditions for what a provider can and cannot do. The Internet is a means of transporting and distributing knowledge... just as with highways, there need to be guidelines for both kinds of traffic."

The Classification of Internet Governance Issues

Internet Governance is a complex new field requiring an initial conceptual mapping and classification. The complexity of Internet Governance is related to its multidisciplinary nature, encompassing a variety of aspects, including technology, socio-economics, development, law, and politics.

The need for an initial mapping of Internet Governance is both academic and practical. On the academic side, an increasing volume of research on Internet Governance is being produced, but it has focussed mainly on ICANN and other issues belonging to the so called "narrow" approach to Internet Governance. A broader theoretical framework is still lacking, in particular on the international aspects of Internet Governance. The practical need for classification was clearly demonstrated during the WSIS process. Many players including nation states, had difficulties grasping the complexity of Internet Governance. A conceptual mapping of the field should contribute towards more efficient negotiations within the context of WSIS as well as other multilateral negotiation processes on Internet-related issues.

A classification may assist Internet Governance players with the following:

- clearer identification of the main issues requiring negotiation;

- reduction of negotiation "noise" caused by inconsistent interpretations of the main concepts;
- avoidance of duplicating efforts by addressing the same issues in multiple fora;
- maintenance of an appropriate balance between a broad perspective and specific issues, thereby avoiding the problem of being "unable to see the forest for the trees."

Ultimately, a careful mapping of Internet issues should make the process of negotiating Internet Governance more efficient. In economic terms, it should reduce the transaction cost—in other words, reduce the total time required for negotiations. This would be of particular benefit to countries with limited financial and human resources, thus enabling their increased participation. Unclear and confusing negotiating processes require disproportionately higher human resources and more time.

Diplo's classification of Internet Governance groups all issues in five classification clusters. Adjusting the terminology to the world of diplomacy, Diplo has adopted the term "basket." (The term "basket" was introduced in diplomatic practice during the Organisation on Security and Cooperation in Europe (OSCE) negotiations.) The following five baskets have been used since 1997, when Diplo started developing its classification scheme:

1) infrastructure and standardisation;
2) legal;
3) economic;
4) development;
5) socio-cultural.

Diplo's classification of Internet Governance is the conceptual basis for Diplo's overall approach to this field, including training/education, research, and the development of tools. Since its introduction in 1997, the classification has been used in courses attended by more than 300 students as well as by many researchers. Regular feedback on this classification scheme has been the basis for constant adjustments. The current classification, therefore, is based on numerous iterations as well as aggregated knowledge and experience.

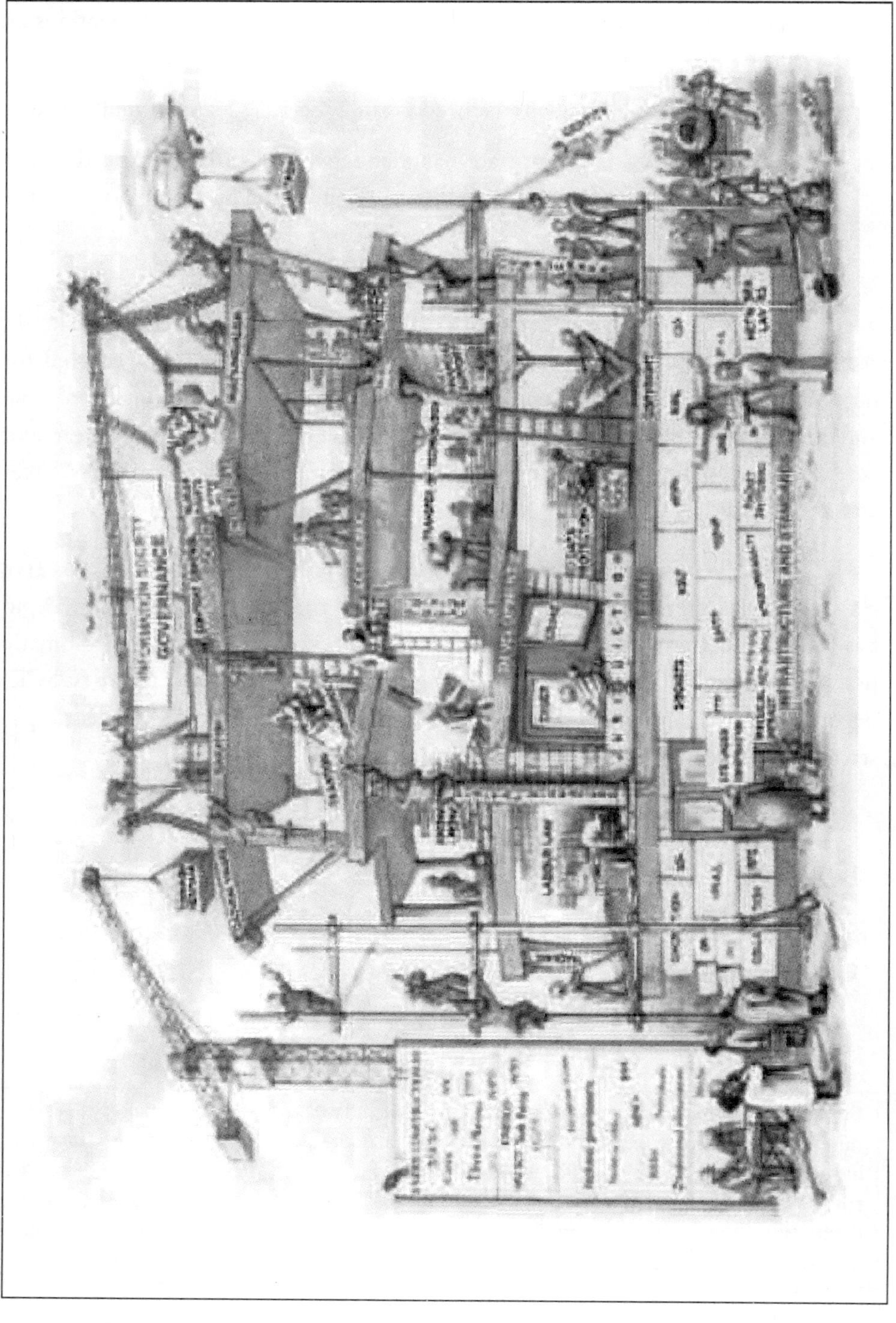

The five-basket model is metaphorically presented through this "Building under Construction" illustration.

"Building under Construction:" Internet Governance – Are We Building the 21st Century Tower of Babel?

A painting by Pieter Brueghel the Elder (1563), displayed in the Kunsthistorisches Museum in Vienna, shows the construction of the Tower of Babel. (Another, smaller, painting of the same year and on the same subject is in the Boijmans Van Beuningen Museum in Rotterdam). The *Bible's* book of *Genesis* (11.7) refers to the construction of the Tower of Babel: "let us go… and confuse their language so that one will not understand each other's language, each will not understand their fellow."

The analogy of the construction of the Tower of Babel seems appropriate when looking at the Internet – or, more specifically, at the structure of the emerging Information Society. This comparison has prompted the authors to consider another building under construction —not aimed at reaching the heavens but at least at reaching everyone on the planet. Diplo has developed a framework for the discussion of Internet Governance, illustrated in the picture on the previous page. It is important to realise that all of the floors in this building are linked, and that construction is on-going and never-ending.

3

Internet Governance: Theory and First Principles

Johannes M Bauer

The paper starts with a brief review on the notion of governance and answers the fundamental question of whether Internet should be governed at all. Later, it explores the conceptual and normative foundations that could help embed the multiple dialogues in an overarching framework. The paper builds on the literature on the governance of large technical systems, the literature on policy design in dynamic environment, and more recent attempts to bridge these strands of thought in the theory of complex adaptive systems. Further, it explores alternative approaches to Internet governance—spontaneous self-governance, forms of self- and co-regulation, the theory of distributed governance and public interest government intervention—and explains their comparative advantages and disadvantages.

1. Introduction

For many years, the Internet was regarded as a space that should not and could not be regulated by governments. This view is poignantly expressed in John Perry Barlow's Declaration of the Freedom of Cyberspace:

> *"Governments of the Industrial World, you weary giants of flesh and steel, I come from Cyberspace, the new home of the Mind. On behalf of the future, I ask you of the past to leave us alone. You are not welcome among us. You have no sovereignty where we gather. ... Your legal concepts of property, expression, identity, movement, and context do not apply to us. They are all based on matter, and there is no matter here."*
>
> – Perry Barlow 1996.

However, even if one were to subscribe to an anarchic view of cyberspace, this does not imply the absence of any forms of governance altogether. Even the anarchic literature acknowledges that forms of coordination between participants in social processes are necessary, although they are envisioned as decentralized, voluntary, emerging forms of harmonization (Nozick 1974). Any social organization is characterized by a set of specific institutional arrangements. With regard to the Internet, Lessig (1999) pointed out that even in the absence of formal regulation code *de facto* serves as quasi-regulator, and often in a less transparent manner than more formal rules. Going beyond Lessig's argument, Mueller (2002) pointed out the many formal and informal rules upon which the Internet community relies in its daily interactions.

The recognition that the Internet in practice is shaped by forms of governance, has freed the Internet community to engage in a more deliberate and creative discussion of different options as to how these processes could be structured. Lessig (1999) suggested that—much like the constitutions of many nations—some form of government intervention could actually serve to safeguard the freedoms of cyberspace. Mathiason (2004) suggests that a framework convention should be organized to design ground rules for Internet governance. Institutional arrangements can, at least to a certain degree, be shaped by deliberate political action, thus raising the question as to how and by whom they should be designed.

With the World Summit on the Information Society (WSIS) and the establishment of the Working Group on Internet Governance (WGIG) a further shift has taken place toward accepting the need for a global, more formal framework (WGIG 2005; WGIG 2005; WSIS 2003; WSIS 2003). While this latest round of talks has brought governments back into the picture, one of the fascinating aspects of the unfolding debate is the strong participation by civic sector groups and, to a lesser degree, industry and its associations.

As a complement to this fascinating international process, this paper explores concepts that could help embed the multiple dialogues in an overarching framework. Internet governance is analyzed as a problem of coordinating a multi-level, adaptive socio-technical system. Such coordination is required to assure the working of large systems. A broad spectrum of alternative coordination mechanisms is available ranging from reliance on norms and traditions, decentralized market decisions, forms of self- and co-regulation, and forms of government intervention and regulation. In contrast to pundits who propose to restrict the term "Internet governance" to domain name and possibly other technical issues, a broader notion is used in this paper. As will become clear in the course of the paper, such a broader notion is the only logically coherent view of governance; it also puts the problem of governance (to design, as far as possible, a "best" set of processes and practices) into sharper light.

The paper builds on the literature on the governance of large technical systems (Mayntz and Hughes 1988), the literature on policy design in dynamic environment, and more recent attempts to bridge these strands of thought in the theory of complex adaptive systems (Bauer 2004; Cherry and Bauer 2004). Starting point is a brief review of the notion of governance and the question of whether the Internet can be governed at all. Answering this question with "yes but", the paper then explores alternative approaches to organize governance and their comparative advantages and disadvantages. This framework is then applied to some of the 21 issues identified by WGIG, in particular to questions related to network infrastructure, network security, and the multi-lingual reconfiguration of the Internet.

2. Internet Governance Defined

The Internet is a large, adaptive socio-technical system. It is, furthermore, a multi-layer system in that it is embedded in and has effects on local, sub-national regional, national, supra-national regional, and global levels (see Hollingsworth, Müller, and Hollingsworth (2002) for a more detailed discussion of multi-layered socio-economic systems). Any large system depends on coordination mechanisms that integrate its multiple sub-systems and assure its working. A broad spectrum of alternative coordination mechanisms is available to solve these coordination tasks. They involve different levels of central planning and range from a reliance on norms and traditions, decentralized market decisions, networks and networked organizations, forms of self- and co-regulation, to forms of government intervention and regulation (Latzer 2002; Ogus 1995).

The notion of governance evolved during the past decades and it may be helpful to define upfront how it will be used throughout this article. After World War II, the emphasis of the debate was on government planning, policy development and implementation (Mayntz 2003). These activities were seen as purposeful actions of the privileged sovereign actor state. Initially, it was neither questioned that the state was capable of steering economy and society nor that it would pursue the public interest. However, beginning as early as in the 1960s but certainly during the 1970s and 1980s, the limits or successful steering became more visible and also shifted the focus of research to a critical examination of actual government behavior.

For example, in the United States, the Chicago and Virginia Schools emphasized different forms of government failure and recommended different remedies. The Chicago School modeled government as a supplier in a market for policies and stressed the capture of public officials by well-organized interest groups. A solution was seen in far-reaching deregulation. The Virginia School argued that the presence of government would inevitably lead to attempts by stakeholders to seek favorable rules and result in a waste of social surplus in unproductive rent-seeking. An appropriate design of constitutional rules was seen as an important remedy of these problems. In Europe, systems theory depicted a polycentric world without any center capable of steering the entire system toward specific outcomes. In parallel with these conceptual currents, forms of coordination other than government, such as voluntary self-regulation, promulgation of codes of behavior by business associations, and co-regulation received renewed attention. These arrangements had existed and were documented for several centuries and were now seen as vehicles to overcome the weaknesses of government. The term "governance" was initially used to describe these non-hierarchical, non-government forms of coordination.

A third, encompassing concept of governance emerged from the new institutional economics literature (see Williamson (2000) for an attempt to take stock). All mechanisms of coordination are seen as forms of governance. Thus, markets, hierarchies, networks, informal norms are all mechanisms of governance. These mechanisms operate at four different levels of society and time-scales. In Williamson's model, higher levels impose constraints on the levels immediately below and lower levels provide feedback to higher levels. At the level of social embeddedness, where informal institutions, customs, traditions, norms and religion are situated, change can take very long periods of time, even hundreds or thousands of years. The next lower level defines the institutional environment and encompasses the formal rules of the game, including the specification of property rights and the organization of political institutions. Change on this level may take ten to one hundred years. One level down is the governance structure of a society (the "play of the game"), most importantly contractual arrangements. Aligning governance structures with the type of transactions is one important task at that level and can take one to ten years. Finally, at the lowest level continuous decisions regarding resource allocation and employment are being made.

The third approach is the logically most consistent view of governance and will be adopted in this paper. It explicitly recognizes that different types of transactions require different types of governance mechanisms. One important problem of governance is to design mechanisms that are appropriate to the problem at hand. However, not all aspects of the institutional matrix are designed and established by deliberate action. Some institutional arrangements evolve from the repeated interaction of individuals and organizations. Thus, while at the micro-level there will be deliberate decisions by individuals, institutions at higher levels emerge and thus cannot be seen as the result of any deliberate policy design. For example, markets often are the outcomes of numerous smaller deliberate arrangements. They are embedded in these arrangements; in that sense, they are not "spontaneous" arrangements, as claimed by Hayek, but frequently they are not deliberate designs either.

Institutional arrangements provide a framework within which shared mental models of the world are developed and perpetuated (Aoki 2001; Denzau and North 1994). At the same time, they function as lenses to identify problems that might require collective action and narrow the set of possible responses to a sub-set compatible with the existing institutional arrangements. The recent definition of "governance" proposed by WGIG reflects these insights:

> *"Internet governance is the development and application by Governments, the private sector and civil society, in their respective roles, of shared principles, norms, rules, decision-making procedures, and programmes that shape the evolution and use of the Internet." (WGIG (2005), p. 4).*

However, this definition does not explicitly recognize (although it does not preclude it) that governance mechanisms not only are designed but also emerge without specific design actions. The institutional matrix of the Internet is a hybrid of governance mechanisms that were designed and some that emerged in an evolutionary process from repeated interactions. This raises the question as to whether a system of Internet governance can be designed, even if there were a will to do so, and at what level it can be designed. Before we address this question, we will briefly discuss whether the Internet should be governed.

3. Should the Internet be Governed?

At a fundamental level, this is a futile question. Even if it were possible that the Internet functioned in a purely decentralized mode, it is likely that some norms and conventions, even if they were local or indigenous to specific social networks, would emerge from repeated interactions. These emergent institutional arrangements would then constitute a governance structure. Even the most radical cyberian would probably not have any qualms with such an emergent governance structure. The contested question is whether deliberate collective efforts should be made to design a governance structure for the Internet and if it is so, how they should be structured. An affirmative answer must rest in the assumption that such a deliberate effort would create a more efficient and/or more equitable Internet or a space that is better suited to the diverse needs of the multiple cultures participating in it. In the heat of the unfolding debate over Internet governance, such basic questions are rarely asked.

There are three main areas where these questions arise: (1) issues related to the network infrastructure upon which the Internet rests; (2) technical coordination issues related to the Internet as a logical layer of protocols, including the organization of the numbering and identifier space; and (3) issues related to the content of the communications, including intellectual property issues. This is not an exhaustive list and other areas that might need explicit governance structures exist, for example, issues related to the applications and services offered using the Internet, including the establishment of legal frameworks for electronic commerce. A detailed discussion of these areas would exceed the scope of the present paper but it is necessary to review briefly the arguments for and against governance efforts in the first three areas.

Policies adopted at the level of the infrastructure, upon which the Internet resides have a direct impact on the Internet. Despite the close interrelation, the policy debates in these areas are not very well linked. In part, this is due to the fact that the traditional regulatory debate is conducted primarily within regulatory agencies that do not have jurisdiction over Internet issues or have voluntarily ceded jurisdiction. Internet policy issues are often discussed in different government agencies and by different stakeholders. This divergence is also due in part to the fact that the intellectual and philosophical underpinnings of traditional telecommunication regulation and Internet governance are quite different. In contrast to earlier periods, traditional regulation is increasingly influenced by relatively specialized economic approaches and a strong focus on efficiency and forms of market failure as the main rationale for public policy.

As these models do not allow for an integrated treatment of equity concerns, the importance of these concerns in the regulatory debates is also receding. If they are recognized as legitimate at all, equity issues are relegated to other policy domains. Moreover, trade-offs between efficiency and equity are often declared, putting efficiency goals in conflict with equity goals. Interestingly, legal scholars have been more creative than economists in proposing alternative frameworks to think though pressing policy issues, such as spectrum policy or policies for the emerging broadband environment (Benkler 2003; Frischmann 2005). In contrast, the Internet policy debate encompasses both efficiency and equity issues, drawing from a much broader body of social, legal, and economic theory.

It is important to realize that few of these conventional wisdoms that prevail in traditional telecommunications regulation have strong support in welfare economics. First, the often-invoked trade-off between efficiency and equity ignores the second theorem of welfare economics, which shows that any point on the efficiency frontier (representing, for example, different combinations of equity and efficiency) can be reached via a competitive equilibrium by varying the initial endowments of agents. These initial endowments will not only include resource endowments but also likely to include the legal and regulatory frameworks within which market processes unfold. This is but another way of stating an insight of institutional economics and economic sociologists, that markets do not exist in a vacuum but need to be embedded in a legal and regulatory framework.

Different such frameworks exist and hence different constellations of institutional arrangements may yield efficient outcomes (North 1990; Swedberg 2003). Second, as Amartya Sen has expressed so eloquently in his prolific writings, comprehensive rationality has to go beyond a given institutional framework and evaluate different designs of such frameworks as well as their consequences. Moreover, it has to critically reflect the values and objectives that are being pursued, rather than rely narrowly on efficiency (Sen 2002). The Internet governance debate thus provides an opportunity to broaden the traditional telecommunications policy discussion.

Within the Internet policy debate, similar arguments can be made with regard to technical issues, domain names, and identifiers. A rationale for deliberate governance is often based in the need to ascertain the functionality of the logical infrastructure of the Internet. This is seemingly self-evident with regard to the need to rely on numbering conventions that are unique (Mueller 2002). However, there are many ways to design and promulgate such a unique identifier space. Market failure as a rational for coordination of the numbering space fails to capture the problem: the design of the numbering space is a precondition for market forces to work at other related layers of the Internet. The early numbering conventions are a good example of a governance mechanism that emerged from the repeated interactions of a relatively small group of people. However, as the number of participants and stakeholders increases, the transaction costs of this process will increase, perhaps even exponentially and the development of shared norms will likely take much longer, if a sustainable solution can be reached at all. It is therefore nearly inevitable that some form of hierarchical coordination is used. ICANN is one such approach but others are feasible.

The most contested issues are related to the content of communications on the Internet. It is this area where virtual space and physical space are in strenuous relations. One extreme position would be to claim with Barlow that cyberspace is a different frontier and a different world. Another extreme position is cultural relativism, the stance that it is impossible to rank order (local) cultures and political systems. Democratic and dictatorial, tolerant or fundamental nations or societies are of equal value and deserve equal respect. Therefore, no general set of values and norms may exist that holds across the global Internet space. Whereas the first position would argue in favor of no or minimal governance, the second would argue for decentralized governance, essentially mapping nation states onto cyberspace. In practice, the two worlds are not separate and many interactions exist. Physical space and virtual space co-evolve and shape each other and the existing frictions will need to be addressed. Furthermore, national cultures are neither fully independent nor does a truly global culture exist. Some degree of differentiation will thus be inevitable and is probably a desirable feature of the global Internet. This implies that some form of governance is found that balances freedom to communicate with the legitimate need of different cultures to adopt specific policies.

In sum, in all three generic areas there are strong reasons to seek to establish governance mechanisms. Some of these reasons are related to the presence of market failure, but there are even more important reasons related to the need to find solutions to important issues that affect a large number of participants in the Internet. Before we will discuss available options for governance mechanisms and their relative advantages and disadvantages in section five, the next section will briefly review whether the Internet can be governed.

4. Can the Internet be Governed?

Some pundits have argued that even if there were a need and the will to govern the Internet, its diversity and global reach prevents effective governance. It is often argued that the spatial structure of the political space does not match the spatial nature of the problems: governments operate on a national scale but Internet problems are global in scope. However, the answer to the question of whether the Internet can be governed is not so straightforward. First, supranational forms of governance already exist or, if the present forms are insufficient, it could be developed (Mathiason *et al.* 2004). Second, not all policy issues raised by the Internet require necessarily a global solution as some may be solved regionally or even locally. Third, there may be trade-offs between the dynamics of the Internet and the limited adaptability of global governance structures; between the adoption of local solutions and the vision of a truly seamless global Internet space; or between the reliance on spontaneous, decentralized processes and legitimacy of the emergent outcomes. These trade-offs need to be examined carefully before a choice in favor of one or the other solution is made.

At the heart of the issue is the more generic question of whether large technical systems that are also complex adaptive systems can be governed. Bauer (2004) and Bauer and Cherry (2004) address problems of governance in complex adaptive systems. Deliberate governance requires knowledge of a valid policy model that establishes a stable relation between policy instruments and outcomes. In complex adaptive systems, several challenges exist:

- First, the requisite policy model may not be known with sufficient accuracy.
- Second, due to the dynamic development of the Internet, the policy model may not be stable.
- Third, even if it the correct model were known and stable, political and economic feasibility constraints may prevent adoption of an effective policy.
- Fourth, as it is unlikely that the correct model is known or stable, policy interacts with the large technical system in ways that typically lead to unanticipated outcomes.

Under these conditions, it may be difficult or impossible to find a sustainable set of policies. Cherry and Bauer (2004) characterize a sustainable policy as "… rules that are politically adoptable and for which the underlying policy goals are reasonably likely to be achievable". It might be added that such policies also need to be in the core of the policy game, so that no actor has an incentive to further change the rules. If not, such policies exist, it might be possible to achieve sustainable processes with which policies are continuously adapted (dynamic sustainability). The question then is whether such sustainable policies or processes can be found for the issues affecting the Internet.

To answer this question in general terms, it is first necessary to briefly discuss the notion of large technical systems and complex systems. The notion of large technical systems was developed by researchers such as Hughes (1983) and the groups of social scientists at the Max Planck Institute for Social Studies in Germany Mayntz and Hughes (1988). One of the key questions raised by this research is whether large technical systems can be controlled or at least steered in certain directions. No unique answer emerged from the research efforts and more optimistic positions were juxtaposed by more pessimistic views (see Hughes (2004) for a high-level discussion of these issues). Nevertheless, the dominant view was that such systems, even if they could not be fine-tuned, could be governed and edged in certain directions.

This discussion was continued by the more recent efforts to describe the dynamics of non-linear systems using computational tools, often clustered under the heading "complexity theory". At an abstract level, any system consists of nodes and vertices (links). These links may be physical links as in a communications network or intangible links, as economic interdependencies. Systems come with different degrees of complexity. A null system is on in which the nodes are not connected at all (Potts 2000). Events affecting one node do not have any effects on other nodes of the system. The other extreme is the fully connected system, in which every node is connected directly with every other node. In such a system, events affecting one node may have wide repercussions. Depending on the strength of the links and the time scale of the interaction, such systems can behave in a very unpredictable way as direct and indirect feedback effects percolate through the entire system. Although there are different definitions of the constituent features of complex systems, a system may be considered complex if its overall behavior cannot be predicted other than in rather general terms.

At a very abstract level, Mesarovic, Macko, and Takahara (1970) have investigated and defined the conditions under which multi-level adaptive systems can be successfully coordinated. In this framework, complex adaptive systems need integrating mechanisms or they tend to be unstable. At present, the main coordinating agent at higher system levels is the regime created to manage domain names. Paradoxically, the monopolistic structure of that regime seems to be the precondition to having any effective governance tools over the Internet. It is not obvious—but also not impossible— that governance mechanisms exist that would achieve successful coordination absent in such a centralized intervention point.

At a technical level, the Internet has many of the features of large technical systems and also exhibits some patterns known from complexity research. For example, Barabasi (2002) and his collaborators have shown that traffic flows and nodes on the Internet follow a power law distribution, which is typical for many complex adaptive systems. Similar results are also reported by Pastor-Satorras and Vespignani (2004) and Dorogovtsev and Mendes (2003). It is hypothesized here that the Internet governance structure also reveals elements of a complex adaptive system. The degree of complexity of governance interactions is reduced by the existence of centralized nodes, most importantly ICANN and the registries accredited by it. A critical issue in assessing how the Internet should be governed is then whether the designed structure will suffice to achieve the minimally required coordination.

5. Alternative Approaches to Internet Governance

This section will review several frameworks that could be used to design Internet governance approaches: (1) spontaneous self-organization; (2) forms of self and coregulation; (3) the theory of distributed governance; and (4) public interest government intervention.

The notions that large systems can spontaneously self-organize has captivated social researchers since Adam Smith created the famous metaphor of the "invisible hand" in his *Wealth of Nations* and in the Theory of Moral Sentiments. Economists and practical policymakers have long relied on this notion that individual self-interest can lead to mutually compatible outcomes that are aligned with the larger public interest, often without concern for the conditions under which the conclusion holds. Mathematical economics of the Arrow-Debreu general equilibrium type has indicated how strong the conditions are that must be met in order to achieve such an ideal outcome. Among others, these include perfect information, the existence of all present and futures markets, the absence of any forms of public goods and externalities, and the absence of increasing returns. In practice, these conditions are never met, seriously challenging the value of invisible hand theorems. Thus, the intellectual underpinnings who often used to hail the superior working of decentralized decision-making processes have an insufficient rationale in support of a similar decentralized approach to the Internet governance.

The notion of spontaneous self-organization has received renewed attention in the work of the Austrian School of economics, in particular F A v. Hayek. He saw the main advantage of decentralized decision-making in its superior ability to process incomplete and localized knowledge, thus coining his notion of competition as a "discovery process" (Hayek 1949). More recently, many of the claims made by Hayek have been replicated in experimental models of market coordination. Indeed, this line of work, for the first time, can replicate how coordination in decentralized systems works and the emergent properties it generates. One could thus ask whether the Internet can be characterized in similar terms and whether such decentralized coordination would work. One important obstacle to fully decentralized decision-making is that important aspects of the Internet, for example, the creation and administration of domain names, are not organized as markets. In fact, market organization is seen by many as inimical to the fundamental philosophical principles upon which the Internet is built. Nevertheless, fully decentralized organization seems to be one principally possible approach. A consequence of such a radical step is that many of the features of the Internet at more aggregate levels will be emergent, that is, not directly designed nor controlled. For many, this might be an impossible leap of faith to make. Most likely, it will lead to a more differentiated Internet space in which cultural and political heterogeneity will be reflected. It is by no means certain, that such an Internet would have the technical coherence and end-to-end functionality that is so critical in the present architecture. In as far as participation in such a space yields benefits, voluntary collaboration can be expected.

One might thus expecte that such a fully self-regulated Internet will retain a substantial degree of coherence, perhaps even develop higher-level coordination organizations. The main difference to today's arrangements is that this would be a bottom-up approach. The biggest objection against the feasibility of this model is that the *status quo ante* cannot be eradicated and it is difficult to describe a transition path from here to there.

A second principal model is to rely on forms of self- and co-regulation rather than government intervention. Self-regulation refers to procedures in which private sector actors voluntarily define rules of engagement, such as codes of ethics, standards, or numbering conventions. The present framework of Internet governance is a form of self-regulation, which is nearly always backed by some form of direct or indirect government authority. Co-regulation refers to procedures in which a government body delegates tasks to the private sector but retains the ability to pass enabling legislation, enforce rules, and possibly revoke the delegation. Thus, in co-regulation arrangements the role of the government is more direct. Both self-and co-regulation are widely used in the Internet. Latzer *et.al.* (2002) discuss the conditions under which they promise effective governance. Among other things, self-and co-regulation work well whenever the stakeholders have congruent interests, when all relevant stakeholders participate, when outcomes are easily measurable, and when there is general public support for these forms of governance.

Two of these four conditions are met with regard to Internet governance: outcomes are measurable and there is broad public support for limited government intervention. It is less clear that the interests of stakeholders are sufficient congruent. However, the most challenging is to assure that all relevant stakeholders participate. Even more challenging is to ascertain that sustainable agreements are found. This is not impossible, but it may well be that the direct and indirect transaction costs of negotiating such agreements are prohibitively high. Thus, self-and co-regulation are not unworkable *per se* but possible victims of the large number as well as different backgrounds and interests of the stakeholders that are involved. Some of these possible pitfalls might be overcome if a hierarchical governance structure were to be established, for example by differentiation between global, regional, and national governance arrangements.

Such a deliberate hierarchical organization is the third generic overall organization of governance. It is also the outcome suggested by the theory of complex adaptive systems to assure a desired level of coherence. However, it raises the question as to how the tasks should be assigned to different layers of the governance structure and how these layers relate to each other. Although a multi-level system does not necessarily have to be a federal system, the theory of federalism may help shed some light on the optimal design of such a framework. A federal system is one in which lower-level actors voluntarily delegate some of their powers to higher-level actors and thus are bound in those areas by higher-level decisions. Another possible configuration is a confederation, where such upward delegation exists but the power to prescribe policies to lower-level units is weakened but nevertheless specified in the specific contractual agreements underlying the confederation. An even weaker form are inter-governmental agreements, which typically come with many reservations and caveats on the part of the signatories. Lastly, a hierarchical system can be based upon voluntary collaboration.

In all these cases, an assignment of tasks to the constituent layers needs to be found. Such an assignment could be based on efficiency and/or equity criteria. One rule that is often used is the subsidiarity principle: decisions should be made at the lowest level at which they can be handled most effectively; only if lower level actors cannot solve issues efficiently, should they be delegated to a higher level. This standard is less clear-cut than would be desirable. Often, it will not be obvious in advance what the optimal level of decision-making is. However, an evolutionary process can be designed that would facilitate discovering the best solution. It would require starting with a fairly decentralized structure; only if it is evident that certain problems cannot be solved in that manner should they be assigned to higher levels. One variant of this approach is to embed the hierarchical structure in the legal framework of the Internet. Proposals to call a constitutional convention to agree of core principles of Internet governance would achieve that purpose. Within that framework, decisions could then be organized initially in a most decentralized fashion with provisions that would govern their re-assignment to higher levels, if necessary.

A fourth way of organizing governance is the traditional system of governmental regulation. At the international level, this system suffers from the absence of global government. All agreements are inter-governmental in nature with national governments serving as the agents of implementing and enforcing agreements. In all intergovernmental treaties, many reservations and caveats are taken by individual governments. One of the most problematic issues is that governments across the world enjoy different levels of legitimacy and trust from those they govern. Thus, as many surveys demonstrate, European citizens typically have a higher level of confidence that governments act in their interests and are thus willing to give government an important role in social and economic affairs. In contrast, American citizens and many citizens of developing countries consider traditional government as an antagonistic force. Furthermore, the capability of governments to act as enlightened technocrats varies quite significantly across cultures, regions, and nations. Overall, embedding the Internet into the traditional government structure would likely undermine its transformational potential. Nevertheless, in certain areas, such as law enforcement, provisions to facilitate ecommerce, privacy, and intellectual property rights, formal government involvement may be all but inevitable.

6. Policy Implications and Conclusions

As Williamson (2000) recognizes, identifying possible alternative governance options alone is insufficient. According to his remediability criterion, unless a feasible transition path from the *status quo* to an alternative arrangement can be identified, the *status quo* has to be considered superior. Doing so in detail would exceed the scope and purpose of this paper (and possibly the capacity of a single author). As a very modest step in this direction, the Table relates the 21 key issues identified by WGIG in its preparatory work to its July 2005 report to the four generic frameworks. In each case, a very cautious and tentative assessment is attempted as to whether the task could be effectively solved using a particular structure. The Table illustrates that different issues need different governance structures, thus recalling for a mix of different forms. This is not surprising, as such mixes also evolved in other areas that require global coordination.

Governance Issues and Structures				
Issue	**Self-organization**	**Self- and co-regulation**	**Multi-level governance**	**Governmental**
Administration of Internet names and IP addresses	~	+	+	+
Administration of the Root Server System	—	+	+	+
Peering and Interconnection	+	+	~	—
Telecommunications infrastructure, broadband access, convergence with NGN	+	+	+	—
Cyber security, cyber crime	~	~	+	+
Competition policy, liberalization, privatization, regulations	—	—	—	+
Multilingualization of Internet naming systems	+	+	+	~
Spam	—	—	+	+
Dispute resolution	+	+	—	—
Security of network and information systems	—	+	+	—
Technical standards	+	+	+	—
Affordable and universal service	—	—	~	+
Social dimensions and inclusion	~	~	~	+
VoIP	~	~	+	+
E-commerce	+	+	+	+
Consumer, user protection and privacy	—	~	~	+
Unlawful content and access protection	—	—	~	+
Intellectual property rights	—	+	+	+
Cultural and linguistic diversity	+	~	~	—
Education and human capacity building	+	~	—	+
National policies and regulations	—	—	—	+
Legend: + probably feasible and effective, — probably not feasible or not effective; ~ unknown				

Given the need to find feasible solutions, a gradual transformation from the *status quo ante* is probably the most appropriate approach. Some issues, such as linguistic diversity, may be easily be delegated to decentralized actors. Other issues, which have high potential externalities, such as security issues, may have to be dealt with in a more centralized fashion, albeit with appropriate representation. Nevertheless, more issues than commonly perceived seem to be eligible for delegation to decentralized decisionmaking. This might even include numbering, as long as a unique framework for allowing the assignment of number to regions and sub-regions is agreed. With the increasing processing power of computers, increased diversity should not pose an obstacle. Proposals such as by McKnight and Mueller (2004) to gradually increase the number of top-level domain names, to introduce more market forces into the numbering regime seem reasonable in this perspective. The highest level of controversy will continue to exist with regard to content and political expression on the Internet. Whereas, the Internet has some elements of a disruptive technology, it is unlikely that it will fully undermine traditional forms of government unless supported by other political movements. In the spirit of remediability, it might, thus, be most advisable to organize a constitutional process to attempt to flesh out a global constitution for cyberspace. Should such an effort fail, it might be a second-best solution to let the Internet develop in a more decentralized fashion. Whereas, this might betray some of the original visions of this space, it would likely maintain a global communications platform of unprecedented reach and transformational power.

(Johannes M Bauer, Professor, Department of Telecommunication, Information Studies, and Media and Co-Director, Quello Center for Telecommunication Management and Law, Michigan State University, and can be reached at bauerj@msu.edu.)

References

Aoki, Masahiko. 2001. Toward a Comparative Institutional Analysis. Boston, MA: *MIT Press.*

Barabási, Albert-László. 2002. Linked: The New Science of Networks. Cambridge, MA: *Perseus Publishing.*

Bauer, Johannes M. 2004. "Harnessing the Swarm: Prospects and Limits of Communications Policy in an Era of Ubiquitous Networks and Disruptive Technologies". *Communications & Strategies* (54):19-43.

Benkler, Yochai. 2003. "Some Economics of Wireless Communications." In *Rethinking Rights and Regulations: Institutional Responses to New Communication Technologies,* edited by L F Cranor and S S Wildman. Cambridge, MA: MIT Press.

Cherry, Barbara A, and Johannes M Bauer. 2004. Adaptive Regulation: Contours of a Policy Model for the Internet Economy. Berlin, Germany: 15th Biennial Conference of the International Telecommunications Society.

Denzau, Arthur T, and Douglass C North. 1994. "Shared Mental Models: Ideologies and Institutions." *Kyklos 47*:3-31.

Dorogovtsev, S N, and J F F Mendes. 2003. Evolution of Networks: From Biology to the Internet and WWW. Oxford: Oxford University Press.

Frischmann, Brett M 2005. "An Economic Theory of Infrastructure and Commons Management." *Minnesota Law Review 89* (4):917-1030.

Hayek, Friedrich A von. 1949. "The Meaning of Competition." In *Individualism and Economic Order,* edited by F A v. Hayek. London: Routledge.

Hollingsworth, J Rogers, Karl H Müller, and Ellen Jane Hollingsworth, eds. 2002. *Advancing Socio-Economics: An Institutional Perspective.* Lanham, MD: Rowman & Littlefield.

Hughes, Thomas P 1983. *Networks of Power: Electrification in Western Society,* 1880-1930. Baltimore: Johns Hopkins University Press.

Hughes, Thomas P 2004. *Human-Built World: How to Think About Technology and Culture.* Chicago and London: University of Chicago Press.

Latzer, Michael, Just, Natascha, Saurwein, Florian, and Slominski, Peter. 2002. Sebstund Ko-Regulierung im Mediamatiksektor. Alternative Regulierungsformen zwischen Staat und Markt. Wiesbaden: Westdeutscher Verlag.

Lessig, Lawrence. 1999. "Code and other Laws of Cyberspace." New York: *Basic Books.*

Mathiason, John. 2004. A Framework Convention: An Institutional Option for Internet Governance: The Internet Governance Project.

Mathiason, John, Milton Mueller, Hans Klein, Marc Holitscher, and Lee McKnight. 2004. *Internet Governance: The State of Play: The Internet Governance Project.*

Mayntz, Renate 2003. "New Challenges to Governance Theory." In *Governance as Social and Political Communication,* edited by H P Bang. Manchester and New York: Manchester University Press.

Mayntz, Renate, and Thomas R. Hughes, eds. 1988. *The Development of Large Technical Systems.* Frankfurt am Main: Campus.

McKnight, Lee, and Milton Mueller 2004. "The Post-.COM Internet: Toward Regular and Objective Procedures for Internet Governance." *Telecommunications Policy* 28 (7- 8):487-502.

Mesarovic, Mihaljo, D Macko, and Y Takahara 1970."Theory of Hierarchical, Multilevel, Systems." New York and London: Academic Press.

Mueller, Milton 2002. "Ruling the Root: Internet Governance and the Taming of Cyberspace." Cambridge, MA: MIT Press.

North, Douglass C 1990. *Institutions, Institutional Change and Economic Performance.* Cambridge: Cambridge University Press.

Nozick, Robert 1974. "Anarchy, State, and Utopia." New York: *Basic Books.*

Ogus, Anthony 1995. "Rethinking Self-Regulation." *Oxford Journal of Legal Studies 15* (1):97-108.

Pastor-Satorras, Romualdo, and Alessandro Vespignani 2004. *Evolution and Structure of the Internet: A Statistical Physics Approach.* Cambridge, UK: Cambridge University Press.

Perry Barlow, John 1996. *A Declaration of the Independence of Cyberspace.* Davos, Switzerland.

Potts, Jason 2000. *The New Evolutionary Microeconomics: Complexity, Competence and Adaptive Behavior.* Cheltenham, UK: Edward Elgar.

Sen, Amartya K 2002. "Rationality and Freedom." Cambridge, MA: Belknap Press of Harvard University Press.

Swedberg, Richard. 2003. "Pinciples of Economic Sociology." Princeton, NJ: Princeton University Press.

WGIG 2005. Background Report. Geneva: The Working Group on Internet Governance.

WGIG 2005. Report of the Working Group on Internet Governance. Château de Bossey, Switzerland: Working Group on Internet Governance.

Williamson, Oliver E 2000. "The New Institutional Economics: Taking Stock, Looking Ahead" *Journal of Economic Literature* 38:595-613.

WSIS 2003. Declaration of Principles: Building the Information Society: A Global Challenge in the New Millennium. Geneva: World Summit on the Information Society.

WSIS. 2003. Plan of Action. Geneva: World Summit on the Information Society.

4

The Taxonomy of Internet Governance*

Jovan Kurbalija

More complex a field is, the greater is the need for its classification for conceptual mapping. Internet governance is a very complex field with its multidisciplinary, multi-national aspects. The paper explains Diplo's taxonomy of Internet Governance under five baskets—Infrastructure and standardisation, Legal, Economic, Development, and Socio-cultural. In addition, all the relevant issues associated with each basket were discussed in detail.

Internet governance is an example of a new and complex phenomenon requiring an initial conceptual mapping and classification. The more complex the field, the greater is the need for its classification. The complexity of Internet governance is related to its multidisciplinary character, which encompasses a variety of aspects such as: technological, social, economic, developmental, legal and political. There is both a theoretical and a practical need for an initial mapping of the Internet

* This paper is the summary of a research project on the taxonomy of Internet governance. The current text is open for hypertext discussion on Diplo's hypertext server. Hypertext-based discussion is one of Diplo's methodological tools. It is used in both teaching and research activities. One of its key features is that texts always remain open for comments and discussions. "Traditional text versions", such as academic papers and official reports, reflect the status of hypertext interaction at a certain point in time. This version of the text reflects hypertext interaction as of 16th February 2004.

Source: www.itu.int/osq/spu/forum/intgov04/vontributions/taxonomy/–internet_govern, International Telecommunication Union, March 2004.

governance field. With regard to theory, it is obvious that in spite of the recent growth in the volume of academic research in the field of Internet governance, a clear delimitation in this field of research is still lacking. The practical need for a taxonomy of Internet governance was clearly demonstrated during the World Summit on the Information Society (WSIS) process. Many players, including nation states themselves, faced a considerable challenge in grasping the complexity of Internet governance. A conceptual mapping of the Internet governance field should contribute towards more efficient negotiations in the context of the WSIS as well as other multilateral negotiation processes. This can be achieved through: 1) the clearer identification of the main issues; 2) the articulation of national interests; and 3) the reduction of negotiation "noise" caused by disparate interpretations of the main concepts. This proposed taxonomy of Internet governance is only a tool. It should not be regarded as being "true" or "false", but as just one of the possible approaches to organising this field.

Terminology

The term "classification" refers to a logical organisation of information, ideas and events. It is used to describe both the process and the end result. Another related term, used in our research, is "taxonomy". The word taxonomy derives from the two Greek words taxis ("arrangement") and nomos ("law"). The closest literal translation of taxonomy would be "the law of arrangement". The most developed use of the term can be found in biology. There, it is used to describe the classification of various plants and animals into various types. In our research, we use the term "classification" to describe the process and the term "taxonomy" to describe the end result.

Evolution of Research on the Taxonomy of Internet Governance

In introducing Diplo's taxonomy research, there follow a few comments about Diplo's overall methodology. Our methodology consists of three main pillars: training/education, research and development tools. First, in the fields of training and education, Diplo focuses on the requirements of modern diplomacy, emphasising Internet governance training. Second, our research addresses the question of modern diplomacy from a theoretical perspective. Third, Diplo develops practical ICT-based tools for diplomats, such as negotiation software and applications for the analysis of diplomatic documents. The need for the first classification of ICT/Internet issues was triggered in the preparation of our first course on ICT and Internet policy, held in 1997. The main aim of the course was to introduce diplomats from developing countries to ICT and Internet policy issues. The classification scheme was the basis of the course curriculum. Since 1997, six academic courses and a number of short courses have been held involving more than 200 participants, mainly diplomats from developing countries.[1] Course participants acquired both theoretical knowledge about ICT/Internet governance and practical negotiation skills. The practical training is implemented through a simulation exercise based on the drafting of global instruments for Internet governance. Since 1997, the initial ICT/Internet governance taxonomy has been adjusted through an iterative process based on feedback from students and experience gathered from the courses.

A new phase in the development of a taxonomy started in 2002 with the WSIS process. This research has been conducted in parallel with the WSIS process. Taxonomy research is one of three projects initiated by Diplo in the context of the WSIS. The other two are titled "Research on the Emerging Language for ICT Diplomacy" and "Research on a Multi-stakeholder Approach". The taxonomy research project has benefited from findings of the other two projects. For example, the language project provided useful information about document analysis and underlying rhetorical patterns. This information was used to identify the key classification concept for the taxonomy research.

Development of the Taxonomy of Internet Governance

Our research on the taxonomy of Internet governance consists of two phases: the creation of an initial taxonomy and a comparative analysis of other taxonomies/ classifications of Internet governance.

First Phase – Creating an Initial Taxonomy

As was previously indicated, the initial taxonomy is the result of Diplo's combined training and research activities since 1997. In order to construct an appropriate level of generalisation capable of accommodating all the specific issues, the field of Internet governance is divided into five main baskets: infrastructure and standardisation, legal, economic, development and socio-cultural. The term

The Initial Taxonomy of Internet Governance				
Infrastructure & Standardisation Basket	**Legal Basket**	**Economic Basket**	**Development Basket**	**Sociocultural Basket**
Technical Infrastructure	Copyright	Electronic Commerce	Digital Divide	Content Control
Technical Standards	Trademarks	Taxation	Technology Transfer	Privacy Protection
Content Standards	Labour Law	Market and Pricing Regulation	Financial Support – Public and Private Sources	Human Rights
Interconnection & Interoperability	Dispute Resolution – Arbitration	Investment	Migration – Brain Drain	Education
Domain Name System (DNS)	Cybercrime	Electronic Money	Access and Telecommunication Policy	Moral and Cultural Values
Security of Information System	Jurisdiction	Online Banking		Multilingualism & Cultural Diversity
Encryption	Digital Signature	Customs		Common Heritage of Mankind – Knowledge & Information on the Internet
		Data and Consumer Protection		

"baskets" was introduced in diplomatic practice during the Organisation for Security and Co-operation in Europe (OSCE) negotiations.[2] Since the taxonomy is used for a simulation exercise in multilateral diplomacy, the term "basket" is appropriate as a reflection of the real diplomatic world and its activities.

The Infrastructure and Standardisation Basket

This basket incorporates the basic issues related to the running of the Internet. A multilayer approach is used very often to describe the operations of computer networks. Professor Benkler has divided the Internet structure into three "layers": the "physical infrastructure layer", the "code" or "logical layer" and the "content layer".

The infrastructure and standardisation basket focuses on all three layers. It deals with the "physical infrastructure layer", which comprises all physical facilities capable of transporting digital signals, including telephone copper wire, fibre-optics and cables. This also includes non-physical media such as satellite, micro-wave and wi-fi. A special emphasis in the field of technical infrastructure is placed on the standards and regulations that facilitate the normal functioning of the global telecommunication system, which, in addition to other services, is also used in Internet communication. Most international standards and regulations in this field are managed by the International Telecommunication Union. The global management of the technical infrastructure will be increasingly affected by the liberalisation of the telecommunication market and increasing competition.

The existence of physical connectivity is a pre-condition, but the Internet "came into being" due to Benkler's second, "logical", layer, which controls the network. The cornerstone of the "logical" layer is TCP/IP and other Internet-specific protocols, which are grouped under the title of technical standards. Numeric addresses, handled by TCP/IP, are translated into familiar Internet addresses (e.g., *www.diplomacy.edu*) through the use of the Domain Name System (DNS). The management and coordination of DNS is one of the key issues of Internet governance. This issue gained even higher importance during the recent WSIS. The restrictive use of the term "Internet governance" focuses solely on the issue of the management of DNS and the basic Internet infrastructure. With the introduction of TCP/IP, the traditionally important question of the interconnectivity and interoperability of various networks became less important than in the past.

The third layer is the "content layer", which regulates the organisation of content and information. The World Wide Web "takes shape" on this layer through the use of HTML. The development of content standards is carried out mainly within the context of W3C.

The infrastructure and standardisation basket contains two additional topics: information system security and encryption. The increasing dependence of modern society on ICT and the Internet has led to increased vulnerability and potential risks. Particularly relevant is the vulnerability of the critical infrastructures of modern society, including electricity grids, transport systems and health services. As damage to these systems causes enormous problems and has high cost factor, hackers often target them. The question of information system security is identified as one of the issues in the taxonomy of Internet governance.

Encryption deals with the tools and other means necessary for the protection of data communications. The discussion on encryption has swung between two extremes. On the one hand, governments and others are concerned that strong encryption could be used by terrorists and criminals to avoid detection. On the other hand, restricted encryption protection—combined with excessive government control—will erode the right to privacy of information. Beside the privacy/national security dilemma, another facet is the linking of the need for stronger encryption to the development of e-commerce. With a growing number of financial transactions being performed online, the question of the protection of communication is of paramount importance.

Legal Basket

Almost every issue related to the Internet Governance has a legal component. Security, content control and e-commerce are all matters requiring legal regulation. A topic is placed in the legal basket if it is predominantly legal in nature. For example, various aspects are associated with cybercrime, including social values, security and e-commerce, but cybercrime remains primarily a legal concept. Similar reasoning is applied to the other topics found in the legal basket.

The shaping of a legal response to the development of the Internet is still in its infancy. The two prevalent views about the way in which laws should be adopted are listed below:

a) "New wine in old bottles"—there is nothing conceptually new about the Internet. Existing legal systems in the fields of telecommunications, intellectual property and jurisdiction could be applied to most issues related to the Internet.

b) "New wine in new bottles"—the Internet effectuates new social realities that cannot be regulated by existing legal rules. There is a need to introduce new laws—cyberlaws.

As is usually the case in such matters, the most viable option will be found somewhere in the middle. While many existing rules could be applied to the Internet governance, there is still a need to introduce new rules to regulate specific features of the Internet—especially borderless communication.

Knowledge and ideas are becoming one of the key resources of the global economy. Their protection is exercised through the system of intellectual property rights (IPRs). The most important IPRs for Internet governance are trademarks and copyrights. Trademarks are closely linked to the regulation of domain names. The Uniform Dispute Resolution Policy (UDPR) for solving trademark disputes in the field of domain names is an example of a multi-stakeholder initiative (WIPO, ICANN, ISPs) employing a variety of innovative techniques (arbitration, use of online tools). With the wide distribution of information, the question of the protection of copyrights has gathered additional importance on the international level. Copyrights have a variety of economic, social, cultural and developmental aspects. Copyrights are becoming one of the most important issues in the field of Internet governance.

Technology is developed to be used, but it is very often also (mis)used or even (ab)used. In general, cybercrime deals with the abuse of technology. While the "crime" part of the term has been clearly defined (e.g., theft, distribution of pornography), various opinions about the meaning of "cyber" do exist. Some authors argue that cybercrime is merely traditional crime committed via computers. Others argue that the unique elements of cybercrime warrant special treatment, especially when it comes to enforcement and prevention.

The relations between jurisdiction and the Internet have a built-in ambiguity. On the one hand, jurisdiction is based predominantly on the geographical division of the globe into national territories. Each national territory forms a state, with the sovereign right to exercise jurisdiction over its territory. On the other hand, the Internet has no such borders. The question of jurisdiction on the Internet exposes one of the key dilemmas associated with it: how is it possible to "anchor" the Internet in legal and political geography?

Although the question of digital signatures is classified in the legal basket it has many "cross-basket" aspects. First, it is related to the broader question of anonymity/authenticity on the Internet, which influences many aspects of Internet governance (cybercrime, taxation, etc.). Second, digital signatures are often used within a very specific framework of e-commerce as a way of demonstrating the authenticity of online transactions.

Dispute resolution on the Internet involves many legal issues. The main dilemmas are related to the two aspects of procedure (jurisdiction) and content (choice of law). The obvious limitations of using national courts (jurisdiction, slow and costly process) led towards the increasing use of arbitration. The dispute resolution mechanisms adopted in the field of domain names could be further used in other fields related to the Internet.

The observation that the Internet is changing "the way we work" is frequently highlighted. Some of these changes, such as teleworking, challenge some of the basic elements of labour law. The main challenge is the alteration of the standard routine of work, free time and sleep (8+8+8 hours). It is increasingly difficult to distinguish where work starts and where it stops. Changes in labour laws should reflect these changes.

The Development Basket

The history of human society provides many examples of technology empowering some individuals, groups and nations, and excluding others. The Internet is no different in this respect. From an individual to a global level, a profound change has occurred in the distribution of wealth and power. The impact of ICT on the distribution of power and development has given rise to many questions. Will the ICT-accelerated affect the already formidable development divide that exists between the rich North and poor South. Will ICT reduce or broaden the existing divide?

The key challenge of any development policy is to reduce the digital divide between those who have the access and capability to use ICT, and those who are either unaware or cannot use it for a lack of resources and/or training. The digital divide is not merely confined to the gap in technological access between the developed and developing worlds, but can also readily be found within developed countries across different ethnic and socio-economic groups. The digital divide could be reduced through the achieving of universal access. The ambitious objective of providing universal access is contingent on various developmental aspects including the development of infrastructure, education, changes of policy, etc. One of the problems related to universal access is the limitation of the last mile or local loop. How could home computers be connected to the local exchange or backbone? The attainment of universal access is also linked to the access and telecommunication policies of developing countries. Their lower levels of monopoly in the field of telecommunications could lead towards both cheaper and more efficient access to the Internet.

Developmental possibilities in many developing countries are limited by the "brain drain"—a movement of high-skilled labour from developing to developed countries. The loss to developing countries can be identified in many fields including: the loss of skilled labour and the loss of investment in the education of skilled labour. The rapid development of ICT has increased the demand for skilled labour in developed countries. Besides this development that could further accelerate the brain drain, there are possibilities that could reverse the brain drain too. Modern communication facilities enable many professions, especially in the service field, to be performed online. For example, many companies from developed countries have back offices in developing countries.

Transfer of technology is a traditional developmental issue that gained a new relevance with the development of ICT and the Internet. The core question is how should intellectual property rights (IPRs) be used in the context of transfer of technology. The link between IPRs and the transfer of technology is discussed within the context of many international initiatives and negotiations.

Financial support from both public and private sources is an important component of development assistance. Various multilateral and bilateral mechanisms facilitate financial support for development in the field of ICT. One of the key issues of the WSIS Geneva stage was the establishment of a fund that would facilitate ICT development.

The Economic Basket

This basket contains all the aspects of economic life affected by the use of ICT and the Internet. The core issue is e-commerce, which could be defined as the process of carrying out business transactions online. E-commerce takes three main forms: business-to-consumer (B2C) transactions, business-to-business (B2B) transactions and business-to-government (B2G) transactions. The US government highlights "the online commitment to sell goods or services" as the key element distinguishing traditional commerce from e-commerce. This means that whenever a commercial deal is concluded online it should be considered an e-commerce transaction, even if the realisation of the deal involves physical delivery. The potential for the fast growth of e-commerce on a global level depends, to a large extent, on the establishment of a proper regulatory framework that would facilitate online transactions. One important issue of the emerging regulatory framework is consumer protection. In the past, customers rarely needed international protection. With e-commerce, an increasing number of international transactions are taking place. This increases the need for international consumer protection. Payment procedures are the key to the faster development of e-commerce. Electronic money and payments should facilitate a more secure and easier transfer of funds. A further facilitation to e-commerce would be provided by the use of online banking.

The taxation of e-commerce transactions is one of the most highly debated issues in this field. One school of thought argues that that there is no difference between traditional and electronic commercial transactions. Thus, e-commerce taxation does not require special rules. Others argue that the taxation of e-commerce requires a special status of its own. On the international level, the latter approach has been adopted.

WTO introduced a temporary Internet tax moratorium, rendering international e-commerce transactions tax free. Besides taxation, customs are also affected by the development of e-commerce. The transaction of digital goods over international borders cannot be controlled in the same way as the transaction of material goods.

This opens many issues related to the applicability of the existing concept of custom control as well as the introduction of some new procedures.

The economic basket includes an additional two issues. The first is investment, especially the regulation of specific features of ICT-related investment such as venture capital. The second is the market and pricing regulation of e-commerce.

The Socio-Cultural Basket

The socio-cultural basket includes some of the most controversial issues in the field of Internet governance, such as content control, privacy protection and multilingualism. Perceptions of the socio-cultural impact of the Internet usually reflect national, religious and cultural differences. One of the main issues in this basket is content control. Content control initiatives are instigated for various reasons. The most controversial reason is controlling access to politically and ideologically sensitive information. Another reason for content control is related to the access of websites that could affect the moral and cultural values of a particular society. The last group of content control initiatives deals with the control of content accessed by children. Interrelated with some aspects of content control are various human rights, including the right to freedom of expression and the right to access to information.

Privacy, commonly interpreted as the "right to be left alone," is considered to be one of the most important rights of modern society. Information technology has provided powerful tools for gathering and analysing enormous amounts of information. These tools are used both by government departments (tax, social security, health, property, criminal records) and the business sector, which gathers assorted information about its customers. Privacy protection is gaining more attention on the international stage as was demonstrated in the recent data protection negotiations between the EU and the USA.

The global impact of the Internet has threatened many languages and cultures. The growing importance of English in Internet life requires concentrated efforts towards the protection of linguistic diversity on the Net. The protection of multilingualism and cultural diversity is becoming an important issue. The question of the common heritage of mankind comprising the knowledge and information found on the Internet also needs to be addressed.

Education is another important issue which is gaining international relevance. The Internet makes online learning possible. With the growing number of individuals participating in courses delivered via the Internet, there arises a need to address the international aspects of these developments.

Second Phase—Comparing the Initial Taxonomy with Other Similar Initiatives and Projects

In the second phase of our research, after making an initial classification, we compare various classification schemes and methodologies with our initial taxonomy. A survey of other projects and initiatives results in the finding that the majority of projects focus on specific fields such as development, cybercrime, e-commerce and the digital divide. The comparative analysis included the following sources:

International, legal and political documents. The main international legal document dealing exclusively with Internet-related issues is the Council of Europe Convention on Cybercrime.[3] Although they are not legally binding, the OECD Guidelines have a high importance too, most of them having been implemented in the domestic laws of member states. Most international official sources dealing with Internet governance issues are non-binding documents—resolutions, declarations and statements. Their international legal importance lies in their being considered a part of "soft law" or establishing practices that could lead to customary international law. These international political documents are adopted within the framework of the United Nations, regional organisations and initiatives as well as some global political initiatives such as G7/G8.[4] The most relevant international documents for taxonomy research are those adopted in the context of the WSIS process, including the final declaration, the action plan and the regional declarations. Most of these documents boast broad coverage, providing some elements for the conceptual mapping of the field of Internet governance. Our taxonomy research tries to identify the underlying classifications in those documents.

Research and policy papers. A second important source includes the various research and policy papers prepared as part of the various multilateral and research initiatives. The most relevant report for taxonomy research is the "Louder Voices", conducted by a group of experts within the framework of the Commonwealth Telecommunication Organisation and Panos Institute. One of the objectives of the "Louder Voices" project was to map the international decision-making structure in the field of Internet and international telecommunications.

Academic publications—books and papers. Internet governance is becoming an increasingly important issue in the academic field. Most publications are focusing on the issues related to the position and role of ICANN. For our taxonomy research, the most interesting studies were those covering a broader framework, such as Marcus Franda's book "Governing the Internet: The Emergence of an International Regime".

The underlying methodology of the academic studies is extracted in order to be compared with Diplo's initial taxonomy.

Information available on websites. The last source for the taxonomy research included the websites of organisations dealing with Internet governance issues. 53 websites dealing with some aspects of Internet governance were identified. This included the websites of the EU, international organisations (WIPO, UNDP, OECD, UNESCO, UNCTAD, WTO, the World Bank, the UN ICT Task Force, ASEAN and APEC), national organisations such as USPTO and various non-governmental organisations such as the Internet Society, GKP, GIPI and EFF.

Data from these four sources was collected, analysed and compared with Diplo's initial taxonomy, which is the starting framework for our research. The comparative analysis resulted in:

a) identifying the similarities between Diplo's initial taxonomy of Internet governance and other taxonomies/classifications;
b) identifying any missing dimensions in Diplo's initial taxonomy structure;
c) checking the validity of the overall taxonomy framework consisting of the five baskets (infrastructure-standardisation, legal, economic, development and sociocultural).

The first report on the Taxonomy of Internet Governance Project should be presented at the Global Forum on Internet Governance (New York, 25-26 March 2004).

(Jovan Kurbalija, Director of DiploFoundation).

Endnotes

1 The list of participants in the postgraduate diploma and short courses in the field of the Internet and Diplomacy is available at: http://www.diplomacy.edu/Edu/Alumni/map.htm.

2 The OSCE (initially CSCE) process consisted of three baskets: politico-military, economic-environmental and human rights.

3 The Convention on Cybercrime is open for signing. It has not yet entered into force.

4 Okinawa Charter on Global Information Society (2000), Report of the Digital Opportunity Task Force (DOT Force).

5

Internet Governance: A Regulative Idea in Flux

Jeanette Hofmann

This paper presents the Internet Governance as an open-ended collective process of searching that aims to fill the global regulatory void both conceptually and institutionally in a legitimate way in a phased manner. The author highlights that the major challenge for having a suitable Internet governance is to have a binding and legitimate regulatory capacity for a dynamically evolving infrastructure, amidst intensified conditions of transnationalism, partial deterritorialization and decentralization.

The Internet also presents new opportunities for dealing with the problems it creates.

– Johnson, Crawford, and Palfrey,
"The Accountable Internet: Peer Production of Internet Governance"

Although the term Internet governance has been in use about ten years now, there is not yet general consensus on its meaning. First of all, the concept "governance" and its relationship to government is unclear; second, it is unclear what extent and form of authority Internet governance has and in future should have. The concept became a popular catchphrase around the mid-1990s (Kleinwächter 2004a). According to William J Drake, Internet governance proved to be a "heavily contested concept ... from the very moment it entered into our collective lexicon" (2004: 123). Don MacLean also has described the "Internet governance question" as "very unstable and highly contestable on every dimension, ranging from the definition of key terms to the selection of appropriate forms of governance and institutional arrangements" (2004: 76–77). One telling indication of the political significance of this conceptually ambiguous state of affairs is the United Nation's establishment in 2004 of a working group to provide some clarification of these issues. Under the aegis of the UN Secretary-General, this working group has been charged among other things with ascertaining what precisely Internet governance encompasses and which public policy issues are relevant in this context.

One could argue that vague, ambiguous terminology is not unique to Internet regulation. Indeed, the production of collective frames of reference and ever-shifting meanings is a constitutive and, above all, continuous part of governance processes. "Anyone involved in governing, in whatever capacity or authority, forms images about what he or she is governing.... Even implicit images govern those who govern. Governing images are always there; however, they can certainly be (re)created and changed. During image formation, governing challenges will be defined and formulated as governing issues" (Kooiman 2003: 29). Thus, the unique aspect of Internet governance is perhaps not so much its vague and fluctuating frames of reference, as the speed with which and extent to which prevailing images, perceptions of problems, and the assumptions based on these images and perceptions change. Because Internet governance is still a very recent field of activity, it provides an ideal opportunity to observe the making of a governance arrangement. As I shall show, the prevalent understanding of Internet governance at any given time is closely related to its changing forums.

MacLean has advanced the theory that in the governance arrangements of international telecommunications policy, long cycles of diversification alternate with long cycles of consolidation. At the beginning of a phase of institutional diversification come the technological innovations—such as those preceding the development of the Internet—together with a political shift in thinking, like the one triggering the demise of the International Telecommunication Union (ITU) as the "single general-purpose forum for governing global electronic networks." As MacLean has pointed out, the outcome of these innovations and political repercussions is by no means certain: "The revolution in governance of global electronic networks … has created a global governance void within which a complex and confusing array of local activities take place without any overall coherence or top-down coordination of the kind formerly provided by the ITU" (2004: 93).

In this sense, Internet governance can be understood as an open-ended, collective process of searching which aims to fill a global "regulatory void" both conceptually and institutionally in a legitimate way. This void arose because the principle of sovereignty, which was an essential component in international regulation of the telephone network, has not been carried over to the Internet. Thus, the practical challenge in the current search for a suitable form of Internet governance is how to generate a binding and legitimate regulatory capacity for a dynamically evolving infrastructure, amidst intensified conditions of transnationalism, partial deterritorialization, and decentralization. So far, attempts to establish a stable governance arrangement have failed. Over the last fifteen years there have only been phases in which the transformation of governance structures has slowed down.

In view of the ambiguous structures and boundaries of this policy area, I present Internet governance in this article as a process of searching that has unfolded in several stages. The three distinct phases that I shall discuss in detail are characterized by their own specific spheres of activity, constellations of actors, policy agendas, and perceived problems. The first phase lasted up to the mid-1990s and can be described as the "technical regime." The main forum of this phase, the Internet Engineering Task Force, was the first standards organization for the Internet, and to this day continues to be the most important. In this period Internet governance was synonymous with the development of standards, and the organizational rules of the engineering community clearly set the tone and approach for other areas of interaction related to the Internet.

The second phase was characterized by the effort to institutionalize self-governance mechanisms on the Internet. Self-governance without direct government interference was seen as the appropriate solution for the proclaimed "ungovernability" of the Internet. The Internet Corporation for Assigned Names and Numbers (ICANN) could not, however, fulfill the high expectations placed on it and eventually initiated a reform process aimed at establishing a public-private partnership.

The third phase is presently—at the time of writing—in its formative stage. It has already become clear that this phase will also be characterized by a process of "forum shifting" and, consequently, a reconfiguration of the actors involved. The UN World Summit on the Information Society in 2003 emphasized the importance of Internet governance as a policy field. Developing countries, in particular, have expressed their dissatisfaction with the current governance arrangement and are demanding an intergovernmental solution for the Internet.

An examination of the different periods of this process of searching could possibly lead to insights into governance processes that extend beyond the Internet. The role and significance of worldviews in the development of governance arrangements are particularly important in this respect. As Jan Kooiman has observed, images constitute the most important frame of reference in the "governing process" (2003: 29). Changes to regulatory structures therefore become most likely when competing ideas or perceptions of problems no longer can be integrated or ignored.

1. The Technical Regime

Toward the end of the 1960s, when the first trial runs of ARPANET, the precursor to the Internet, were being completed, communication networks were operated in most countries as a state monopoly by the national postal and telephone administrations. Control over the development of communications technology fell to standards organizations, which basically are made up of the former monopolies and national suppliers (Abbate 1999; Genschel 1995). Because they faced no competition, the postal companies could model the architecture and functionality of the telephone networks on their own organizational structures. Thus, telephone networks became just as nationally and hierarchically structured as the companies that were running them (Genschel 1995: 46), and the international coordination of telephone networks came to be determined by the principle of sovereignty. The national operators are brought together in the ITU, a sub-organization of the United Nations, which resolves technical and financial questions of international importance by arranging agreements between sovereign states.

Unlike the public telephone networks, the Internet initially attracted hardly any state interest in its control or oversight. At the time, it had emerged as one of many data networks, and even into the early 1990s it was regarded as an academic toy by many experts from the world of telephones, a plaything that would soon vanish into thin air. In fact, if the European governments had had their way, the data network never would have attained its current status. The European postal ministries rejected the Internet because they preferred a different network architecture, one more similar to the telephone networks (see Abbate 1999).[1]

Europe's indifference and the United States' liberal market policy on data networks meant that the Internet was left to its own devices—or, more precisely, to the engineers who developed it. Up to the mid-1990s, its technical development and infrastructure management were for the most part in the hands of an informal group of engineers, which in the course of the 1980s had grown into the most important standards organization for the Internet, the Internet Engineering Task Force (IETF). If there was a generally accepted decision-making entity at all up to the mid-1990s, then it was concentrated in the technical authority of the IETF. What characterized the IETF was not only its technical know-how and eagerness to innovate but also its rather academic structure, which was intentionally fashioned as an alternative model to state and intergovernmental standards institutions. For a time even the ITU considered the IETF to be "one of the most successful paradigms of the post-industrial age" (Shaw 1999). The IETF was the only standard organization for the Internet until the privatization of the network infrastructure and the development of the World Wide Web (WWW) in the early 1990s. In hindsight, the governments' indifference gave the IETF unparalleled decision-making power.

The original management structure of the Internet was very informal and reflected the university setting in which it arose. The first experiments with the transmission technology characteristic for the Internet were carried out in the late 1960s at the University of California, Los Angeles. Up to 1992 the Internet had been a research network to which only universities and research centers had access. The technical standards as well as the namespace and address space of the Internet were considered to be goods in the public domain, which were to be administered in the interest of the entire academic community of users.

The informally organized Internet Assigned Numbers Authority (IANA) was the central authority in the administration of the Internet. Established under the umbrella of the Information Sciences Institute of the University of Southern California and at times financed through public funds of the National Science Foundation (NSF), the IANA administered the Internet's namespace and address space and also edited Internet Standards. At its core the IANA consisted of just one person, Jon Postel, who died in 1998. The only supervision of Postel's position—which by today's standards would be considered quite powerful—was of an informal nature as well. It resulted in large part from his function within the IETF, in which he played a leading role as one of its founders.

Unlike classic standards organizations in communications technology, the IETF is a private organization: to this day the IETF is an informal community without legal form.[2] There are not and never have been the rules on membership and national representation found in conventional standards committees. Each and every participant—in principle, at least—speaks only for him or herself. The IETF sees itself as a "meritocracy" that is based on consensus and a specific professional culture. The precondition for the acceptance of a draft standard is a broad majority, which is determined by means of communication and compromise in an open, public setting. As the IETF motto under the leadership of Dave Clark in the early 1990s declared, *"We reject kings, presidents and voting. We believe in rough consensus and running code."*

The Internet's pioneers eschewed the typical "telephone mentality" not just in an organizational but in a technological sense as well. Their interest in communications technology arose from a bottleneck in the development of computers typical for that time: the computing capacity which in the 1960s was costly and therefore quite scarce. Time-sharing systems made it possible for several users to simultaneously access one central computer, thus enabling more efficient use. The idea that became the basis for the Internet was to extend the time-sharing principle to real-time connections between computers over a broad geographic area. The networking of computers was to enable a virtual work environment irrespective of actual physical distance.

The idea of developing a special communications network for the transfer of data was not a new one. Telephone companies had been working on their own network architectures. The paradigmatic fight that broke out between the telephone world and the relatively young Internet community essentially revolved around a question that remains open to this day: Who should have control over the data flow, the network operator or the user?[3]

The architects of the Internet opted for a radical decentralization and minimalization of the network concept. At its core the Internet consists of an open, nonproprietary technical standard that defines how computers communicate with each other.[4] In accordance with the Internet's characteristic end-to-end principle, the control of data flow resides not with the network operator but with the users, or, to be more precise, with the respective applications. In the words of its creators: "The Internet, a loosely-organized international collaboration of autonomous, interconnected networks, supports host-to-host communication through voluntary adherence to open protocols and procedures defined by Internet Standards. There are also many isolated interconnected networks, which are not connected to the global Internet but use the Internet Standards" (RFC 2026).

The engineering community's motives for doing without a centralized control point were both technical and operational in nature. The decentralized network architecture not only promised greater system stability, it also reduced the amount of network administration required. The Internet Protocol thus constitutes a network of autonomous networks which delegates control over data exchange to the end user.

Outside the engineering community, too, the network's architecture was viewed as a major break with the principles of organization and development of modern infrastructures. Early generations of users were fascinated by the regulative implications and practical consequences of this decentralized form of organization.

The first wave of academic works on the Internet placed a great deal of emphasis on technological aspects. Many legal and social science scholars who dealt with the Internet in the 1990s studied its technological aspects in detail, because these were viewed as the key to understanding coordination structures of the future: "The Internet is built on a simple suite of protocols—the basic TCP/IP suite.... Like a daydreaming postal worker, the network simply moves the data and leaves interpretation of the data to the applications at either end. This minimalism in design is intentional. It reflects both a political decision about disabling control and a technological decision about the optimal network design" (Lessig, 1999: 32).

One popular belief (also held by members of the IETF) was that there is an equivalent relationship between technical architecture and social organization. The IETF emerged as a prototype for new "postgovernmental" forms of coordination: "Perhaps the best current example of 'nongovernmental governance' is the Internet Engineering Task Force.... Like the Internet itself, the IETF has no official governmental charter or formal membership requirements.... While it is not obvious how broadly the IETF model might be used to deal with other GII [Global Information Infrastructure, a project initiated by the US government] technical and nontechnical issues, it does serve as an impressively successful contrast to slowmoving, formally chartered international standards bodies.... More generally, nongovernmental governance may be the default scenario for the GII" (Baer 1996).

One quality frequently attributed to the Internet in the 1990s was its ability to undermine social hierarchies and state forms of intervention. At first, this aspect concerned the Internet itself. Its decentralized structure, oblivious of borders, promised considerable immunity against state or private-sector intentions to control it: "The very design of the Internet seemed technologically proof against attempts to put the genie back in the bottle" (Walker 2003).

However, users also experienced the sphere of digital communication as a place of incomparably great freedoms, against which political authority proved to be more or less powerless. In the mid-1990s, John Henry Barlow self-confidently proclaimed, "Governments of the Industrial World, you weary giants of flesh and steel … On behalf of the future, I ask you of the past to leave us alone. You are not welcome among us. You have no sovereignty where we gather" (Barlow 1996).

It was widely held in the mid-1990s that state sovereignty could not be effectively exercised on the Internet (see Hofmann & Holitscher 2004). One reason often named—in addition to the network's architecture—was the territorial constitution of political rule: the exercise of political authority necessitates control over a physical territory. Laws are valid only within clearly defined geopolitical boundaries, and the Internet basically negates such boundaries.[5]

In view of the lack of borders, uncertain identities, and locations in digital space, the only plausible way forward seemed to be to disallow the validity and jurisdiction of territorial forms of regulative authority with respect to the Internet. From the point of view of cyberspace, the end or death of "geographical tyranny" had moved at least within the bounds of possibility: "The Net thus radically subverts a system of rule-making based on borders between physical spaces, at least with respect to the claim that cyberspace should naturally be governed by territorially defined rules" (Johnson & Post 1997: 6).

The generally perceived ungovernability of the Internet, however, opened up the question of who or what could legitimately replace the regulatory authority of governments, the "weary giants of flesh and steel." If the Internet truly did defy traditional forms of rule-making, which actors, institutions, and procedures would be suited to replace a nation-state or intergovernmental authority? The growing international interest in the mid-1990s in appropriate forms of coordination for the Internet, marked the beginning of Internet governance as a research topic and a policy field.

The discussion about suitable forms of governance acquired both its empirical frames of reference and a certain degree of practical urgency through the transformation of the Internet at the beginning of the 1990s. After the US government withdrew its funding of the infrastructure, the Internet became accessible to private users as well. Explosive growth followed just a few years later. One reason for this growth was the creation of a new communications service that both simplified and considerably expanded potential use of the Internet: the World Wide Web (WWW). The WWW gave the Internet, which up to then, had been strictly ASCII-based, a graphic user interface. Moreover, it enabled new forms of presentation and visibility, which then made the Internet interesting for retail.

The WWW makes use of an element of the network infrastructure, that until then had played a rather peripheral role: the domain name system. Up to the mid-1990s domain names primarily functioned as a user-friendly mnemonic for the far from memorable numeric Internet addresses. As the Web spread, their meaning changed virtually over night. The IETF conceived of domain names as an arbitrary string of characters, whose ambit was to be exclusively limited to the Internet. They were assigned on a "first come, first served" basis, and claims of ownership to domain names were explicitly ruled out: "Domain names provide convenient addressing mechanism for people and machines to identify resources without having to remember long strings of numbers. Registration … confers no ownership or legal rights to the name beyond establishing the relationship for Internet addressing purposes" (Mitchell *et al.* 1997: 262).

Jon Postel defined the status of domain names in similar terms: "Concerns about 'rights' and 'ownership' of domains are inappropriate. It is appropriate to be concerned about 'responsibilities' and 'service' to the community…. The registration of a domain name does not have any Trademark status. It is up to the requestor to be sure he is not violating anyone else's Trademark" (Postel 1994). Domain names were viewed as a public good, and Postel appealed to the reason and morals of the Internet community—which was still small in 1994—to use this good in an appropriate way.

The WWW used domain names in a new way by utilizing them as "locators" of content. The unforeseen consequence of this addressing method was that domain names no longer primarily served the identification of organizations, but instead were discovered to be a way to designate any resources and individuals. The hierarchical utilization of individual domain names—the usual practice up to then—had become a thing of the past;[6] domain names were "promoted" to symbolic addresses and "became a big deal" (Oppedahl 1997).

One consequence of this "webification" (Mueller 2002) was a rapidly increasing demand in the mid-1990s for attractive domain names. Because there are only so many easy-to-remember domain names, they quickly became a scarce good that could fetch high prices: dealing in domain names became a lucrative business. The first legal battles over domain names began in 1994. Claims to trademark protection challenged the principle of assigning domain names on a "first come, first served" basis and thus, as well, its status as any arbitrary string of characters. However, in the mid-1990s it still was by no means decided that claims to trademark rights actually could be enforced with respect to domain names.[7]

The increased significance of the domain name system brought a number of different economic interests into the picture. Demands for effective, Internet-wide trademark protection stood in direct opposition to interests in a complete liberalization of the namespace. The differences between the two camps came to a head on the question of whether or not additional top-level domains (TLDs) should be created in order to satisfy the undeniable demand. Whereas trademark protection agencies were against an expansion of the namespace, "cyber liberties" groups and those selling domain names voiced their support for such expansion.

The dispute about the future of the domain name system revealed a power vacuum and lack of decision-making authority on the Internet. The growing pressure for a reorganization of the domain name system came to nothing because there was no institutional address for the requests of the parties involved. The engineers who had developed the domain name system, and to some extent still administered it, stood firmly by their conception of domain names and refused to recognize legal claims in protecting trademarks. But the more the Internet grew and the controversy about the right to domain names became an important issue, the more the IETF's status as a widely accepted arbiter eroded. In the dispute over future rules for the domain name system, the IETF came to represent only one of many competing special interests.

The call for a formal regulatory structure for the namespace which would reflect the transformation of the Internet both advanced and shaped the emerging discussion about Internet governance. However, it should be noted that the domain name system represented, by no means, the only problematic issue on the Internet. There was a serious shortage of Internet addresses in the early 1990s, necessitating a speedy reform of the existing allocation procedure. Moreover, the carrier agreements on data exchange ("peering agreements"; see Cukier 1998; Peake 2004) raised doubts about the ability of the market's regulatory capacity. Then, in the mid-1990s, there were already the first signs of "digital divides" within and between regions. Each of these issues could have become the catalyst for reflection on governance structures on the Internet—and shaped these structures each in their own way. Thus, the generally perceived need for action and the complete absence of authority should not be interpreted as self-contained "facts" that preceded the governance arrangement. Rather, both the choice of "problem" to be solved and the perception of this "problem" are constitutive elements of Internet governance.

Perhaps the most important assumption in early discussions on Internet governance was the notion that the Internet would generate a new kind of social space subject to its own rules, which would differ considerably from those of the physical world. "Global computer-based communications cut across territorial borders, creating a new realm of human activity and undermining the feasibility—and legitimacy—of applying laws based on geographic boundaries. While these electronic communications play havoc with geographic boundaries, a new boundary, made up of the screens and passwords that separate the virtual world from the 'real world' of atoms, emerges. This new boundary defines a distinct Cyberspace that needs and can create new law and legal institutions of its own" (Post & Johnson 1997: 3).[8]

"Lex mercatoria" became a popular analogy for conceptualizing this new form of spatial ordering. These rules had been developed in the Middle Ages in response to trade across territorial borders.[9] In allusion to this commercial law, Reidenberg (1998) proposed the legal concept of *"lex informatica"* for the Internet. One of lex informatica's defining characteristics would be that law and regulatory practices would not constitute the only source of regulation. Much like legal regulations, network architectures are able to enforce as well as obviate certain kinds of action and behaviors on the Internet: "Technological capabilities and system design choices impose rules on participants ... the set of rules for information flows imposed by technology and communication networks form a *'lex informatica'* (Reidenberg 1998: 553). Thus, the network architecture was regarded as an important element of Internet governance in two ways: On the one hand, it constituted the object of regulation, as, for example, in the case of the domain name system (DNS). On the other, it was viewed as a resource for governing conduct. What remained uncertain, however, was what conclusions could be drawn from a *"lex informatica"* for the generation of a political authority on the Internet.

There was widespread agreement on two points: first, that there is no predestined actor for governing functions on the Internet; second, that this task should not be left to either governments or intergovernmental organizations such as the ITU. As the OECD stated, "At present there is no consensus among the Internet community and all sectors of the Internet industry on how a governance structure will evolve for the DNS. There is increasing agreement that decisions over reforms to the DNS should involve all stakeholders and in particular industry" (OECD 1997: 6).

In hindsight, it appears that the negative attitude toward governmental "interference" in the "domestic affairs" of the Internet was one of the few—albeit fundamental—points of agreement in the conflict-filled beginnings of Internet governance. The modus operandi of governments was equated with hierarchy, bureaucratic slowness, and thinking in terms of territorial nation-states, and was portrayed as the antithesis of the unbridled and innovative Internet. "So while we believe that there is a role for collective judgments, we are repulsed by the idea of placing the design of something as important as the internet into the hands of governments," was how Larry Lessig (1998) summarized the Internet community's mood toward the end of the 1990s. Representatives from science, business, and technology denied governments the right, and above all the ability, to develop suitable and legitimate governance structures for the Internet.

The term "self-governance" became a counter-concept of the intergovernmental regime. "Self-regulatory structures" like those developed by the IETF—and which were springing up in a similar form in countless online communities—were thought to provide the most promising strategy for the future management of the Internet. Positive attributes of the self-governance concept included openness and inclusiveness, a bottom-up orientation based on consensus, and, in particular, decentralization of authority. Hence, all stakeholder groups would be permitted to take part in coordination of the Internet, and only decisions reached by means of consensus would have a realistic chance of commanding compliance. At the same time, centralized decision-making would be kept to the absolute minimum necessary.

The high level of optimism in the second half of the 1990s was reflected in the expectation that the Internet would give rise to lasting, sustainable alternatives to the governance practices of nation-states. The Internet's technical architecture seemed to guarantee that enforcement of the principle of sovereignty on the Internet would be impossible in the long term as well. The hypostatization of the network technology as a "countervailing force against the centralization and concentration in government and the mass media" (Walker 2003) became a key conceptual component in the understanding of Internet governance as self-governance.

As an idea, Internet self-governance enjoyed a strong base of support, particularly because it seemed to include all stakeholders—except governments. In practice, however, differences of opinion soon emerged with respect to the actual configuration of actors and the authority, objectives, and values of the organizational structure to be created.

2. Internet Self-Governance: The Rise and Fall of a Concept

In terms of time and objectives, the institutionalization of governance structures for the Internet was almost entirely determined by conflicting claims of rights to the Internet's namespace.[10] The IETF came up with the first initiative for the founding of a coordinating body for the Domain Name System which would also be acceptable at the international level. The authority over the Internet that had already been lost was to be regained through strategies of integration. The International Ad Hoc Committee (IAHC) was formed in 1996 and comprised representatives from standards organizations (IETF, ITU), trademark associations (WIPO, INTA), and a US federal agency (the Federal Network Council, or FNC). In its recommendations, the IAHC proposed a moderate expansion of the domain name system and itself as the new supervisory body.

This model, which would have given authority over the namespace to standards setting organizations and trademark associations, was rejected not least by the US government. One IAHC member—anticipating things to come—described the political defeat of the IAHC as the price to be paid for the Internet's success: "For the past decade or more we've been slaying the giants of old, preaching a new utilitarian form of technology.... But the price of such a victory is to become the mainstream of the technology industry, and the price, like it or not, is to recreate all the institutions and their associated ponderous weight and political awareness which we so vehemently criticized in a past lifetime" (anonymous; quotation in Shaw 1999).

In 1997, the US government decided to step out from the "shadow of hierarchy" and redirect further efforts to reform the domain name system to itself. Its first move was to announce that it wished to withdraw from oversight of the DNS. In a document from summer 1997 designated "Request for Comments,"[11] the US Department of Commerce (DOC) asked interested experts from the Internet community to give opinions and advice on reform of the namespace (DOC 1997). The first proposal for an "Improvement of Name and Address Administration" of the Internet followed in early 1998. In this document, the Department of Commerce announced its intention to hand over political supervision of the DNS and address space to a private organization that should include international participation but operate on the basis of California law (DOC 1998a).

The so-called Green Paper triggered a wave of criticism around the world. Many stakeholders interpreted the Green Paper as an usurpation of power by the US government in the face of an Internet community that had been managing the Internet relatively free of government involvement. In Europe, too, it was feared that "the current US proposals could, in the name of the globalisation and privatisation of the Internet, consolidate permanent US jurisdiction over the Internet as a whole" (Council of the European Union and the European Commission 1998). And it was not just the European Union that clearly preferred an intergovernmental organization on the model of the telephone regime for management of the Internet. However, a few months later, the US government presented a White Paper which defended the main features of the proposed course of action and made only minor amendments (DOC 1998b).[12]

According to the White Paper recommendations, the engineering community's informal supervision of the network infrastructure was to be replaced by a formal nonprofit organization, which would include international involvement, but be based in the United States. The private sector was to be given the leading role in this organization, though a reasonable amount of participation by other stakeholder groups would also be incorporated.

Governments, on the other hand, were to be kept as far from the Internet as possible. The language and line of reasoning in the US government's recommendations contained various references to the antigovernment discourse on Internet Governance: "The new corporation should operate as a private entity for the benefit of the Internet community as a whole. The development of sound, fair, and widely accepted policies for the management of DNS will depend on input from the broad and growing community of Internet users" (DOC 1998a). The White Paper set forth four general principles for the development of this governance structure:

1. *Stability:* The privatization of Internet management must not disrupt the reliability and security of the domain name system.

2. *Competition:* Network administration should be left as much as possible to market forces.

3. *Private, bottom-up coordination:* Coordination of the Internet should be carried out in a private-sector organization that reflects the grassroots governance tradition of the Internet.

4. *Representation:* The governance structure should reflect the functional and geographic diversity of the Internet. Mechanisms that ensure international participation should be developed (DOC 1998b).

The US government also specified the organizational structure of the corporation to be established: representatives from the various operations related to infrastructure,[13] representatives from trademark protection agencies, and commercial and noncommercial users "from around the world" should be integrated into the policy-making process. "The Internet community is already global and diverse and likely to become even more so over time. The organization and its board should derive legitimacy from the participation of key stakeholders.

Since the organization will be concerned mainly with numbers, names and protocols,[14] its board should represent membership organizations in each of these areas, as well as the direct interests of Internet users" (DOC 1998b).

In addition to the Internet industry and standards-setting bodies, Internet users now appeared to emerge as a third force in regulation of the Internet. Ordinary Internet users, not governments, were expected to represent the interests of society. The US government explicitly excluded governments from any decision-making responsibility; their participation was to be permitted only in an advisory capacity, as fellow users: "Restrict official government representation on the Board of Directors without precluding governments and intergovernmental organizations from participating as Internet users or in a non-voting advisory capacity" (DOC 1998b). With respect to inclusiveness and legitimation, the new organization was supposed to not only fulfill the demands of international organizations, but even surpass them—as individual citizens are only indirectly represented in international organizations through their respective governments.

In a Memorandum of Understanding in late 1998, the US Department of Commerce officially recognized the newly created Internet Corporation for Assigned Names and Numbers (ICANN; DOC 1998c). Prior to this, there had been negotiations lasting several months on the future structure and composition of ICANN, and a broad spectrum of interested parties from the private sector, technology, civil society, and international organizations had participated in this process. One issue had especially provoked irreconcilable differences of opinion: the relative influence of the various interest groups. The role of individual users and of governments had been contentious from the very beginning (see Hofmann 2004). The participating companies and standards setting organizations clearly would have preferred a self-regulatory model free of any state or civil-society involvement.[15]

Yet, in spite of these conflicts of interest, the organizational structure of ICANN that emerged in 1999 and 2000 initially appeared like a small wonder on the international policy-making scene. The agreement reached between the US government and ICANN called for roughly equal representation of industry and users on the Board of Directors. The absence of state authority was to be compensated by new, legitimizing forms of representation and consensus based decision-making. Moreover, in response to international pressure, a Governmental Advisory Committee (GAC) for governments and international governmental organizations also was established. The US government continues to this day to have a special role: it is a member of the GAC and at the same time oversees ICANN.[16]

The agreements between the US Department of Commerce and ICANN did leave one rather weighty question open: by what means Internet users were to decide on nine board directors in future. There were no organizations, neither within nor outside the Internet, that could claim to represent in any credible way the cultural and geographic diversity of users worldwide. After considerable delay and under pressure from the US government, ICANN at last saw no other choice but to establish a membership organization for individual users—the "At-Large Membership"—despite growing opposition among its own ranks.

Without a doubt, the creation of a transnational user organization as a step toward the institutionalization of regional and functional diversity in regulation of the Internet represented new territory. From the perspective of those directly involved, however, this task was confined to the next, most obvious goal of filling a number of seats on the Board of Directors: "ICANN faces the daunting goal of seeking a fair ballot, free from capture or fraud, from a potential electorate of millions of Internet users worldwide who have little knowledge of ICANN and little understanding of its mission, in order to select a high-quality board of technically-capable members" (Common Cause & CDT 2000). In a contested decision-making process within ICANN, those who supported a direct election of board of directors through voting over the Internet, won out.

The first and to date, only global election on the Internet, in 2000, ran quite differently than expected. One surprise was the number of people who voted. ICANN was largely unknown in the late 1990s, watched by only a small number of specialists around the world. Yet, instead of the expected few thousand voters, about 170,000 users registered to vote. The cause for the election's sudden surge in popularity lay in national rivalry for seats on the board. ICANN had divided up the Internet into five regional constituencies,[17] each of which was to elect one director. But what had been conceived of as constituencies based on world regions was soon undermined in some countries through national voting attitudes. Because the national majority among voters determined the chances of the respective candidates, there was a storm of voter registrations in the spring of 2000 (Hofmann 2002).

In the opinion of the organizers and many skeptical observers, the election of At-Large Directors was a complete disaster. One telling indication of this was said to be the number of voters (first criticized as too large, then as too small).[18] Thus, once the election was over, the question again arose of what the future role of individual Internet users within ICANN should be. The recommendations forwarded by a committee of top-ranking experts appointed by ICANN to specifically consider this question were not implemented (At-Large Study Committee 2001). The tripartite model of self-governance consisting of representatives from industry, technology development, and civil society, with some role for advisory participation by governments, had shattered by the end of the two-year term of the At-Large Directors.

With respect to its actual coordination tasks, too, ICANN was confronted with almost insurmountable challenges. It soon became evident that the conflicts surrounding domain names were no easier to resolve through the self-governance approach. In addition, cooperation with the various infrastructure providers also turned out to be extremely difficult. To this day, a significant number of operators of name and address registries refuse to submit their functions to contractual oversight by ICANN. And, finally, there was disagreement about the financing of ICANN. Because of these problems, ICANN failed to meet the conditions set out in agreements with the US government, which, in turn, were prerequisite for a complete privatization of its tasks. One telltale sign of this failure were the perpetual renewals and constant revisions of the Memorandum of Understanding with the US government. As one skeptical observer of the self-governance process asked, had it ever been realistic to think "that ICANN, an ICANN with no statutory or regulatory authority, will be able to implement and enforce decisions based on a belief that the Internet will be some idyllic island of private-sector cooperation?" (Shaw 1999).

In the third year of its existence ICANN initiated its first fundamental reform process. ICANN's president had presented an analysis of the organization's situation at the beginning of 2002, which bluntly and unceremoniously certified ICANN as dysfunctional. In his report, the president interpreted the source of ICANN's failure as a governance problem. ICANN's private-sector structure based on voluntariness and self-imposed obligations was, in his view, too weak to cope with the tasks entrusted to it: "If one thing is clear from the past three years, it is that a purely private entity that must depend on the voluntary cooperation of many other entities is not likely to be able to coordinate anything globally without significant governmental support" (Lynn 2002).

The role of governments in Internet administration became the linchpin in both the diagnosis of the problem and the suggested approach toward reform. The self-governance model had proved to be a wrong choice that now had to be replaced by a "true public-private partnership." Whereas consensus among stakeholders was the "driving notion" in ICANN's early years, effectiveness would now have to come to the fore. Ironically, ICANN hoped to gain authority and legitimacy on the Internet by ensuring a more active role for the governments it so recently had scorned. Three years of experience had shown, Lynn claimed, that a purely private model cannot work: "It is not workable because it leaves ICANN isolated from the real-world institutions—governments—whose backing and support are essential for any effective global coordinating body to accomplish its assigned tasks. Though many in the traditional Internet community react strongly against the very mention of governments, it is simply unrealistic to believe that global coordination of the DNS can succeed without more active involvement of governments.... What is needed at this stage if ICANN is to carry out its mission is neither a totally private nor a totally governmental solution, but rather a wellbalanced public-private partnership" (Lynn 2002).

Because ICANN was unable to gain the authority to act through consensus, governments were now supposed to step in and help establish some kind of order in the Internet's namespace. The concept of public-private partnership essentially called for a reapportioning of the relative influence of the various actors. The participation of individual users on the Board of Directors was reduced to a liaison function without entitlement to vote. The standard organizations voluntarily relinquished any further collaboration. In contrast, the role of governments was strengthened, though not on the scale desired by ICANN. In fact, governments rejected the role that ICANN had envisioned for them.[19] As Shaw has noted, governments have "their own machinery and processes to make mutually acceptable agreements—this is an intergovernmental context; it is not on ICANN's turf" (Shaw 1999). Indeed, the discussion about Internet governance did leave "ICANN's turf" and went on to conquer new, intergovernmental territory.

3. Internet Governance as a Multi-Stakeholder Process

In 1998, the year that ICANN was founded, the ITU took the initiative to organize a World Summit on the Information Society (WSIS).[20] The formal resolution of the UN General Assembly to have ITU organize and hold the summit followed in late 2001, that is, around the time that ICANN was preparing to announce its intent to give up the self-governance model. The first phase of the two-part summit conference took place in Geneva in late 2003.

The UN Summit on the Information Society shifted the discussion on Internet governance to a new organizational and thematic context, thereby opening up new perspectives on regulation of the Internet. World Summit conferences constitute designated UN territory; thus, governments are the key speakers and negotiators, whereas representatives from the private sector and civil society are only allowed to speak in circumstances specified by the "rules of procedure."[21] In contrast to typical Internet forums, developing countries enjoy strong representation among the governments at UN meetings. Two types of document constitute the product and practical terms of reference of the World Summit: the Declaration of Principles and the Plan of Action. These documents structure the activities of the preparatory conferences and form the discursive frame of reference for the negotiations.

The Summit threw a comprehensive, all-embracing light on the concept of the information society.[22] Contrary to the expectations of most observers, Internet governance proved to be one of the most contested topics in the preparatory phase. In particular, the prevailing equation of Internet governance with the administration of namespace and address space was questioned. Many participants called for a broader definition that would include issues such as Internet access, interconnection costs, cultural diversity, and the digital divide.

But the main issue of contention in the debates over Internet governance was the question of nation-state control over the network infrastructure. The organization of the Internet's administration in the form of a public-private partnership overseen by the US government drew especially sharp criticism. Many developing countries regard the Internet as an encroachment on their sovereignty, and thus demand greater leverage than the current governance structure provides.[23] In particular, they consider unacceptable the special role that the United States has created for itself in the coordination of the network architecture. A representative of China's Ministry of Information Industry, commenting on governmental negotiations during the WSIS, described the situation as follows: "This governance structure, whatever it refers to, ICANN or US government, is illegitimate. For ICANN, it is not an international organization and is constantly at the state of discarded, by US government, if it couldn't get the continued contract from US government.... Facing the fact that the Internet has evolved into a global infrastructure, there came the urgent need that all the concerned governments, including the US government, should govern the Internet in a collective and coordinated manner.... Today's governor is not the ICANN, nor the private sector, not the individual netizens, nor the governments around the world. It is solely the government of the United States" (Zicai 2004). Many countries share the position of China's government.

A large number of developing countries view ICANN as an exclusive organization dominated by wealthy industrial countries. Because they lack funds and expertise, they are excluded from any meaningful participation. In their view, a private governing body such as ICANN was acceptable as long as the Internet was in its early developmental stage. But now the Governmental Advisory Committee within ICANN is no longer seen as sufficient to articulate national interests. UN organizations such as the ITU would not only guarantee recognition of the principle of sovereignty, but also offer developing countries relatively greater opportunities for participation.[24] For their part, developed countries defended the existing governance arrangement. In response to demands for an intergovernmental solution, they countered with the "multistakeholder approach," which was becoming increasingly popular in the course of preparations for the Summit. In its current form this approach incorporates the private sector and civil society, in addition to governments and international governmental organizations.[25] The open, participatory multistakeholder approach, ICANN's supporters argued, complemented the Internet's tradition and structure better than any form of intergovernmental organization could.

The conflict between the governments over the most suitable form of governance concentrated on a passage in the draft version of the summit declaration which dealt with international problems. While it was easy enough to reach a consensus that the protection of public interests in connection with the Internet falls under the sovereign right of nation-states, no agreement could be reached on the question of jurisdiction with regard to international affairs. In the summer of 2003, a number of governments had presented suggestions on wording, which were included as "alternatives" in the draft declaration:

"[Policy authority for Internet-related public policy issues should be the sovereign right of countries.

[Internet issues of an international nature related to public policies should be coordinated Alternatives:

a) between governments and other interested parties.

b) through/by appropriate intergovernmental organizations under the UN framework.

c) as appropriate on an intergovernmental basis.

d) through/by appropriate international organizations.

e) through appropriate and mutually agreed international organizations.]]"[26]

Whereas the meaning of the five options was clear to all participants, the point that actually needed to be resolved, the "Internet issues of an international nature related to public policies," remained decidedly nebulous. The object of negotiation clearly was institutional jurisdiction, but the substance and scope of public policy issues remained vague. One reason for this indeterminacy is that the governments could not come to an agreement on a common interpretation of

Internet governance. The governments that associate Internet governance primarily with the tasks of ICANN do not see any impending encroachment on their national sovereignty. Those governments, however, that understand Internet governance in broader terms including communications services and Internet content rightly point to problems of sovereignty. In the opinion of one diplomat involved: "In Geneva, we accepted that there was a role for governments, but we were not really ready to discuss what we meant with these 'public policy issues,' in particular we were unable to spell out whether we were thinking about a narrow, technical definition, or whether we were referring to a broad definition, including issues such as network security, intellectual property rights, consumer and data protection" (Kummer 2004: 55; also see Kleinwächter 2004a).

Just a few days before the summit a tentative compromise was put together in order to move beyond the unyielding fronts of both governance camps. The substantive conflict was bypassed by means of procedures: "Delegations were firmly entrenched in positions that were diametrically opposed and it would have been overoptimistic to find a far-reaching solution. The only way out was to establish a process to deal with these issues and in order to reach agreement we had to concentrate on the modalities of the process we hoped to initiate" (Kummer 2004: 54).

The governments battled it out over the principle, political conflict, Internet governance, exclusively among themselves. Access to the working level of the Summit, the "drafting groups," was denied the "stakeholders" (including ICANN). Behind closed doors the delegates wrote, in contradiction to their own actions, "The international management of the Internet should be multilateral, transparent and democratic, with the full involvement of governments, the private sector, civil society and international organizations. It should ensure an equitable distribution of resources, facilitate access for all and ensure a stable and secure functioning of the Internet, taking into account multilingualism" (WSIS 2003a).

The reference to democracy here is particularly noteworthy: in this form, at least, it was new to the discussion of Internet governance. ICANN had always preferred terms like "bottom-up" processes, and previous demands for democratization were emphatically rejected. Yet now, even though it is not clear what exactly is meant by democratic, international management, this yardstick will have to be held up to any future governance models.

The process intended to reconcile the governments' contrary positions, involves the creation of a working group on Internet governance. It was formed under the UN Secretary-General—consensus could not be reached on any other option—and has been charged with preparing the ground for decision-making in the second phase of the Summit. The working group's mandate consists of three quite formidable tasks, challenging in terms of policy and technical expertise. First, it is to develop a working definition of Internet governance; second, it must identify the public policy issues that are relevant to Internet governance; and, third, it is to propose a common definition of the roles and responsibilities of the stakeholder groups in both developing and developed countries (governments, international organizations, the private sector, and civil society). In line with the multistakeholder concept, the working group is to include representatives from governments, civil society, and the private sector (WSIS 2003b).

Just setting up the working group proved to be an extremely long process, taking up more than half the total time allotted in the Action Plan. The process of forming the group, keenly watched everywhere, spawned a discursive life of its own, which in many respects seemed to anticipate the functions and responsibilities of the working group. A large number of international events took place—prompted by the announcement of the nascent working group—ensuring that systematic public reflection on Internet governance was set in motion even before the group began its actual work. The papers and other contributions that have been presented in connection with these events have already shown that the "common" understanding of Internet governance is once again in flux, and that a new phase of conceptual change is underway. In its future form, Internet governance will probably be embedded in more comprehensive regulatory contexts that have a direct or indirect impact on the Internet. Examples might be international agreements on trade and competition, guidelines on copyright protection, data privacy protection, and cyber crime, as well as national measures on consumer protection and the regulation of telecommunications (see MacLean 2004; Mueller, Mathiason, & McKnight 2004; Drake 2004; Kleinwächter

2004b). Meanwhile, the prevention of state interference—once the leitmotif of debates on Internet governance—has been quietly pushed to the side.

The forty-member Working Group on Internet Governance (WGIG) will present its final report in July 2005. The road leading up to this point has been rocky: WGIG members have depicted the current issues and state of affairs in about twenty broad "issue papers."[27] As its basis for an assessment of existing governance structures, the WGIG has now devised criteria for the conceptualization of terms like transparency, accountability, and democracy, as well as presented a discussion paper on the role of the respective stakeholders.[28] There are already indications that the administration of names and numbers on the Internet will be just one of many topics.

Overall, there are now signs of an expansion of Internet governance's frame of reference and, furthermore, of a reappraisal of the stakeholders in this field. This shift in emphasis concerns the role of governments in particular: state intervention is no longer automatically equated with the suppression of innovation and of freedom to communicate. Rather, one can observe an increasing willingness to reflect on the desirability and conditions of a more comprehensive form of political coordination for the Internet. Accompanying (but not preceding) this trend is a growing sense of urgency about the unintended consequences of another, less positive meaning of "unbridled" communications: the spread of spam, viruses, identity theft, and other forms of Net abuse are leading to a sense—in no way trivial in the context of Internet governance—that "unconstrained online interactions can lead to highly undesirable results. There are bad guys out there who do not care what effects their actions have on others" (Johnson, Crawford, & Palfrey 2004: 7). To the extent, however, that self governance runs up against the limits of its regulatory capacity, the traditional leitmotif in the debates on Internet governance—the prevention of state intervention—loses its power of persuasion.

Even if, in the development of Internet governance, particular attention has been paid to questions of process, one can in all certainty count on an intensified regulation of data traffic and communications infrastructure in coming years. In this light, the development of the Internet has turned out to be more similar to that of other communications infrastructures than initially expected. In retrospect, the diagnosis of the Net as "different" and ungovernable will probably be attributed in part to its novelty. Nonetheless, future governance structures could differ from traditional arrangements, particularly with respect to the relative importance of the principle of sovereignty and the role of nongovernmental actors. It is quite possible that an increase of state intervention will take place in the context of a "privatization of governance" (Zangl & Zürn 2004).[29] Up to now, at any rate, governments have been relatively open in terms of their role in coordination of the Internet: "Now we are at the beginning of a reflection process on how best to coordinate Internet Governance.... The Summit agreed on no more no less than the need to adapt traditional models of governance to the needs of the 21st Century and find new forms of cooperation which allow for the full and active participation of all stakeholders" (Kummer 2004: 55). Thus, the political challenge in coming years will be to establish institutionally safeguarded forms of participation that are capable of creating favorable synergies between legitimation and effective problem-solving, without recourse to exclusive principles of sovereignty.

4. Conclusion: Internet Governance as a Process of Searching

To observe the development of Internet governance is to follow an endlessly winding and intricate path of negotiation. As I have argued in this article, this process can be understood as a process of searching. The ever distant—and perhaps unattainable—vanishing point of this search process is a stable regulatory arrangement accepted by all sides, which can adequately accommodate the changing set of problems in transnational data traffic as well as the desire of stakeholders to be involved. Up to now questions of process have been front and center in this development. Regardless of whether it concerns oversight of the DNS, the allocation of Internet addresses, or the battle against spam, public attention is focused on the legitimacy of the respective claims to authority. In the collective struggle for suitable forms of coordination, the Internet has become an experimental domain where visions of transnational democracy clash with the rights of sovereignty reflected by the territorially defined nation-state.

The prevailing responses to the question of suitable regulatory arrangements for the Internet have changed many times over since the 1980s. Above all, this change reflects the growth and transformation of the Internet over this period.

I have differentiated three phases characterized by specific perceptions of the problems to be tackled, specific regulatory forms, and specific constellations of power and actors. The transition from the first to the second phase was instigated by opening up the Internet to private use: the private sector and individual users wished to have stronger representation of their interests in name and number administration. At the beginning of the third phase there are unmistakable signs of a certain disillusionment with the effectiveness of self-regulatory structures. Governments are referring to the public interest in Internet governance and are considering—not for the first time—proposals aimed at the internationalization of the central resources of the DNS.

One conclusion to be drawn from this development is that the ongoing transformation of Internet governance cannot be adequately understood as a reaction to existing governance problems. Rather, the perception and assessment of problems are themselves constitutive parts of governance arrangements. From the perspective of the IETF, the conflict over domain names in the mid-1990s represented at most a temporary sideline.[30] In contrast, ICANN's reading of Internet governance is so closely connected to the administration of domain names and Internet addresses that topics extending beyond it, like those playing such a visible role at the UN Summit on the Information Society, are systematically ruled out from consideration. Thus, definitions of Internet governance, either narrow or broad, always implicitly include preliminary decisions about institutions, constellations of actors, and forms of authority.

The option of strengthening intergovernmental authority is preferred mainly by countries in the southern hemisphere. Though industrial countries are critical of the United States' unilateral position, nearly all of them reject the notion of a UN solution. Thus, the ancient regime of telecommunications (Drake 1994), which left all international coordination up to sovereign states, seems to have come to an end. Its institutional successor, however, is still uncertain, and the process of searching might continue indefinitely. One interesting new facet in the discussion of Internet governance to emerge from the UN Summit is the question of democracy. The concept sets very ambitious standards for organizational structures, which neither UN agencies nor public-private partnerships such as ICANN satisfy. In democratic theory it is a contentious issue whether democracy can be practiced beyond the nation-state at all. Internet governance could evolve—in part by design, in part unintentionally—into an ongoing pilot project.

(Jeanette Hofmann is program leader for Internet Governance at the Wissenschaftszentrum Berlin für Sozialforschung (WZB) (Social Science Research Center Berlin) and conducts research at the project group "Kulturraum Internet" which she co-founded in 1994. She is co-coordinator of the WSIS Civil Society Internet Governance Caucus, and a member of the WSIS German Civil Society Coordination Group, providing representation to the German Government Delegation at the World Summit on the Information Society. She can be reached at jeanette@wz-berlin.de)

Endnotes

1 "X.25," the rival model to the Internet, defines a centrally managed network architecture for a uniform public data network; the architecture reflects nation-state boundaries. It would have given the postal authorities far-reaching control over the physical wires and the available communication services as well as the data flow. However, in its "First Computer Inquiry" the Federal Communications Commission (FCC) in the United States decided against public regulation of data transmission networks (see Oxman 1999).

2 Since its founding in 1992, the Internet Society has functioned as a legal umbrella for the IETF and also holds the rights to Internet Standards.

3 Paul Baran's work was particularly influential for the design of the Internet. Taking up a position opposed to the precepts of the telephone world, Baran argued that robust and reliable data transmission could be achieved by replacing the hierarchical structure of the telephone networks with a local and distributed system of loosely connected nodes. While the telephone companies viewed such ideas as heresy and fought against them, the US military found them interesting and supported the development of an experimental research network through ARPA, the Advanced Research Projects Agency.

4 More precisely, the so-called Internet Protocol specifies an addressing system for the identification of computers. In addition, it defines a data transmission process known as "packet switching."

5 The Internet operates on the basis of logical, not physical, addresses; there is thus no direct link between the address and the geographic location of a node. Moreover, the enforcement of state sovereignty is made that much more difficult because the identity and, hence, the nationality of users cannot always be ascertained.

6 Originally, domain names were used to identify universities and research organizations, which in turn delegated namespace to individual fields or departments.

7 In the opinion of the IETF, the domain name system was not designed to map other naming systems and, because of its flat structure, was not in the position to represent the product- and region-specific differentiations in trademark law. "As John Gilmore said, you just cannot pour ten pounds of trademarks into a one-pound domain sack" (Johnson & Post 1997: 88).

8 The working group "Kulturraum Internet," which ran from 1994 to 1998 at the Wissenschaftszentrum Berlin für Sozialforschung (WZB), also started out from the assumption that the Internet represented a novel place for interaction, distinct from the material world, which could be examined from an insider perspective (see Helmers, Hoffmann, & Hofmann 1998).

9 Because traders could not resolve their disputes by means of existing law, a new legal framework tailored to transactions across geographic boundaries developed, supplementing local law. Some observers assumed that a comparable development could be expected for the Internet.

10 The timeframe was already set by the approaching end of the monopoly on domain name registration in the top-level domains .com, .org, and .net, which the US company Network Solutions had turned into a lucrative business.

11 Among other things, a Request for Comments is the term for Internet standards and thus explicitly tied in with the communication rituals of the Internet community.

12 One of the few significant changes concerned the role that the US government assigned to itself. The US government distanced itself from its original intention to specify the structures of the corporation to be founded.

13 These functions included, *inter alia,* the Regional Internet Registries for the allocation of Internet addresses, the DNS registrars, the standards organizations, and the Internet service providers (ISPs).

14 A "protocol" is a term typically used on the Internet to mean "technical standards."

15 A list of founder organizations, including multinational corporations such as AT&T, MCI, and IBM, can be found in Mueller (2002: 166–172).

16 In addition, the US government is in charge of the authoritative root server, the Root Master File, and thus has the power both to set up and to delete Top-Level Domains (TLDs).

17 Africa, Asia/Australia/Pacific, Europe, Latin America/Caribbean Islands, North America.

18 According to ICANN's president at the time, the number of votes cast amounted to onehundredth of all Internet users. "These are not numbers which meet any test related to

democratic legislative elections" (Roberts 2001). However, representative voter participation among users on a global scale had never been the declared aim; it first gained acceptance as an assessment criterion after the election.

19 The governments did accept the offer of greater involvement and influence, but decided on the Board of Directors (and the responsibility connected with it) and against participation in the financing of ICANN.

20 Resolution 73, Minneapolis, 1998 *[http://www.itu.int/council/wsis/R73.html]*.

21 The definition of these circumstances is usually the responsibility of the first preparatory conference on the World Summit, which establishes the rules of procedure. In the case of the WSIS, the delegates primarily dealt with the question of whether or not the private sector and civil society should be granted the status of observers. The rules were later modified several times over the course of the process.

22 One of the strengths of the final documents is how they draw conceptual and normative links between areas that at first glance seem unrelated, such as the advancement of human rights and the development of telecommunications. The declaration stresses the effective realization of human rights as a precondition for the creation of an inclusive and global information society. It therefore became clear in the course of the Summit that a proper interpretation of the right to information and freedom of expression includes access to communication networks.

23 There is some truth to the impression of a loss of sovereignty through the spread of the Internet. In many developing countries, state-controlled telecommunications are an important source of income. New communications services such as Internet telephony (VoIP) threaten to bypass state monopolies. For that reason VoIP is illegal in some countries. The proponents of an intergovernmental regime for the Internet expect that a UN organization such as the ITU could devise an Internet equivalent to the international Accounting Rate System, which aims to ensure a fair cost distribution in international telecommunications.

24 Whether developing countries are in a position to make use of these opportunities for participation is another matter entirely. As studies on ITU's standardization activities show, it is developed industrial countries that normally set the tone (see Schmidt & Werle 1998).

25 In this context civil society is defined as a network consisting of nongovernmental organizations and individuals who actively participate in Summit preparations.

26 Whereas the United States wished to accept option A exclusively, many developing countries insisted on option B. The position of the United States was supported by, among others, the European Union, Canada, Mexico, Senegal, and Malaysia, though these countries also would have accepted option D as a compromise. Among the strongest supporters of an "intergovernmental" solution were Brazil, South Africa, India, and China (also see Hofmann 2003).

27 The "issue papers," the list of roughly forty "public policy issues" on which they are based, and the "clusters" derived from this list are available on the Internet at the WGIG Website: *[http://wgig.org/]* (accessed April 23, 2005).

28 All of these texts can be found on the WGIG Website.

29 The German term is Vergesellschaftung, which is not quite the same as privatization.

30 In the opinion of three IETF members, which was quite representative of the organization's position: "... it is at best unhelpful, and most likely destructive, to delineate the DNS as a central focus in discussions of the future of Internet governance and sustainability, to which we believe it is largely irrelevant" (Mitchell, Bradner, & Claffy 1997: 269).

References

Abbate, Janet (1999) Inventing the Internet, Cambridge, MA, MIT Press.

At-Large Study Committee (2001) "Final Report on ICANN At-Large Membership" [At Large Membership Study] *[http://www.atlargestudy.org/final_report.shtml]*.

Baer, Walter S (1996) "Will the Global Information Infrastructure Need Transnational (or Any) Governance?" RAND/RP-603, reprinted from *National Information Infrastructure Initiatives: Visions and Policy Design,* pp. 532–552.

Barlow, John Perry (1996) "A Declaration of the Independence of Cyberspace" *[http://www.eff.org/~barlow/Declaration-Final.html]*.

Common Cause & CDT (2000) "ICANN's Global Elections: In the Internet, For The Internet" *[http://www.commoncause.org/icann/icannstudy.pdf]*.

Cukier, Kenneth (1998) "Peering and Fearing: ISP Interconnection and Regulatory Issues" *[http://www.ksg.harvard.edu/iip/iicompol/Papers/Cukier.html]*.

Department of Commerce (DOC) (1997) "RFC on the Registration and Administration of Internet Domain Names" *[http://www.ntia.doc.gov/ntiahome/domainname/dn5notic.htm]*.

Department of Commerce (DOC) (1998a) A Proposal to Improve Technical Management of Internet Names and Addresses, Discussion Draft 1/30/98 (Green Paper) *[http://www.ntia.doc.gov/ntiahome/domainname/dnsdrft.htm]*.

Department of Commerce (DOC) (1998b) "Management of Internet Names and Addresses" (White Paper) *[http://www.ntia.doc.gov/ntiahome/domainname/6_5_98dns.htm]*.

Department of Commerce (DOC) (1998c) Memorandum of Understanding Between the US Department of Commerce and Internet Corporation for Assigned Names and Numbers *[http://www.ntia.doc.gov/ntiahome/domainname/icann-memorandum.htm]*.

Drake, William J (2004) "Reframing Internet Governance Discourse: Fifteen Baseline Propositions," in: Don MacLean (Ed.) *Internet Governance: A Grand Collaboration* (ICT Task Force Series 5), New York, pp. 122–161.

Council of the European Union and the European Commission (1998) "Reply of the European Community and its Member States to the US Green Paper" *[http://europa.eu.int/ISPO/eif/InternetPoliciesSite/InternetGovernance/MainDocuments/Reply toUSGreenPaper.html]*.

Genschel, Phillip (1995) Standards in der Informationstechnik. Institutioneller Wandel in der internationalen Standardisierung, Campus: Frankfurt.

Helmers, Sabine, Ute Hoffmann & Jeanette Hofmann (1998) "Internet ... the Final Frontier: eine Ethnographie. Schlußbericht des Projekts: Interaktionsraum Internet: Netzkultur und Netzwerkorganisation in offenen Datennetzen," WZB Discussion Paper FS II 98-112, Wissenschaftszentrum Berlin.

Hofmann, Jeanette (2002) "Verfahren der Willensbildung und der Selbstverwaltung im Internet – Das Beispiel ICANN und die At-Large-Membership," WZB Discussion Paper FS II 02-109.

Hofmann, Jeanette (2003) "Erfahrungsbericht über die Teilnahme an der dritten Vorbereitungskonferenz zum Weltgipfel über die Informationsgesellschaft (PrepCom 3) im September 2003," *Internationale Politik,* 58, 12, 103–109.

Hofmann, Jeanette (2004) "Der kurze Traum von der Demokratie im Netz – Aufstieg und Fall von ICANNs At-Large-Membership," in: Dieter Gosewinkel, Dieter Rucht, Wolfgang van den Daele & Jürgen Kocka (Ed.): *Zivilgesellschaft – national und transnational* (WZB Jahrbuch 2003), pp. 359–382.

Hofmann, Jeanette & Marc Holitscher (2004) "Zur Beziehung von Macht und Technik im Internet," in: Udo Thiedeke (Ed.) *Soziologie des Cyberspace,* pp. 411–436.

Johnson, David R., Susan P. Crawford & John G. Palfrey, Jr. (2004) "The Accountable Internet: Peer Production of Internet Governance," *The Virginia Journal of Law and Technology,* 9, 2–33.

Johnson, David R & David G Post (1997) "And How Shall the Net Be Governed?: A Meditation on the Relative Virtues of Decentralized, Emergent Law," in: Brian Kahin & James H Keller (Ed.) *Coordinating the Internet,* Cambridge, pp. 62–91.

Kleinwächter, Wolfgang (2004a) "Internet Co-Governance – Towards a Multilayer Multiplayer Mechanism of Consultation, Coordination and Cooperation," paper presented at the Informal Consultation of the Working Group on Internet Governance (WGIG), Geneva, September 20–21, 2004 *[http://www.itu.int/wsis/preparatory2/wgig/kleinwachter.doc]*.

Kleinwächter, Wolfgang (2004b) "Beyond ICANN vs. ITU: Will WSIS Open New Territory for Internet Governance?" in: Don MacLean (Ed.) *Internet Governance: A Grand Collaboration* (ICT Task Force Series 5), New York, pp. 31–52.

Kooiman, Jan (2003) Governing as Governance, Sage, London.

Kummer, Markus (2004) "The Results of the WSIS Negotiations on Internet Governance," in: Don MacLean (Ed.) *Internet Governance: A Grand Collaboration* (ICT Task Force Series 5), New York, pp. 53–57.

Lessig, Larry (1998) "Governance," Keynote speech at CPSR Conference on Internet Governance, October 10, 1998 *[http://cyber.harvard.edu/works/lessig/cpsr.pdf]*.

Lessig, Lawrence (1999) "Code and Other Laws of Cyberspace," *Basic Books,* New York.

Lynn, Stuart (2002) "President's Report: ICANN – The Case for Reform" *[http://www.icann.org/general/lynn-reform-proposal-24feb02.htm]*.

MacLean, Don (2004) "Herding Schrödinger's Cats: Some Conceptual Tools for Thinking about Internet Governance," in: Don MacLean (Ed.) *Internet Governance: A Grand Collaboration* (ICT Task Force Series 5), New York, pp. 73–99.

Mueller, Mathiason & Lee McKnight (2004) "Making Sense of 'Internet Governance': Defining Principles and Norms in a Policy Context," in: Don MacLean (Ed.) *Internet Governance: A Grand Collaboration* (ICT Task Force Series 5), *New York,* pp. 100–121.

Mueller, Milton (2002) Ruling the Root: Internet Governance and the Taming of Cyberspace, Cambridge, MA, MIT Press.

OECD (1997) Internet Domain Names: Allocation Policies, Paris *[http://www.oecd.org/pdf/M000014000/M00014302.pdf]*.

Oppedahl, Carl (1997) "Trademark Disputes in the Assignment of Domain Names," in: Brian Kahin & James H Keller: *Coordinating the Internet,* Cambridge, pp. 154–186.

Oxman, Jason (1999) "The FCC and the Unregulation of the Internet," OPP Working Paper No. 31. Federal Communications Commission (Office of Plans and Policy Federal Communications Commission), Washington DC.

Peake, Adam (2004) "Internet Governance and the World Summit on the Information Society" *[http://rights.apc.org/documents/governance.pdf]*.

Postel, Jon (1994) "Domain Name System Structure and Delegation" [*http://www.cis.ohiostate. edu/cgi-bin/rfc/rfc1591.html.*].

Reidenberg, Joel R (1998) "Lex Informatica: The Formulation of Information Policy Rules Through Technology," *Texas Law Review,* 76(3), 553–584.

Request for Comments 2026 (1996) "The Internet Standards Process – Revision 3," Scott Bradner *[http://www.ietf.org/rfc/rfc2026.txt]*.

Roberts, Michael M (2001) "Towards Improved Representation in ICANN" *[www.atlargestudy.org/roberts_paper.html]*.

Schmidt, Susanne & Raimund Werle (1998) Coordinating Technology: Studies in the International Standardization ofTelecommunications, Cambridge, MA, MIT Press.

Shaw, Robert (1999) "Reflection on Governments, Governance and Sovereignty in the Internet Age" *[http://people.itu.int/~shaw/docs/reflections-on-ggs.htm]*.

Walker, John (2003) "The Digital Imprimatur: How Big brother and Big Media Can Put the Internet Genie Back in the Bottle" *[http://www.fourmilab.ch/documents/digital-imprimatur]*.

World Summit on Information Society (WSIS) (2003a) "Declaration of Principles. Building the Information Society: A Global Challenge in the New Millennium" *[http://www.itu.int/dms_pub/itu-s/md/03/wsis/doc/S03-WSIS-DOC-0004!!MSW-E.doc]*.

World Summit on Information Society (WSIS) (2003b) "Plan of Action" *[http://www.itu.int/dms_pub/itu-s/md/03/wsis/doc/S03-WSIS-DOC-0005!!MSW-E.doc]*.

Zangl, Bernhard & Michael Zürn (2004) "Make Law, Not War: Internationale und transnationale Verrechtlichung als Baustein für Global Governance. Verrechtlichung und Vergesellschaftung als Elemente von Global Governance —Verrechtlichung durch Verfahren – Verrechtlichung durch Konstitutionalisierung," in: Bernhard Zangl & Michael Zürn (Ed.) *Verrechtlichung -Baustein für Global Governance?*, Bonn *[http://www.sefbonn. org/download/publikationen/eine_welt/ewb_18_einleitung_zangl-zuern_de.pdf]*.

Zicai, Tang (2004) "Core Issues for the UN Working Group on Internet Governance."

Section II

Principles and Models

6

Advocacy Position for Internet Governance*

The Global Knowledge Partnership (GKP) Executive Committee says that the initial stage of any negotiations on Internet Governance requires a mapping of the field, based on the following questions: What? (issues), Who? (actors), Where? (fora), and How? (methods). The article advocates some principles that should be actively advanced and well articulated, as appropriate, in relevant fora for the discussion of Internet Governance. It also suggests some Working Guidelines that should be used in Global Knowledge Partnership (GKP) advocacy on Internet Governance.

* The GKP Executive Committee has decided that GKP will not adopt a formal advocacy position and plan of action at institutional level on areas other than Multi-stakeholder Partnerships. The various thematic advocacy documents prepared by members and in consultation with members serve as input and a guide for GKP members to formulate a shared view on the issues and to embark on collaborative action based on shared interests.

– GKP Secretariat, May 2004.

Source: www.globalknowledge.org/gkps_portal/view_file.cfm?fileid=1943, DiploFoundation & Global knowledge, May 2004.

The World Summit on the Information Society (WSIS), held in Geneva in December 2003, officially placed the question of Internet Governance (IG) on global diplomatic agendas. The Declaration of Principles and Action Plan adopted at the WSIS, proposed a number of actions in the field of IG, including the establishment of a Working Group. Convincing answers to the following and related questions are expected: Who governs the Internet, if anyone? Which actors are likely to influence its future development? What will their policies be with regard to infrastructure, e-commerce, content, funding, spam, security, and other issues central to the emerging Information Society?

The initial stage of any negotiations on IG requires a mapping of the field, based on the following questions: What? (issues), Who? (actors), Where? (fora) and How? (methods).

WHAT: So far two main approaches have been taken to defining the scope of IG. The narrow approach focuses on issues concerned with the technical infrastructure of the Internet (infrastructure and standardisation). The broad approach adds policy issues. Together, these issues can be divided into five baskets:

- **Infrastructure and standardisation basket** (running of technical infrastructure, technical standards, content standards, interconnection and interoperability, IP numbers, Domain Name System (DNS), security of information systems, spam and encryption);
- **Legal basket** (copyright, trademarks, labour law, dispute resolution, cybercrime, jurisdiction and digital signature);
- **Economic basket** (electronic commerce, taxation, market and pricing regulation, investment, online banking and financial transactions, customs, data and consumer protection);
- **Development basket** (digital divide, technology transfer, financial support —public and private sources, migration—brain drain, access and telecommunication policy);
- **Socio-cultural basket** (content control, privacy protection, human rights, education, moral and cultural values, multilingualism and cultural diversity, youth, common heritage of mankind—knowledge and information on the Internet).

Work on the above baskets should be guided primarily by the following principles:

a) ensuring the stable and secure functioning of the Internet;

b) promoting universal access;

c) protecting public interest by promoting the Internet as a global public good and reducing its negative public aspects;

d) promoting development aspects of IG; and

e) preserving the free flow of ideas and knowledge on the Internet.

WHO: The mix of technical, legal, economic and social aspects of IG makes it very difficult for one group of players to govern the Internet exclusively, whether these are states, international organisations or technical communities. IG requires a broad and functional multi-sector approach. The legitimacy and implementation of decisions reached will depend on the level and nature of the involvement of various actors.

WHERE: IG issues are addressed on different governance levels (local, national, regional and global). The particular nature of the Internet requires adjustments to the traditional geo-political parameters of a state-centred system. Generally speaking, the Internet requires global solutions. However, many issues need more customised regulation on regional, national or even local levels, in particular culture-specific aspects of the Internet such as regulation of content and protection of children. The promotion of subsidiarity presupposes awareness and capacity building on all levels, especially national and local ones.

HOW: The IG negotiation process should take into account and possibly accommodate the various institutional and professional cultures represented in this process. The most critical aspect will be a convergence of the procedures and working methods developed by the founding communities of the Internet (e.g. IEFT, Internet Society) on the one hand and multilateral diplomatic circles on the other. The process of IG negotiations should also rely more on the use of online negotiations and consultation facilities. Online negotiations should broaden the number of participants in IG negotiations. It would also be appropriate to promote the use of the Internet for negotiations on Internet-related issues.

Internet Governance: Recommendations for the GKP Plan of Action

1. Advocacy

The following PRINCIPLES should be actively advanced and well articulated, as appropriate, in relevant fora for the discussion of Internet Governance (Working Group on Internet Governance, ICANN, ITU, regional meetings, etc.):

- Promote a development agenda as well as interdependence between IG and development issues.
- IG consists of a wide range of issues with different relevance for development. The IG survey should assign to each IG issue a development indicator specifying short, middle or long-term relevance for developing countries. The IG process should be guided by overall WSIS development objectives. One of the cornerstones of development assistance should be the promotion of universal access on the global level.
- Promote basic values and principles including the free flow of ideas and knowledge.
- The future IG regime should promote basic values and principles including the free flow of ideas and knowledge. Particular attention should be paid to technological and policy aspects of the promotion of basic values. For example, while technology should facilitate the free flow of ideas and knowledge, these principles should be clearly stated and promoted on the policy level. Technological solutions are not sufficient.
- Protect public interest by promoting the concept of the Internet as a global public good and reducing its negative public aspects.
- The Internet is a public/private hybrid. Both public and private institutions have contributed to the development of the Internet. With the growing involvement of the private sector in the Internet, the private/public sector balance must be protected, mainly through the more active protection of public interest. The main focus should be on promoting various aspects of the Internet as a global public good (e.g., easier communicaiton among people worldwide, contribution to economic development, socio-cultural empowerement) and reducing its negative public aspects (e.g., cyber-crime, spam).

The level of stakeholders' responsibility and contribution to the IG process should reflect their use and abuse—if any—of the Internet (for example: application of "the polluter pays" principle in the case of reducing Internet's negative public aspects).

The following WORKING GUIDELINES should be used in GKP advocacy on Internet Governance:

- "Do not re-invent the wheel": start from existing regulations and IG mechanisms.
- A clear understanding of existing global, regional, national and local regulations and mechanisms for IG is necessary. This understanding could be developed through an IG survey focusing on three groups of regulations and mechanisms: a) those invented for the Internet (e.g., ICANN); b) those that required considerable adjustment in order to address Internet-related issues (e.g., trademark protection, e-taxation); and c) those that could be applied to the Internet without significant adjustment (e.g., freedom of expression). The survey should also make a clear distinction between prescriptive and enforcement regulations. Prescriptive jurisdiction (e.g., do not distribute pornographic materials to children, do not commit crime) does not differ substantially between "real" and "Internet" life. The main differences exist in the enforcement of rules, given the particular nature of the Internet.
- "Do not fix what is not broken": maintain the current functionality and robustness of the Internet; yet remain flexible enough to adopt changes leading towards the increased functionality and higher legitimacy of IG.
- A general consensus recognises that the stability and functionality of the Internet should be one of the guiding principles of IG. The stability of the Internet should be preserved through the early Internet approach of "running code," which involves the gradual introduction of well-tested changes in technical infrastructure. The slogan "do not fix what is not broken" should be used more as a criterion for the evaluation of specific IG-related issues (e.g., introduction of new protocols, changes in decision-making mechanisms, etc.) than as general approach towards IG.

- Promote a holistic approach and prioritisation.
- A holistic approach should facilitate addressing not only technical but also legal, social, economic and development aspects of Internet development. This approach should also take into consideration the increasing convergence of digital technologies, including the migration of the majority of telecommunications towards TCP/IP based networks. The other side of the holistic approach is the necessity to prioritise dealing with particular issues by participants in IG negotiations. Neither developing nor developed countries are homogenous groups. Among developing countries there are considerable differences in priorities, level of development and IT-readiness (e.g., between ICT-advanced countries such as India, China, and Brazil, and some least-developed countries in sub-Saharan Africa).

A holistic approach and prioritisation of the IG agenda should help stakeholders from both developed and developing countries to identify topics of direct interest and relevance for them. This should lead towards more substantive and, possibly, less politicised negotiations. The stakeholders would group around issues rather than around the traditional highly politicised division-lines (developed—developing countries, governments—civil society, etc.).

- Increase awareness of the relationship between technical and policy aspects of IG.
- One of the main challenges will be to address the interplay between technical and policy aspects of IG in an appropriate way. It is difficult, if not impossible, to draw a clear distinction between technical and policy aspects. Many technical problems require a technical solution. Yet many technical solutions are not neutral. They promote certain processes, empower some groups and influence social, political and economic life. It is difficult to say where technology stops and policy starts or where they overlap. Ultimately this interplay will be managed not by clearly defined scientific rules but by the political process.
- Promote innovative negotiating techniques and the use of online tools for negotiation—“walk the talk approach”.

- The IG negotiation process will present a considerable challenge in multilateral diplomacy and global governance. The design of the process should address the following main groups of requirements: a) an open, collaborative, consensus-driven, bottom-up approach; b) effective participation of various stakeholders including the business community and civil society; and c) effective participation of governments and other entities from developing countries. Addressing these requirements will call for both the use of well-proven and efficient negotiating techniques and the introduction of new innovative approaches. One of the main innovative techniques should be the use of online tools for negotiations. Internet-based negotiations should facilitate the participation of a broader group of stakeholders, especially those who cannot afford to participate in traditional diplomatic conferences.

One priority will be to assist developing countries to participate meaningfully in the IG process. This assistance should include: awareness building among decision makers; training and capacity building; development of national institutional frameworks for IG, assistance in participating in a variety of international fora dealing with IG (e.g., ICANN, ITU, WIPO, WTO, Internet Society, etc.); establishment of an "Internet Governance Advisory Center" (a "one stop" center where stakeholders can find information about events, background information, and policy advice); and "just-in-time training" aimed at providing necessary skills and knowledge when they are needed – usually prior to important meetings.

2. Training

The need for training and capacity building in the field of Internet Governance was clearly stated at recent meetings on this topic (the ITU Workshop and the UN-ICT Task Force Global Forum). Training should address the following priority problems: a) the lack of awareness among decision-makers; b) the lack of understanding of the complex issues involved in IG; c) the lack of a coordinated multidisciplinary approach.

Training should provide an understanding of the holistic approach to IG, focusing on the five main IG baskets: infrastructure and standardisation, legal, economic, development and socio-cultural. The standard length of a training course should be five weeks (one week per basket), with the possibility of delivering shorter courses with more focused coverage. Training courses should make use of a variety of examples and case studies to help partsicipants make the necessary link between the overall context and practical problems. Most of the training should be delivered online.

3. Research

Currently most of the research conducted on Internet Governance takes place in developed countries, mainly the United States. Few studies address the development aspects of IG. Further research on development aspects of IG should help to create a better understanding of the role of developing countries in the IG process.

GKP-led research should focus on the following main questions:

- What are the IG issues of direct relevance for developing countries?
- What is the interplay between IG and development issues?
- How should IG and development issues be approached in the context of the WSIS?
- How can the participation of developing countries in the IG process be strengthened?

Research should be organised as an online collaborative effort of GKP-members, with the participation of researchers and students from developing countries. Research should result in the development of an "Internet Governance Development Portal", policy papers and a publication: "Development Aspects of Internet Governance".

7

WSIS, Internet Governance and Human Rights – Background Material

Johan Hellström

Human rights like 'privacy' and 'freedom of expression' etc., are fundamental aspects of Internet governance. Irrespective of the model that is adopted for Internet Governance, it should address the human rights issues to gain acceptability. The paper enumerates WGIG's (Working Group on Internet Governance) four Internet Governance models. It also highlights some of the Internet governance violations.

WSIS and WGIG

The first phase of the United Nations World Summit on the Information Society (WSIS) was held in Geneva during 10-12 December 2003. It addressed a broad range of themes concerning the Information Society and adopted a Declaration of Principles, which outlines a common vision of the values of an information society, and a Plan of Action, which outlines the steps that need to be taken (see Appendix 1 for more information).

Source: www.kus.uu.se, 2005. Collegium for Development Studies, Uppsala University.

Despite these essential commonly agreed principles, the first Summit failed to agree on issues concerning Internet governance. In order to come up with a solution on the second issue, UN Secretary-General established a Working Group on Internet governance (WGIG, sometimes pronounced "Wig-gig"), a multistakeholder working group including representatives from governments, civil society and the private sector. WGIG was asked to present the result of its work in a report "for consideration and appropriate action for the second phase of the WSIS in Tunis [16-18 November 2005]" (www.wgig.org).

> The WGIG report provides the following consensus working definition of internet governance:
>
> Internet governance is the development and application by Governments, the private sector and civil society, in their respective roles, of shared principles, norms, rules, decisionmaking procedures, and programmes that shape the evolution and use of the Internet *(WGIG, 2005).*

On 14 July 2005, WGIG released their report. Among the most difficult and political decisions discussed in the report are; 1) the identification of the respective roles and responsibilities of governments, existing intergovernmental/international organisations, the private sector and civil society; 2) the choice between the four

> **Upcoming Paper from Avri Doria:**
> **Human Rights and the Role of Civil Society in WGIG**
>
> Given the diversity of participation in the World Summit on Information Society (WSIS) and Working Group on Internet Governance (WGIG), and the participation by some governments that are frequently cited for Human Rights abuses, engaging in open dialog concerning Human Rights is difficult and often impossible. This has affected both the government and the civil society sectors of the WSIS throughout the process.
>
> With the recent refusal of the WSIS secretariat to grant the NGO *Human Rights in China (NRIC)* accreditation, the issue of human rights has again been brought into the foreground. Additionally there is evidence that the human rights situation in Tunisia, the site of the final conference of the WSIS, is worsening instead of improving as the summit approaches. While this is being discussed somewhat in the WSIS preparatory meeting, especially with the civil society caucuses, it is difficult to reach any ameliorative conclusions, because a great number of Tunisian government approved 'human rights' organizations and some governments impede the discussion whenever it is brought up.
>
> The paper will review some of the pertinent human rights issues and will discuss the events in the WGIG and the WSIS. The paper will also explore the current reactions and the possible reactions of northern states, civil society and human rights activists to events in the WSIS.

options for governance mechanisms that are provided and; 3) the decision to call for the creation of a forum for dialogue (regardless of the four models).

Four Internet Governance Models*

Model 1: Global Internet Council (GIC)

Governments as members; private sector and civil society advising

GIC consists of members from governments with appropriate representation from each region (and closely tied to the UN) and with involvement of private sector and civil society. GIC would take over the functions relating to international internet governance currently performed by the US Department of Commerce. It would also replace the Internet Corporation for Assigned Names and Numbers (ICANN) Governmental Advisory Committee (GAC).

Model 2: No specific oversight organisation

Possibly enhanced role for existing GAC

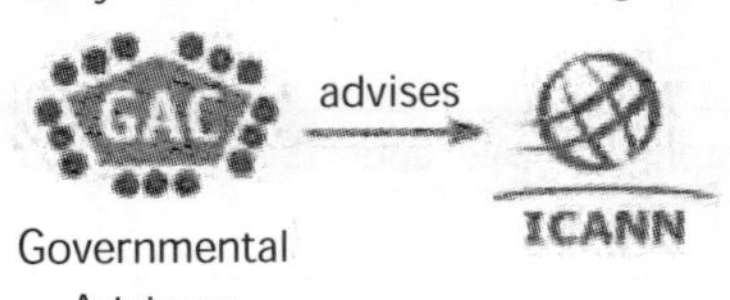

ICANN would stay in its current role (see Appendix 2) and even be significantly strengthened due to the general world consensus. This model would also mean an enhanced role for GAC. According to Mathiason, 2005, this model implies that there is no need for a specific oversight organisation since "everything is fine, and existing institutions can adapt to solve any remaining problems".

Model 3: International Internet Council (IIC)

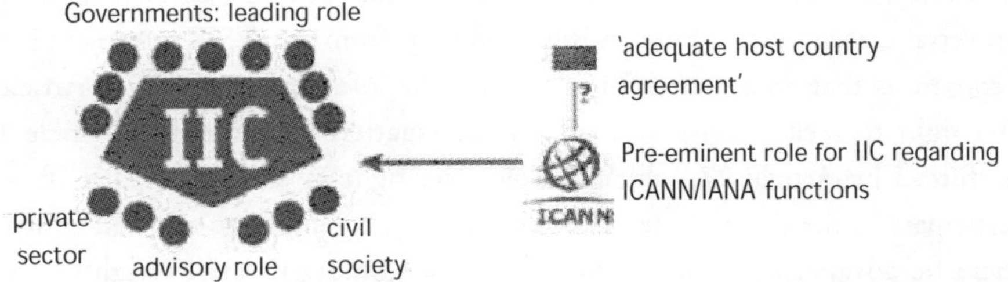

Given that no single Government should have a pre-eminent role in relation to international internet governance, an International Internet Council (IIC) would fulfil the corresponding functions for policy issues involving national interests especially in relation to ICANN/IANA (Internet Assigned Numbers Authority) competencies. This model would likely leave ICANN a purely technical body.

Contd...

Contd...

Model 4: Public Policy and Oversight Separated

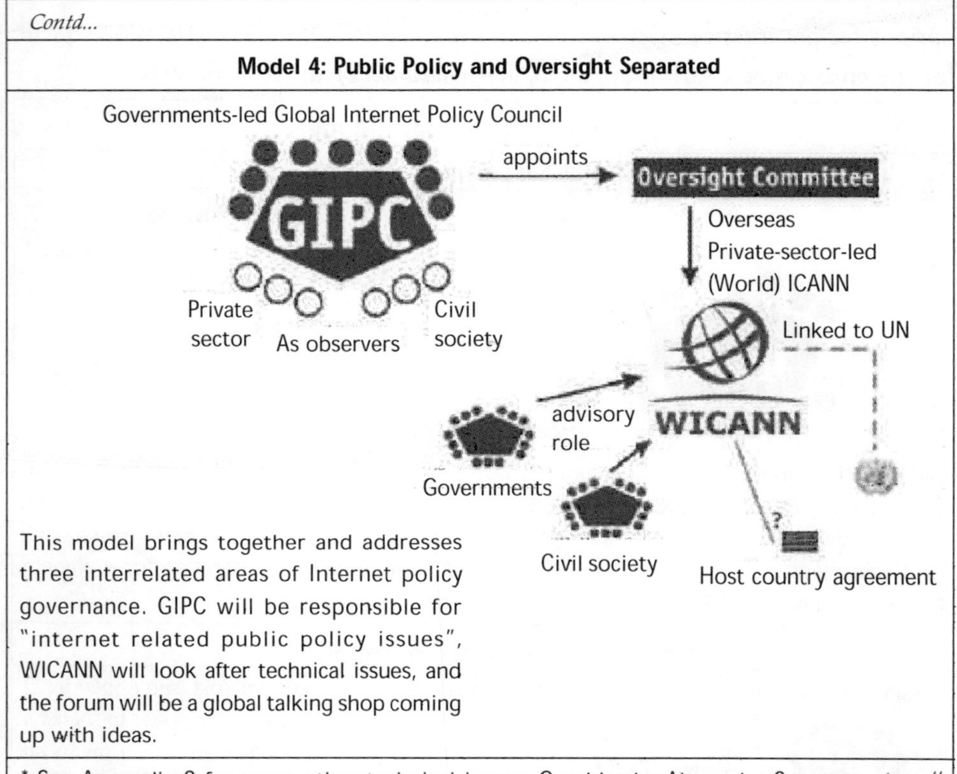

This model brings together and addresses three interrelated areas of Internet policy governance. GIPC will be responsible for "internet related public policy issues", WICANN will look after technical issues, and the forum will be a global talking shop coming up with ideas.

* See Appendix 2 for some other technical issues. Graphics by Alexander Svensson, *http://www.wortfeld.de/images/wgigmodels-02.pdf*

ICT and Human Rights

The right to freedom of opinion and expression was first proclaimed an international norm by the then-members of the United Nations in the 1948 Universal Declaration of Human Rights. Results from the WSIS agreement include a consensus that an essential foundation of the information society is Article 19. The right to seek, receive and impart information guaranteed in Article 19 is reinforced by Article 27, which upholds the right of each individual "freely to participate in the cultural life of the community, to enjoy the arts and to share in scientific advancement and its benefits" (www.un.org/Overview/rights.html).

As new information societies (yes, societies) emerge and new policy and legislation comes into effect, human rights must be at the heart of the WSIS. Alfonso Gumucio-Dagron, 2005, states that:

The digital divide issue and the access to new technologies of information and communication, which is presented as the main thrust of the information society, cannot be discussed outside the democratisation of society. We could hardly accept an argument that only values the expansion and generalisation of new technologies, outside of communication rights and freedom of expression.

Not only that the Internet is developed from a democratic tradition and hence embodies strong democratic tendencies, the Internet has become crucial for the flourishing of freedom of expression and, in a non geographic sense, of freedom of assembly (Article 20 of the Universal Declaration). The Internet promises enhanced capabilities towards living a better life and with access to ICT in general and the Internet in particular, informed people can, among other things:

- Promote good governance and include democracy
- Expose corruption
- Facilitate participatory development
- Expand access to information
- Support equitable economic growth
- Strengthen civil society through the building of networks among individuals
- Boost media capacity
- Enhance fast communication between individuals and groups.

Internet and Censorship (Chappatte, 2005)

Source: The International Herald Tribune, May 11, 2005

However, there are numerous examples of Internet governance violations. Two examples are Myanmar's (Burma) "cut-the wire" policy—limiting Internet access by strictly controlling physical links to the Internet—and China's great firewall ("Golden Shield") of censorship. China's strategy for blocking and regulate objectionable content on the Internet is highly controversial, and has been the object of strong protest and criticism, from outside as well as inside of China.

Ibrahim Moose Luthfy: Oppressive Governments and the Need for International Internet Governance – a Maldivian Example

Ibrahim Luthfy, the co-founder of the e-mail newsletter Sandhaanu, was condemned to life imprisonment in 2002. After escaping from police custody and fleeing to Switzerland, he obtained political asylum but is still one of the top most wanted persons to the Maldivian* government.

Sandhaanu made history in Maldivian journalism by creating the first and totally independent internet publication in the local language "dhivehi". Sandhaanu immediately obtained nationwide support and material from dissident journalists, intellectuals and the general public, and was therefore able to openly criticize the oppressive government. Because of the electronic format, Sandhaanu also reached the out-islands where the government controlled printed media did not reach.

Until May 2003, the national telecommunication company Dhiraagu, was the only Internet Service Provider (ISP) and had the exclusive right to provide internet services. In December 2003, the government opened up the Internet access sector to competition and Focus Computers, a privatelyowned ISP with its own international gateway via satellite, began operating. It is not clear why, but this ISP is following the government's internet censorship policy and the government continues its campaign to block independent and opposition websites.

In late 2000, a special Internet Surveillance Unit was set up at the police headquarters. It is believed that the unit is under the full control of the president, who is also the police chief. The government has also hired foreign experts and invested in expensive equipment, software and surveillance training in order to be able to trace and monitor the content of the e-mail messages passing through internet servers. A privacy law is supposed to protect e-mail but it is not respected. When it comes to cracking down on dissent, there is no law that can protect the privacy of internet users in the Maldives.

Although the Internet is under constant surveillance by means of sophisticated equipment and software, and although dissidents are severely punished for just expressing their views over internet, Sandhaanu fans have challenged the regime again. After an interruption of nearly two years, Sandhaanu was relaunched from Europe on March 11, 2004. In 20 days, the number of subscribers grew to 5,350.

* Maldivia is a nation consisting of a group of islands south-west of India

Is China's human rights policy an internal matter or should foreign governments and international organisations bother? And seen from an Internet governance point of view, should China be forced to respect the open nature of the Internet?

Two weeks before WGIG released the report, the United States Department of Commerce, National Telecommunications and Information Administration (NTIA) released the "US Statement of Principles on the Internet's Domain Name and Addressing System". The message is clear: the unilateral US-stand regarding the "control of the Internet", i.e. the 13 "root" servers, and its exceptional role as unilateral contracting and oversight authority for ICANN will remain. However, also WGIG is clear on this issue: "No single Government should have a pre-eminent role in relation to international Internet governance" (WGIG, 2005).

The US rejection of the WGIG report indicates that the Internet governance discussion at WSIS in Tunis will be tough. Despite the fact that the European Union wants to change certain things regarding Internet governance, the EU does not seem to be pushing hard for change or to confront the US. How should Sweden react? And how should Sweden respond to the fact that all of the four models on Internet governance call for an increased say by more governments, including countries known to favour strong domestic Internet content control, and other Internet related human rights violations? What do the four models of institutional arrangements suggested by WGIG imply in terms of human rights protection? Is there an inadequate comprehension of Internet technology in Internet governance discussions? Who should represent Sweden in the new multistakeholder forum (if it is created)? These are some of the questions that need to be discussed.

(Johan Hellström works in the Collegium for Development Studies, Uppsala University, Uppsala, Sweden and can be reached at johan.hellstrom@kus.uu.se)

Note: The Collegium for Development Studies is a unit within Uppsala University. The objectives of the Collegium are to facilitate cross-disciplinary cooperation on development issues as well as a critical and constructive dialogue among researchers and other development actors. www.kus.uu.se

References

Auerbach, K 2004. Questions and Answers About The Internet and Internet Governance. *URL: http://www.cavebear.com/rw/igov-qa.html*

Gumucio-Dagron, A 2005. Right to Communicate – From the summit to the people in Information for Development – *Human Rights and ICTs.* Vol. 3, No. 7

Lessig, L 2001, The Architecture of Innovation presented at the Conference on Public Domain, Duke Law School, November 10-11 2001. URL: *http://www.law.duke.edu/pd/papers/lessig.pdf*

Mathiason, J 2005. Where do we go from here? Statement by the Internet Governance Project, Syracuse University. URL: *http://www.wgig.org/docs/Syracuse-JULY.doc WGIG,* 2005.

Report of the Working Group on Internet Governance, Château de Bossey. URL: *http://www.wgig.org/docs/WGIGREPORT.pdf*

WSIS, 2003. Declaration of Principles – Building the Information Society: a global challenge in the new Millennium. URL: *http://www.itu.int/dms_pub/itu-s/md/03/wsis/doc/S03- WSIS-DOC-0004!!PDF-E.pdf*

WSIS, 2003. Plan of Action. URL: *http://www.itu.int/dms_pub/itu-s/md/03/wsis/doc/S03-WSIS-DOC-0005!!PDF-E.pdf*

General references to websites

http://www.un.org/Overview/rights.html

http://www.wgig.org/

http://www.icann.org/

http://www.isoc.org/

Cartoon

Chappatte, P. 2005. Internet and Censorship in The International Herald Tribune, May 11 2005

Graphics

Svensson, A 2005. Organizational models for global public policy and oversight, Version 0.2. *URL: http://www.wortfeld.de/images/wgig-models-02.pdf*

Appendix 1: An Information Society for All: Key Principles and Steps that Must Be Taken

The two documents adopted in Geneva; the Declaration of Principles and Plan of Action, set the parameters for the WGIG and contain its Terms of Reference. The paragraphs related to Internet governance and WGIG are mainly under the section *Enabling environment* (§48, 49 and 50 in the Declaration of Principles and §13 a, b and c in Plan of Action).

Key Principles	Action Lines
1) The Role of Governments and All Stakeholders in the Promotion of ICTs for Development	
Governments, private sector, civil society, and United Nations and other international organizations have an important role and responsibility in the development of the Information Society and in the decision-making processes	Develop national e-strategies and when implementing; take into consideration local, regional and national needs and concerns Countries should establish at least one functioning Public/Private Partnership (PPP) or Multi-Sector Partnership (MSP) International organisations should publish reliable information submitted by relevant stakeholders on successful experiences of mainstreaming ICTs
2) Information and Communication Infrastructure: An Essential Foundation for an Inclusive Information Society	
Connectivity and access; universal, ubiquitous, equitable and affordable; adapted to regional, national and local conditions, making greater use innovative technologies where possible. Establish ICT public access points in disadvantaged areas for ensuring universal access; in places such as post offices, schools, libraries and archives	Governments should support an enabling and competitive environment for the necessary investment in ICT In the context of national e-strategies; support technical, regulatory and operational studies by the International Telecommunication Union (ITU) and other relevant international organisations; address the special requirements of disadvantaged and vulnerable groups Design and produce ICT so that everyone has easy and affordable access Encourage the use of unused wireless capacity and the creation and development of regional ICT backbones and Internet exchange points
	Contd...

Contd...	
3) Access to Information and Knowledge	
Universal Declaration of Human Rights, Article 19 Removing barriers to equitable access to information for economic, social, political, health, cultural, educational, and scientific activities Preservation of documentary records Affordable access to software	Development and promotion of public domain information Promote research and development to facilitate accessibility of ICTs for all Governments, and other stakeholders should establish sustainable multi-purpose community public access points, providing affordable or free-of-charge access Promote awareness among all stakeholders of the possibilities offered by different software models, and the means of their creation, including proprietary, open-source and free software, in order to increase competition, freedom of choice and affordability Governments should actively promote the use of ICTs as a fundamental working tool Fostering worldwide cooperation between libraries
4) Capacity Building	
Literacy and universal primary education, so that each person has the opportunity to acquire the necessary skills and knowledge in order to understand, participate actively in, benefit fully and see the new opportunities offered by ICTs Major factors in determining development and competitiveness, i.e. positive integration into the knowledge economy, depends largely on increased capacity building in the areas of education, technology know-how and access to information	Develop domestic policies to integrate ICTs in education and training at all levels Designing and offering courses for public administration, taking advantage of existing facilities such as libraries, multipurpose community centres, public access points Develop pilot projects to demonstrate the impact of ICT based alternative educational delivery systems Promoting equal training opportunities in ICT-related fields for women and girls Training of teachers should focus on the technical aspects of ICTs, on development of content, and on the potential possibilities and challenges of ICTs. Activate volunteer programmes to provide capacity building on ICT for development
	Contd...

Contd...	
5) Building Confidence and Security in the use of ICTs	
Strengthen the trust framework, prevent the use of information resources and technologies for criminal and terrorist purposes, while respecting human rights	Promote cooperation among the governments at the United Nations and with all stakeholders to; prevent, detect and respond to cyber-crime; promote user education and awareness
6) Enabling Environment	
ICTs should be used as an important tool for good governance Existence of a policy and regulatory framework Improving global affordable connectivity, intellectual property issues, and knowledge sharing Development and adoption of international standards (like radio frequency spectrum) Secure, safe and healthy working environment 48. ... The international management of the Internet should be multilateral, transparent and democratic, with the full involvement of governments, the private sector, civil society and international organizations. It should ensure an equitable distribution of resources, facilitate access for all and ensure a stable and secure functioning of the Internet, taking into account multilingualism. 49. The management of the Internet encompasses both technical and public policy issues and should involve all stakeholders and relevant intergovernmental and international organizations. In this respect it is recognized that: a) Policy authority for Internet-related public policy issues is the sovereign right of States. They have rights and responsibilities for international Internet-related public policy issues;	13. To maximize the social, economic and environmental benefits of the Information Society, governments need to create a trustworthy, transparent and non-discriminatory legal, regulatory and policy environment. Actions include: a) Governments should foster a supportive, transparent, procompetitive and predictable policy, legal and regulatory framework, which provides the appropriate incentives to investment and community development in the Information Society. b) We ask the Secretary General of the United Nations to set up a working group on Internet governance, in an open and inclusive process that ensures a mechanism for the full and active participation of governments, the private sector and civil society from both developing and developed countries, involving relevant intergovernmental and international organizations and forums, to investigate and make proposals for action, as appropriate, on the governance of Internet by 2005. The group should, *inter alia:* i) develop a working definition of Internet governance; ii) identify the public policy issues that are relevant to Internet governance; iii) develop a common understanding of the respective roles and responsibilities of
	Contd...

Contd...	
b) The private sector has had and should continue to have an important role in the development of the Internet, both in the technical and economic fields; c) Civil society has also played an important role on Internet matters, especially at community level, and should continue to play such a role; d) Intergovernmental organizations have had and should continue to have a facilitating role in the coordination of Internet-related public policy issues; e) International organizations have also had and should continue to have an important role in the development of Internet-related technical standards and relevant policies. 50. ... We ask the Secretary-General of the United Nations to set up a working group on Internet governance, in an open and inclusive process that ensures a mechanism for the full and active participation of governments, the private sector and civil society from both developing and developed countries, involving relevant intergovernmental and international organizations and forums, to investigate and make proposals for action, as appropriate, on the governance of Internet by 2005.	governments, existing intergovernmental and international organisations and other forums as well as the private sector and civil society from both developing and developed countries; iv) prepare a report on the results of this activity to be presented for consideration and appropriate action for the second phase of WSIS in Tunis in 2005. c) Governments are invited to: i) facilitate the establishment of national and regional Internet Exchange Centres; ii) manage or supervise, as appropriate, their respective country code top-level domain name (ccTLD); iii) promote awareness of the Internet. ITU and other regional organisations to ensure rational, efficient and economical use of, and equitable access to, the radio-frequency spectrum by all countries, based on relevant international agreements
7) ICT Applications: Benefits in All Aspects of Life	
ICTs should create benefits and sustainable production and consumption patterns	Promote the use, existence, and benefits of e-government, e-business, e-learning, e-health, e-employment, e-environment, e-agriculture, and e-science
8) Cultural Diversity and Identity, Linguistic Diversity and Local Content	
Promotion, affirmation and preservation of diverse cultural identities and languages as reflected in relevant agreed United Nations	Develop local cultural industries suited to the linguistic and cultural context of the users
	Contd...

Contd...	
documents including UNESCO's Universal Declaration on Cultural Diversity Creation, dissemination and preservation of content in diverse languages and formats, including people living in rural, remote and marginal areas	Support local content development, translation and adaptation, digital archives, and diverse forms of digital and traditional media by local authorities
9) Media	
Commitment to the principles of freedom of the press and freedom of information, as well as those of the independence, pluralism and diversity of media, which are essential to the Information Society. Freedom to seek, receive, impart and use information for the creation, accumulation and dissemination of knowledge are important to the Information Society	Encourage the media—print and broadcast as well as new media—to continue to play an important role in the Information Society Encourage traditional media to bridge the knowledge divide and to facilitate the flow of cultural content
10) Ethical Dimensions of the Information Society	
Respect peace and uphold the fundamental values of freedom, equality, solidarity, tolerance, shared responsibility, and respect for nature Use of ICTs and content creation should respect human rights	Promote the common good, protect privacy and personal data and take appropriate actions and preventive measures, as determined by law, against abusive uses of ICTs such as illegal and other acts
11) International and Regional Cooperation	
The worldwide agreed objective is to contribute to bridge the digital divide, promote access to ICTs, create digital opportunities, and benefit from the potential offered by ICTs for development. Core competences of the International Telecommunication Union (ITU) are of crucial importance	International cooperation among all stakeholders is vital in implementation of this plan of action and needs to be strengthened with a view to promoting universal access and bridging the digital divide, *inter alia,* by provision of means of implementation.
Source: WSIS, 2003.	

Appendix 2: Technical Issues

In general, public policy matters are the responsibility of governments. However, considering the complexity of the Internet governance issue, policy discussions must also include the active part of private sector and civil society.

There are several private sector led organisations that play a critical role in the technical coordination of the Internet including:

- Internet Architecture Board (IAB), *http://www.iab.org/*
- Internet Engineering Steering Group (IESG), *http://www.ietf.org/iesg.html*
- Internet Engineering Task Force (IETF), *http://www.ietf.org/*
- Internet Corporation for Assigned Names and Numbers (ICANN), *http://www.icann.org/*

The Internet SOCiety (ISOC) is a "professional membership society with more than 100 organizations and over 20,000 individual members in over 180 countries. It provides leadership in addressing issues that confront the future of the Internet, and is the organization home for the groups responsible for Internet infrastructure standards, including the Internet Engineering Task Force (IETF) and the Internet Architecture Board (IAB)." *(http://www.isoc.org/)*

The ICANN is an "internationally organized, non-profit corporation that has responsibility for Internet Protocol (IP) address space allocation, protocol identifier assignment, generic (gTLD) and country code (ccTLD) Top-Level Domain name system management, and root server system management functions. These services were originally performed under US Government contract by the Internet Assigned Numbers Authority (IANA) and other entities. ICANN now performs the IANA function." *(http://www.icann.org/general/)*

Governments provide advice to ICANN through the Governmental Advisory Committee (GAC). *(http://gac.icann.org/)*

Infrastructure

The Internet is a "layered" system and layers are crucial for the understanding of the Internet infrastructure. However, for the purpose of the Internet Governance debate, Lawrence Lessig's three-layer model will do (Lessig, 2001):

1) At the bottom, the physical layer; computers and the wires that link them; mostly private property

2) On top of the physical layer is the logical (code) layer; the set of protocols; commons

3) Content layer; material; both free and controlled (copyright protected).

Karl Auerbach, 2004, states that:

"Many people consider services and applications such as the World Wide Web (WWW), Voice Over IP (VOIP), and the Domain Name System (DNS) to be part of the Internet. One may, however, consider them as layered-on services and applications rather than mechanisms that are necessarily embedded into the core of the Internet. Clarity of thought regarding matters of Internet governance may be enhanced by considering these services as distinct applications and not part of the core Internet."

Human Rights and Internet Governance

– Meryem Marzouki and Rikke Frank Jørgensen

We welcome the creation of a global Internet governance forum, and hope for this forum to contribute to greater awareness of the urgent need to respect and protect international human rights standards in a number of policy areas related to Internet. We wish to stress the importance of creating an inclusive, non-discriminatory, and transparent discussion space, with real means of civil society participation not least from the developing countries. We also recognise a need for greater human rights awareness and capacity building across the many issue-specific arenas of Internet policies, which currently exist.

We wish however to remind that the tendency to address any Internet related policy aspect within the framework of Internet governance may result in a lawless zone escaping international human rights protection and diluting responsibility and accountability of States towards their citizens.

Throughout the WSIS process it was time and again reaffirmed that the information society must foster and protect human rights as stipulated in the Universal Declaration of Human Rights, and the vast array of Human Rights Conventions, at international and regional level. Thus, compliance with international human rights law as well as effective human rights protection must be a baseline for assessing both national and international regulation related to information society policies.

The system of human rights protection is built on citizens being able to claim protection and enforcement of human rights by their governments, and if this fails through the international human rights system. The fact that the international community can hold states accountable for national human rights protection is key to the whole system of protection. Within the trans-national policy arena of Internet regulation, it is crucial that citizens' basic rights and freedoms remain protected, and that there are concrete measures to enforce these rights and freedoms.

We wish to point to two main areas related to Internet policies, where we are very concerned with current policy developments:

- *Privacy.* As stressed in the contribution to the Internet Governance Forum from the WSIS Civil Society Working Group on Privacy and Security, there is no international legal framework for online privacy protection and enforcement. In the current political climate driven by the so-called "war on terror", international human rights privacy standards are under the strongest pressure since their adoption, and are currently being restricted in a number of areas with little or no legal safeguards to ensure check and balances. Another area of concern is the level of privacy protection for user data in the "Who is" database, which is currently set by US domestic standards, and thus do not comply with the level of data protection guaranteed to citizens in i.e. Europe.
- *Freedom of expression.* It is well documented that online freedom of expression are being violated around the globe, both in the form of outright censorship but also by more subtle measures including privatised censorship and state measures to protect against so-called harmful content. Areas of concern include state filtered information access, ISP self-regulation of harmful content, state/commercial censorship of search terms, criminalisation of content that are fully legitimate under international freedom of expression standards including when leading to imprisonment of online journalists and bloggers, extended copyright regimes, etc.

We encourage the Internet Governance Forum to address, unfold, and raise greater awareness on these issues among all stakeholders. We call the Forum for cooperation with existing UN bodies in charge of Human Rights issues, especially the UN Office of the High Commissioner for Human Rights, with a clear goal to strengthen human rights protection related

Contd...

Contd...

to Internet policies, and to ensure that all Internet policies have human rights protection as their baseline. To this end, we hope that the Internet Governance Forum will endorse the WSIS Civil Society Human Rights Caucus proposal to establish an Independent Commission on the Information Society and Human Rights, composed of highly qualified experts in various relevant fields, with a broad geographical representation, to monitor and assess relevant legislation and policies to ensure that these are compliant with international human standards.

The WSIS Human Rights Caucus was set up in June 2002 to ensure that human rights are firmly placed on the information society agenda. It has more than 65 member organisations.

Note: For more information on the WSIS Human Rights Caucus see: *http://www.iris.sgdg.org/actions/smsi/hr-wsis* or Contact: *Meryem Marzouki, IRIS, marzouki@ras.eu.org and Rikke Frank Jørgensen, Danish Human Rights Institute, rfj@humanrights.dk*

Source: www.article19.org. The WSIS Civil Society Human Rights Caucus To The IGF Open Consultations, February 16-17, 2006. This article is an integral reproduction of the document. Reprinted with permission.

8

Community Node-Based User Governance (CNBUG): Applying Craigslist's Techniques to Decentralized Internet Governance

Alice Goldmann

In the 'Accountable Internet: Peer Production of Internet Governance,' Cyberlaw-scholars Professors David R Johnson, Susan P Crawford, & John G Palfrey Jr. suggest decentralized governance and user accountability as a means of governing the Internet. While advantageous over existing centralized models, Peer Production model also suffers from significant practical shortcomings that would make it unlikely to be adopted as a global means of Internet governance. A new model, Community Node-Based User Governance (CNBUG), inspired by Peer Production's decentralized model, consists of three principal components that establish its effectiveness: decentralized user-dependent governance, geographic nodal-centered communities, and quorum flagging, similar to that employed by Craigslist.org, an online

community information Web site. These three components work together to establish a means of Internet governance that unlike its predecessors, does not chill speech or isolate users, integrates decision-making, accountability, allows for the participation and integration of developing nations, represents global community standards, allows for concurrent online and territorial enforcement, and protects users from bad actors; all while preserving the Internet's fundamental purpose and nature, and also leaving intact its considerable business and technical infrastructure.

Should the Internet be Governed?

Cyberscholars, governments and users have been faced with the looming question of whether the Internet can and should be governed. Since the Internet's inception and its subsequent evolution into an inexpensive and omnipresent means of global public communication, users have been resistant to the idea of being governed online. When President Clinton signed the Telecommunications Act of 1996[1] into law, John Perry Barlow responded with his now infamous *A Declaration of the Independence of Cyberspace.*[2] In it he decreed that territorial governments have no business governing the Internet, and that it would be governed from within.

For years, various governments have attempted to govern the Internet through the creation of new laws, online borders, and extraterritorial enforcement, yet very few have succeeded. At the same time, there has been a proliferation of "bad actors"[3] online, and it has become evident that something must be done to protect users.[4]

The Accountable Internet: Peer Production of Internet Governance[5] (and its follow-up submission to the International Telecommunications Union Workshop on Internet Governance[6]) attempts to solve the problem of governing the Internet by proposing a new model of Internet governance that is meant to supplant the two existing models known as the Benevolent Dictatorship Model ("Benevolent Dictatorship") and the Democracy Model ("Democracy").[6] *The Accountable Internet's* proposed Peer Production Model ("Peer Production")[7] rejects the idea of a centralized Internet government inherent in Benevolent Dictatorship and

Democracy. Instead it proposes that each individual user be responsible for governing the Internet.

Building on the strengths and advantages of Peer Production, this paper proposes Community Node-Based User Governance ("CNBUG"), a new model that maintains the decentralized aspects of Peer Production while enhancing it with the administration aspects of Craigslist.org ("Craigslist"), a community information and classifieds Website (see Appendix' A).

Three Models of Internet Governance

While all three models of Internet governance reviewed in The Accountable Internet: Peer Production of Internet Governance[5] embody certain advantages, they also suffer from significant practical shortcomings that would make them unlikely to be adopted as a global means of Internet governance. Note that these three models apply to governing the Internet as a whole rather than on a per-Website basis.

Benevolent Dictatorship Model

A walled garden is a pre-defined area on the Internet that is subject to the control of an overseer, referred to as the "benevolent dictator" ("dictator"). Walled gardens can be private such as AOL.com, where users that choose to participate in AOL's online community agree to subject themselves to its rules; or public, such as exists in the Peoples Republic of China, where online communications within the country are regulated internally, and those originating from outside its geographic borders are filtered by a customized firewall.[8]

In a Benevolent Dictatorship, the Internet is a walled garden where all those inside the wall are protected by the dictator but are also subject to his/her discretion, rules, policies, and enforcement control. Users typically participate in the walled garden with the expectation that the dictator is ensuring that unsuitable content and malicious actions are not occurring within its walls. In certain private sector controlled walled gardens, such as AOL, users defer to the dictator's technological prowess in keeping their Internet safe and free of problems, indecencies, viruses, and spam. In furtherance of this goal, AOL provides its subscribers with email filtering, firewalls, parental controls, anti-virus and anti-spyware software, identity theft protection, and an army of overseers (employees) entrusted with keeping the walled garden safe and secure.[9]

A longstanding problem with the Benevolent Dictator Model is its historical reputation for dissatisfactory customer service. Even though participants can report non-compliant content to the dictator, each posting must be reviewed on an individual basis to determine whether or not it is compliant with corporate policy and the law. This approach is inefficient and expensive: "Although users registered a steady stream of complaints, they saw little reduction in bad behavior since individualized *ad hoc* attention to each reported problem could not put a significant dent in wrongdoing."[10] To stay in business, the company in question had to eventually move away from the Benevolent Dictator Model, by shifting power and decision-making to its clients.[10]

While safe within their walled garden, the Benevolent Dictatorship's participants effectively consent to the dictator's unbounded authority to shape their Internet experience. Their "best interests", and thus the content and information they are able to access online, are determined according to the dictator's discretion. Users often do not even realize that the content they are exposed to is filtered, missing, or censored,[11] as the dictator has full discretion and capability to restrict information without notice, accountability, or scrutiny.

Despite the private Benevolent Dictator having so much unaccountable control, US courts have nonetheless found that by participating in a private enterprise such as an online walled garden, subscribers implicitly consent to such rules. Where the private enterprise is not a monopoly, US courts have been reluctant to void the enforceability of boilerplate contracts, suggesting instead that the consumer had the option to accept those terms or go elsewhere.[12] In China, the Chinese government has cited morality and public welfare in justifying their strict and yet undefined rules on Internet content.[8]

Democracy Model

In a Democracy, users elect a body of representatives that is entrusted to govern the Internet.[5] Democracy has the advantage of reflecting the will of the voters and, unlike in a Benevolent Dictatorship, makes the decision-makers periodically accountable for their actions. Ideally, users can elect a body of representatives that reflect their values and take action on their behalf, instead of relying on the judgment of a pre-appointed unaccountable governing body.

One of the biggest challenges evoked by Democracy is compliance with differing global values, customs and attitudes. Even if a representative body were successfully elected to govern the Internet, it would have the impossible task of establishing a set of uniform global Internet rules that would be able to satisfy the enormous variations and often passionately and violently conflicting contradictions of community standards[13] across the globe.

For example, while some countries legally mandate sexual education classes for children in public school,[14] the mere suggestion of sexual education would be unthinkable in certain cultures and belief systems. A globally elected body of representatives would have difficulty passing judgment on a safe sex Website for teenagers, or an AIDS and HIV or birth control information Websites for adults, that would satisfy communities that view this information as essential and those that are adamantly opposed to its open availability and dissemination.

In China for example, Web sites about Falun Gong or the Tiannamen Square Massacre are strictly prohibited, with violators imprisoned for posting or even viewing such content on the Internet.[10,15] In Iran, filtering extends to Farsi-language blogs, e-mail, and online discussion forums with prohibited content, including but not limited to gay and lesbian, politically sensitive, and women's rights Websites.[16] Both exemplify content that does not typically offend the community standards of many other countries, and demonstrates how on a global scale, the enormous variation of social and religious values would necessitate an infinite set of diverse community standards.

In an online Democracy, problems would also arise if the majority of users were to elect a particularly conservative Internet government that would chill online content and speech; or an overly liberal government that would permit content and speech that some communities found objectionable (or even illegal) such as the sale of Nazi memorabilia in France.[17]

Paradoxically, a freely elected Internet government could potentially create a global imbalance of representation, resulting in global rules and standards made by the select few, likely the richest economies or most developed nations. Certain localities that are currently restricted from online participation due to the digital divide[18] could be prevented from voicing their needs.[19] By the time these localities established a significant online presence, they would be forced to conform to an existing governance infrastructure. The less powerful participants would inevitably resent global rules made on their behalf but without their input, which would cause conflicts rather than lead to cooperation and compliance.[20]

Finally, even if it were elected democratically, certain nations could refuse to recognize the rulemaking and decisional power of a global Internet government. Since it would be unlikely that an Internet-based government would have the authority and police power to enforce its rulings, it would have to rely on traditional territorial regimes for such enforcement. As it stands today, due to conflicting laws, territorial governments do not always have their rulings in Internet-related matters enforced by other governments.[21]

Even if a group of countries were to successfully create and implement a Berne Convention-type treaty[22] to enforce the rulings made by the Internet government, any nation that did not join the treaty would become a global haven for bad actors and thus create a "race to the bottom".

Peer Production Model

Peer Production eschews the idea of a centralized Internet government, and instead lets individual users to govern the Internet on their own behalf, by enabling them to permit or block contact from other. users. By controlling their personal exposure to informational flows, individual users exclude bad actors that contact them, while also lowering the danger of "chilling" content on the Internet as a whole. In determining whether or not to permit a contact to reach a user, Peer Production usually relies on a "trust" system, built on the recommendation of others that are somehow trusted to certify the value of a communication.[5]

Despite Peer Production's revolutionary shift to a decentralized model, it suffers from several significant disadvantages that make it an unlikely candidate for Internet-wide implementation. Conceptually, a collective of individuals, each working on their own, are inefficient in governing a complex system like the global Internet.[23] As well, in creating a self-imposed "microcosmic walled-garden", individual users could enable a "reverse-chilling" effect, where the user would inadvertently deprive themselves of content they would want to see, but could not, because they unknowingly set overly broad filtering criteria.[24]

Another weakness of the Peer Production's trust-based system is that it hinders the interconnection of strangers—one of the Internet's most fundamental and beneficial attributes. The Peer Production trust-based system would create a barrier to online participation, as new users would have to already "know" someone and be 'trusted' before being permitted to participate.[25,5]

The proliferation of the Internet has allowed for communication between users thousands of miles away, without delays or substantial costs. It enables people to create a virtual online identity (MySpace, Friendster), make romantic real-life connections (Match, Lavalife), buy and sell (eBay, ioffer), blog (blogger, livejournal), and be involved in infinite other online 'actions' on a global scale. In contrast, Peer Production endorses a system that requires authentication prior to intra-user communication. Limiting online communications between strangers simply because trust requirements have been set too stringently, or because intra-user trust has not been established, could create user isolation or, possibly, alter the fundamental nature of the Internet as an open global communications medium.[26]

An implementation of Peer Production that relied on other users' recommendations of trust instead of one from a neutral third party could be insecure. Even in an online system where trust is "earned", nothing would prohibit trusted users from later emerging as bad actors.[27] By the time a once trusted user committed an attack and appropriate corrective action was taken, the damage would have already been done.

Worse still, if the Peer Production "trust" model were implemented on a network consisting of open connections between numerous trusted users, the effect of just one bad actor could swiftly overwhelm the entire network with devastating results. There exists no foolproof or definitive way either online or offline to forever ascertain someone's character. Moreover, trusting a stranger online because they have established trust with someone you trust does not serve to eliminate this problem. There is no guarantee that your "friend" has exercised diligence or discretion in opting to make a connection. For instance, on the popular social networking site MySpace.com, users purposefully accept friendship requests from as many people as possible for the sole purpose of feigning online popularity.[28] Often they have absolutely no reference point for accepting a particular user into their personal network, as the request for being "added" as a friend is completely random and the users do not know each other beforehand. Online, a user can make friends with hundreds of people and then purposefully send them spam, or even a virus, which would then get distributed across their "trusted" user base.[29] A trust-based black-and-white list system is unlikely to prevent bad actors from participating on the Peer Production Internet.

The deficiencies of the above-described governance models illustrates the inherent difficulties in creating a means of global Internet governance that could reconcile numerous incongruous requirements, such as avoiding chilling speech and user isolation, ensuring accountability, including developing nations, representing global community standards, allowing for concurrent online and territorial enforcement, and protecting users; all while preserving the Internet's fundamental purpose and nature, and also leaving intact its considerable business and technical infrastructure.

Proposal for a Fourth Model of Internet Governance: Community Node-Based User Governance

The method of content administration that exists on Craigslist (see Appendix A), in conjunction with the decentralized advantages of Peer Production, evokes a fourth model of governance that I have named Community Node-Based User Governance ("CNBUG"). CNBUG consists of three principal components that establish its effectiveness: decentralized user-dependent governance, geographic nodal-centered communities[30] and quorum flagging.

In a CNBUG implementation, real life localities would exist on the Internet as community "nodes", where a node can be a city, state, country, or a permutation of these.[31] Each node's participant makeup would mainly comprise that of the node's corresponding geographic location.

CNBUG's decentralized governance takes the form of providing decisional and enforcement powers to all users that choose to participate in a CNBUG node. Node participants govern by quorum flagging, which is a type of voting. When community node participants encounter content (i.e., text, an image, or a subject category) that they believe is inconsistent with their node's norms, terms of use, or laws, they can voice their disapproval by clicking a button that corresponds to a reason why the post should be removed or reviewed ("flagging the post"). The post is not removed unless its predefined flagging threshold has been met (i.e., flagged by a predefined quorum of users). After the flagging threshold has been reached, the person who posted the offending content receives an email notifying them that the posting has been removed and for which violations. (i.e., which flag has triggered the post's removal).

How CNBUG Compares to the Other Three Models

Even though it looks quite simple, CNBUG provides a powerful and easily understandable governance mechanism that embodies positive elements from Benevolent Dictatorship, Democracy, and Peer Production, while creating an entirely new model. Unlike Benevolent Dictatorship and Democracy, CNBUG does not rely on a central body to govern the Internet. Like Peer Production, it utilizes a decentralized form of governance, empowering individual users to govern their Internet node—by independently deciding what content should or should not be removed from their online community. In essence, CNBUG is sufficiently flexible to allow users to govern any type of content that a particular online community would deem necessary to regulate via collective action.

The table in Appendix B compares the principal advantages and disadvantages of the aforementioned Internet governance models, as well as the Craigslist community service.

CNBUG versus the Benevolent Dictator Model

In a private Benevolent Dictatorship such as AOL.COM, the walled garden's rules take the form of the "terms of use" that outline acceptable and unacceptable behaviors. When the terms of use in a private dictatorship are violated, a concerned user must bring the violation to the attention of the dictator's representative and then wait for a response and/or corrective action, if any.

In AOL's walled garden, the dictator (via employees that act as administrators) enforces the terms of use by warning, penalizing, or banning users for certain behaviors. As in a private Benevolent Dictatorship, CNBUG would also incorporate a written "terms of use" defining acceptable and unacceptable community behaviors. However, unlike the Dictatorship, CNBUG enables participants to make "collective enforcement decisions" independently of any overseeing body. The substantive difference between an implementation of CNBUG and a Benevolent Dictatorship is that CNBUG allows participants to "vote" (via flagging) on issues that directly affect them and their community, thus enforcing their community's norms. In contrast, on AOL, users do not have the ability to govern the walled garden, instead of relying on the dictator. When AOL's employees do govern (i.e., remove content that violates their terms of use), they are required to do so according to the company's policies rather than community's norms. Hence, when a violation occurs that is not against corporate policy, service administrators might be slow to act, or not act at all.

Such a situation occurred in Zeran v. AOL.[32] In Zeran, an AOL member began posting offensive pro-Oklahoma City bombing t-shirts for sale, and provided Zeran's name and contact information, urging people to call him with orders. Resultantly, Zeran became the victim of thousands of harassing and threatening phone calls, appealing to AOL to remove the posts and suspend the violator's account. As AOL was slow in deleting both the posts and the offender's AOL account, the postings and the harassment continued. The same post on an implementation of CNBUG would have likely been flagged immediately on account of its tasteless nature, thus sparing Zeran a bulk of the harassment he suffered waiting for AOL to take it down. The post's removal would be based on its non-compliant content, and would not have to be illegal or even explicitly in violation of the community's written terms of use in order to be removed.

Since CNBUG allows for governance according to community's norms as well as the law, there is no requirement that a removal action be justified in compliance with a policy. Under Lawrence Lessig's model of behavioral regulation,[33] Lessig distinguishes between normative punishments as those enforced by the community and legal ones as those enforced by the government. By allowing both types of enforcement to take place concurrently, CNBUG permits an increase in the effectiveness of legal enforcement, because it frees up law enforcement officers from dealing with insignificant matters so they can focus on egregious violations.

For example, experienced users might be familiar with postings that embody certain Internet scams, which might be non-obvious to less savvy users. Since CNBUG's first line of defense is flagging, users can promptly remove such postings on behalf of their community before others even have a chance to be victimized. Such an approach, while preventing would-be victims from falling prey to the scam, does not preclude coexisting legal enforcement by local authorities, which might take place without notification to a CNBUG node's participants.[34]

On an implementation of CNBUG, while the rules might be echoed in the terms of use ("thou shall not infringe on thy neighbor's copyright"), it is the users that ultimately determine when and if these rules are enforced online, thus relying on fluid norms rather than just law for the purposes of governing their community. For example, if Paris, France's users have refused to enforce copyright law by not flagging posts that contained unauthorized reproductions of copyrighted material, they would simply not be flagged. No centralized Europe-wide or France-wide decision is made or required and the decision itself would be reflected in the community's unwillingness to fulfill the flagging threshold that would remove the legal violation.

If an insufficient number of users flag a post and the pre-determined flagging threshold has not been met, then the post would not be removed until it expires[35] or unless a legal action is independently forthcoming. CNBUG's means of normative enforcement would not however, prevent the lawful intellectual property holder from bringing a legal cause of action for copyright infringement.

Unlike a Benevolent Dictatorship, which conceptually, is not obligated to have accountability, CNBUG integrates decisional accountability into every removal action via a peer-review mechanism (manifested as quorum flagging), which requires a certain predefined threshold to be met prior to allowing the posts' removal. By distributing the responsibility to flag content among multiple users, the abuse of power is less likely.

Not only is CNBUG's flagging threshold set automatically but also, additional technological safeguards can be integrated into the system to ensure that any one user could not repeatedly flag a post. These safeguards further serve to validate the removal decision and reflect the true will of the community rather than that of a pro-active minority forcing its radical values on others. Since an insufficient quorum could not remove a post, this creates a strong implication that it is not offensive to the community's norms.

While the protection of the walled garden is solely entrusted to the dictator, under CNBUG the ability to protect a nodal community is distributed equally among all its participants. A decentralized system allows for faster response to problems because, unlike in a hierarchical centralized private entity, community participants are not required to wade through several bureaucratic layers in order to comply with a corporate policy before making a decision. CNBUG permits participants to respond by voting as soon as they spot a violation, whereas a complainant in a walled-garden would be powerless to remove a post, even if it affected them directly.

Despite relying on decentralized enforcement, CNBUG is not dependent on full member participation. The system would still function if particular users were always proactive (consistently flagging posts that do not comport with the rules); if certain users were flagging just some of the time (removing only the posts with egregious violations or that were personally offensive); or even if the majority was never flagging (in case the subject was obscure or users were apathetic —"someone else will do it"). In CNBUG, users are constrained from acting only by their own willingness to do so, and not because they are lacking the ability to act. Hence, proactive and interested users can reliably act on behalf of and in the best interests of their community.

CNBUG versus the Democracy Model

One of the main problems faced by Democracy would be implementing governing Internet standards on a global scale. Taking into account that even in the United States these standards vary considerably within states (New York City v. New York State standards)[36] and between states (Utah v. Massachusetts),[37] the possibility of implementing a global standard that could satisfy all participating nations would be nearly impossible (Singapore[38] v. Holland).

CNBUG solves this problem by creating communities that are online manifestations of geographic locations.[39] Such a means of online community representation is effective for two principal reasons. First, people's community standards are significantly linked to their geographic origins;[40] and second, because laws are linked to the physical locality where they are meant to rule. Having online communities exist as city/state nodes, permits participants from those localities to project their community's norms and laws onto the Internet and vice versa. Therefore, a poster on the Kansas City node searching for marijuana would likely be subject to a stricter community standard than one on Amsterdam's node because of the latter city's more liberal laws and social norms.[41,42]

Unlike Democracy, CNBUG would accommodate users and communities stuck in the digital divide. Because CNBUG communities exist as online manifestations of their physical locations, no existing community can make decisions or set standards on behalf of others. As each nodal community grows and establishes a firmer online presence, they can apply their own norms, even if they are nested within a larger online community. With the narrowing of the digital divide, new participants would have the opportunity to establish an online presence that is reflective of their norms and laws, rather than be forced to conform to pre-existing regulations.

Even if users were to elect a global Internet government, there is no guarantee that territorial governments would recognize or enforce this government's power or decisions. This danger is not at issue with CNBUG because it does not remove legislative, jurisdictional, or enforcement power from territorial governments. CNBUG simply empowers individual users to govern their community node according to norms that coexist alongside legal enforcement. Giving users normative enforcement power is also effective where societal norms and the law overlap, as bad actors can still be punished by both.[43] Any government, online or offline, typically, only has the time and capability to address a limited number of pressing issues. Hence, the creation of a means to empower individuals to govern on matters that affect them personally removes the need to defer to a central online representative to govern the Internet. CNBUG is a viable manifestation of this power, both in the acceptance or rejection of individual content and, cumulatively and indirectly, managing the Internet as a whole.

Creating online communities that correspond to territorial localities significantly reduces the fundamental confusion as to choice of law applicable in legal enforcement determinations, such as notice and jurisdiction (i.e., in the US, fulfilling minimum contacts for personal jurisdiction[44]). For example, a node in Winnipeg, Manitoba, Canada is clearly subject to Canada's federal laws, Manitoba's provincial laws, and Winnipeg's municipal laws, in addition to the normative standards of all three.[45] CNBUG would adopt Craigslist's policy on encouraging users to participate only on the online manifestation of their territorial community,[46] although it would not prevent them from participating in other communities of their choice. Participation within one's online community node creates knowledge of the community's norms, as well as familiarity with its laws, rules, jurisdiction, and enforcement.[47] Even participation within a community node that was not one's own, would nonetheless create the expectation of being subject to that community's norms and laws. An American, posting on Sydney, Australia's node, would know by virtue of participation on that node that they would not have the benefit of protection from the First Amendment.

It should be noted that there would be cases where geographic/jurisdictional boundaries would not always strictly correspond to the nodal community created on CNBUG. This situation might arise in the areas where community borders crossed over and created hybrid "super communities". Overlapping jurisdictions often occur in areas that share fundamentally the same values, for example, northern New Jersey as a part of New York City (although New Jersey and New York State have different state laws), or the overlap between Switzerland and France in the vicinity of Geneva (both countries have different federal laws). The existence of a hybrid super community would not necessarily destroy the effectiveness of the proposed CNBUG Model, even if the legal systems were, different. For example, there is cooperation between New York and New Jersey, such that a criminal who crossed state lines would not be immune from prosecution. Normative enforcement would unlikely be affected by a hybrid 'super community' because super communities are often based on areas that share similar community norms.

CNBUG versus the Peer Production Model

Unlike the first two models, Peer Production relies on decentralized Internet governance by placing full responsibility and accountability on the individual user. Decentralization presents many advantages over a centralized government, such as not having an overseeing body in charge of making decisions for all users, eliminating over-inclusive or under-inclusive regulation of speech, and settling concerns regarding accountability. Because Peer Production users can decide whether they allow a communication to go through, they are fully accountable for their exposure to online communications. Finally, since Peer Production does not rely on the bureaucratic decision-making practices of a central authority, it allows users to block online threats as soon as they appear.

Despite its strengths, Peer Production's successful implementation depends on a fundamental change in the Internet's structure because it relies on the creation of a trust-based global communication infrastructure. Allowing or disallowing communications to flow according to whether the communicating user is trustworthy is flawed for two reasons. First, because establishing trust online is challenging and never one hundred percent foolproof; and second, because limiting exposure to communications based on trust has the potential to create online isolation.

The Accountable Internet's authors have conceded that the required widespread adoption of authentication (trust) would necessitate "a major state change" for the Internet that could amount to the "addition of a new social layer to the Internet protocol stack". Such a significant change would somehow be based on the Internet users selecting software code "that reliably serves our social values" (presumably defined globally, democratically, and within a reasonable time frame). Conversely, a successful implementation of CNBUG would not require changes to the Internet's architecture; this system of online governance could be enabled to function with minimal disruption to the existing infrastructure. One means of implementing CNBUG would be by creating a "dot node" (.NODE), a new online community space via top-level domain.[48]

Governance accountability depends on trusting the system. Trust is even more important in a decentralized governance model than in a centralized governance model because in the latter model the users always know who is ultimately accountable. To function effectively, Peer Production requires a high degree of accountability, which would be impossible to establish without a trustworthy online voting mechanism. According to the Accountable Internet's authors[5], new "...technologies will enable both end users and access providers to accept messages and establish connections based on trust in the originating party." Trust in their article has been defined as "...the ability to decide with whom to communicate" (i.e., as a two-party decision process), rather than the more conventional Internet definition of trusted systems as "...centralized means of administering permissions for access to particular documents", which they also cite in the same article. In very large transactional systems like the Internet, a two-party decision process is unreliable. E-commerce experience[49,50] stresses that three-party trust is much stronger, especially where the third party is a neutral and reputable third-party certifier. Additionally, "In an environment where third parties are omnipresent and technologically required, their effect becomes a dominant factor in the dynamic accountability equilibrium."[51]

In effect, the CNBUG architecture (implemented via a .NODE top-level domain) acts as a third party certifier, and in addition, distributes the responsibility of third party certification among numerous actors rather than relying on two parties. It is possible to distribute the responsibilities of a third-party certifier among more than three parties, and still achieve adequate levels of trust.[52] Governance based on two-party trust or authentication would not serve as an effective means of reducing the amount of bad actors online.

In addition to problems related to online security, limiting interaction to certain "authenticated" or "trusted" users creates the potential for online self-isolation. As in real life, the majority of Internet users are 'good actors' and, therefore, online isolation effectively stifles one of the Internet's principal benefits: the interconnection of strangers and new ideas. Instead of opening themselves to boundless communications with seemingly infinite users, users would effectively shut themselves off to most online strangers.

The main reason why CNBUG is a more effective means of centralized governance than Peer Production is because instead of punishing the actor by blacklisting, CNBUG only for the removal of the individual posting. CNBUG participants do not govern the Internet by banning users; instead they govern by banning individual postings that do not comply with their community's norms. By dealing with the credibility of the posting rather than credibility of the person who created the posting, CNBUG does not rely on trusting either governments or private enterprises to govern the Internet, a concern raised by critics of an early version of the Accountable Internet.[53] This governance concept embodies three principal benefits: it allows for the preservation of online anonymity, it permits a good actor who committed a bad act to rectify the problem, and it integrates accountability into each removal decision in the form of quorum flagging.

CNBUG's flagging system allows for the preservation of online anonymity, which is an important means of disseminating speech protected under the First Amendment.[54] A good actor, for example, might want to retain their anonymity (perhaps for political purposes in places like China or Iran) and refuse to go through a verification system or self-tagging. Communication with such unidentified users in Peer Production would be barred, because they would not have established "trust" and there would be no means for them to appeal their status ("Hey, I'm not bad, I just want to remain anonymous"). Even if they were to become a part of a trusted network, trusting an anonymous user undermines the fundamental character of any trust-based system. CNBUG allows for anonymity because it substitutes Peer Production's trust "tagging" concept with consensus "flagging", which means that users do not need to identify themselves in order to communicate. On CNBUG, communications can be removed, but not the speakers themselves.

By allowing for the removal of communications instead of the banning of users, CNBUG effectively creates an integrated rectification mechanism. In Peer Production, if a good actor made a bad judgment and was resultantly banned (for example by forwarding a link to a *"Free Ipod Referral"* that they genuinely believed to be legitimate), by virtue of being banned, they would be unable to appeal their status. Conversely, on CNBUG, the offending post would be flagged and then removed, and the poster would be automatically notified via e-mail that their post was removed and which of the flags[55] triggered its removal.

This form of notice allows inadvertent bad actors to modify their behavior, thus avoiding future removals. As it stands under Peer Production, once a user is blocked/blacklisted, it would be difficult for them to remedy the issue and re-integrate themselves to the online community. The *Accountable Internet's* authors have acknowledged the risk of overreaction and collateral damage from "guilt by association" and through "the power of banishment" as potentially the most undemocratic characteristics of Peer Production.[5]

Finally, CNBUG integrates decisional accountability by requiring a quorum to meet a flagging threshold prior to removing a post from the system. Removal by quorum minimizes the danger of overzealous enforcement, especially when technological safeguards are integrated to ensure that users are not flagging maliciously. CNBUG's flagging system would work without human review, with the offending post automatically deleted as soon as the pre-defined flagging threshold were reached. The flagging threshold would be dynamically set by a basic algorithm that calculated the threshold value according to objective[56] inputs, such as the volume of posts in the category/site, frequency of visits, frequency of new posts, and the "volatility" of the category (e.g., sexual encounters would be more volatile than lost pets[57]).

On the whole, CNBUG overcomes the problems posed by Peer Production's outright banning of noncompliant participants while preserving the Internet's open communications character and fundamental architecture.

Disadvantages of the CNBUG Model

Despite having many benefits over the previous three models, CNBUG encompasses certain weaknesses. One of its residual disadvantages is that despite a CNBUG node being organized as a decentralized peer-governed entity, there must still be an overseeing body to determine the community node's terms of use and to re-examine removal decisions challenged by the post originators. Having a governance board make these decisions might revive some of the problems prevalent in Benevolent Dictator and Democracy. However, unlike in the other models, local representatives elected to oversee a node under CNBUG would have a better understanding of their own community's norms and values, and can still be held democratically accountable to their community.

Another limitation of CNBUG is that, at least initially, it would be difficult to implement it on an Internet-wide basis. Since the model's main advantage stems from dividing the Internet into geographical locations,[58] multinational corporations (such as Amazon or eBay) that might like to have a presence on each community node would have to comport with each node's community standards. Under the CNBUG model, this can be achieved by having each individual Web site integrating itself into the flagging system and allowing themselves to be governed (See CNBUG article 2, implementation).

Despite overcoming the danger of individual user isolation on Peer Production, CNBUG might create certain level of nodal city/state/country isolation. Encouraging users to center their Internet experience locally rather than globally might curb the Internet's objective of global interaction.[59] A practical way to offset this problem is to have the CNBUG nodal system exist as a subset of the "regular" Internet, meaning that users participating in their own community node would be subject to all its rules and safeguards, but would not necessarily have the same expectations when leaving the node to surf the open Web.

Finally, CNBUG would have to diligently safeguard against those users that would form an "angry online mob" that could collectively fulfill the flagging threshold requirements of posts that they disagreed with, thus censoring community speech that was not actually violating its normative standards. As noted above, this problem could likely be remedied with an arsenal of sophisticated technological safeguards that limit the amount an individual user can flag in a day and also allow for review of appealed removal decisions.

Conclusion

By evolving and modifying the beneficial aspects of Peer Production, CNBUG manages to create a viable alternative to governing the Internet that resolves many outstanding issues present in the three other models of Internet governance.

Acknowledgements

The encouragement and thoughtful comments of Prof. Susan Crawford and Prof. David R Johnson are much appreciated. I am also thankful to Mr. Craig Newmark for his review of the manuscript and expression of support.

(Alice Goldmann, Benjamin N. Cardozo School of Law.)

Appendix A: A Brief Introduction to Craigslist.org

In 1995, Craig Newmark observed virtual communities of Internet users helping each other out on various Websites and newsgroups. He decided to join the cause and created a Website whose initial purpose was to inform people about events in San Francisco, California. The site became popular by word of mouth and eventually required a devoted server. Newmark wanted to call it "San Francisco Events" but his friends urged him to name it "Craigslist", reflecting the site's personal and down-to-earth nature. Newmark wrote code that enabled users to automatically add postings, evolving the site into craigslist.org ("Craigslist").

The current version of Craigslist is a simple, text-only interface that serves as an enormous global classifieds hub composed of cities and states, spanning six continents (See Figure 1). Craigslist's popularity grows every day and is due entirely to word of mouth.[60] It has become a global online phenomenon, changing cities, impacting newspapers, and at one point ranking as the seventh most visited site on the Internet.[61,62]

Figure 1: Screenshot of Craigslist New York City Main Page

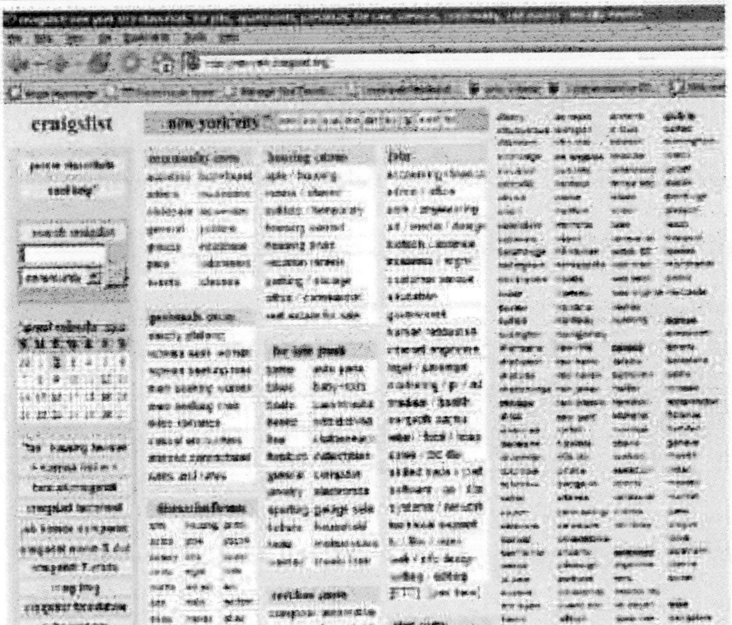

How Craigslist Works

On Craigslist, users have the ability to browse ads, search the system, post in discussion forums, and contact other users. By and large users conduct their searches and postings in the city where they live or work. Some of the cities are themselves divided up into smaller regions. New York City, for example, is subdivided into the five boroughs (Manhattan, Brooklyn, Queens, Bronx, Staten Island), but its Craigslist's community also includes upstate New York, Long Island, and even nearby areas of Northern New Jersey.

Similarly, Switzerland's Geneva Craigslist community includes the adjacent region of France. To post a listing on the system, users must select their community area ("node") and from their node's main page, choose the category corresponding to their posting and click the "post" button. If they have an account and are logged in at the time, the listing is immediately posted. Otherwise, the users are e-mailed a confirmation notice that they must activate by clicking on a link and selecting "publish" before the listing is posted to the site. A posting on Craigslist can be made whether or not a participant is a member, which lowers the threshold for participation. In addition, users have the option to use their real e-mail address or an "anonymized" address,[63] or even have the option to include a phone number but no e-mail.

Essentially, Craigslist functions as a simple to use, convenient and free online town square where users interact with each others in their local community.

The Craigslist's Method of Post Removal: Flagging

On a monthly basis, users from around the globe post approximately 10 million classified ads and 40 million discussion postings.[64] Craigslist, however, has only 19 employees, making any kind of staff content review and moderation unfeasible. Instead of relying on its employees to govern the site, Craigslist has implemented a flagging system that allows all users (participants) to act as moderators. At the top of each Craigslist posting are five flag buttons; four of which remove the listing from the system and one that nominates it for the "best of" Craigslist (See Figure 2).

Figure 2: Screenshot of Craigslist's Five Flags

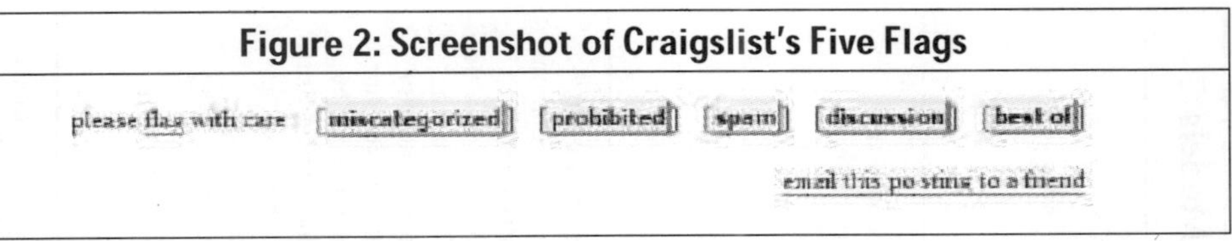

- If a listing is flagged as miscategorized, it means that it was posted in the incorrect category, such as posting a watch for sale in "cars and trucks".
- Prohibited includes items that are not allowed to be sold, as well as any kind of improper (libelous, invasive, abusive, harassing, etc.) statements, misrepresentations, deception, infringement, legal violations, or posts that are a violation of netiquette (such as viruses or attacks).
- The spam button is for flagging multiple posts advertising the same item in different categories, links to eBay auctions, pyramid schemes, chain letters, and links to online businesses for which there is a separate category.
- The discussion button flags posts that comment on other posts, such as if something is a scam, or someone posts an argument regarding a seller or an item's price.
- The final "best of" button is the only one with positive connotations and is used to indicate a funny, entertaining, well-written, or well-liked post. "Best of" is the only category that is reviewed by staffers after being flagged to ensure that it is truly deserving of inclusion in this category.

Figure 3: Post Flagging Notice: Removal Statistics

Thanks for flagging!

- If you flagged by mistake, don't worry—it takes more than one flag to affect a posting.
- Approximately 5% of all craigslist postings are removed through community flagging.
- 98% of postings removed by flagging are in violation of the craigslist terms of use

On behalf of craigslist and the entire free world, thanks for taking the time to flag!

Continue browsing free stuff on new york craigslist

(Please share your suggestions for improvement in our feedback forum)

For a post to be deleted, it must receive a certain amount of flags. The flagging threshold that triggers post's deletion is determined by the Craigslist staff, and varies according to city and category, with the exact threshold value kept secret.

Appendix B: Principal Advantages/Disadvantages of Different Internet Governance Models

#	Principal Characteristics of Internet Governance Models	Benevolent Dictatorship	Democracy	Peer Production	Craigslist (Local Information and Classified Service)	CNBUG
1.	**Governance**	Centralized non-democratic	Centralized democratic	Decentralized	Decentralized, but with centralized non-democratic aspects	Decentralized democratic
2.	**Service Administration Method**	Appointed by the dictator	Democratically elected	Self-governed by user	Appointed by the company	Self-governed
3.	**Method of individual record's removal**	Notification sent to the 'dictator' who ultimately makes and enforces decisions. Dictator determines compliance according to guidelines or even by arbitrarily changing guidelines time to time or in response to the external pressure (i.e., from the media)	Notification sent to the government body, which makes the decision of compliance according to democratically determined guidelines	Blacklisting from self-selection process	Triggered upon flagging threshold. Some most important decisions made by the central body	Triggered upon flagging, violations determined by 'community norms', as defined by the quorum majority within a predefined time frame, or by a similar time-sensitive peer/quorum decision mechanism

Contd...

Contd...

1	2	3	4	5	6	7
4.	**Number of people typically involved in an individual post's removal**	Typically 1 (Administrator appointed by the dictator) The number of people necessary to make a removal decision is static	Typically 1 (Administrator appointed by the board) The number of people necessary to make a removal decision is static	Typically 1 (The user self-administers) The number of people necessary to make a removal decision is static	The exact number of flags required to remove a post is kept secret (i.e. 6 flags), and varies depending on the category. Flag threshold number is determined by a Craigslist administrator The number of people necessary to make a removal decision is dynamic (it varies depending on the category and other factors)	The exact number of flags required to remove a post is kept secret (i.e. 6 flags), and varies depending on the category. Flag threshold number is determined algorithmically The number of people necessary to make a removal decision is dynamic (it varies depending on the category and other factors)
5.	**Notification of an individual post's removal**	Dictator sometimes notifies but there is no obligation to do so	Administrator sometimes notifies but there is no obligation to do so	No notification	System automatically sends notification e-mail to violator	System automatically sends notification e-mail to violator
6.	**Sanctions upon violation**	Varies from warning to banning from system	Varies from warning to banning from system	Inability to interact with this particular user	Warning, no banning from system	Warning, no banning from system

Contd...

Contd...

1	2	3	4	5	6	7
7.	**Legal Enforcement**	Dealt with according to internal policies, then authorities are contacted if necessary	Legal action might be deferred to territorial enforcement authorities	User must contact the authorities to trigger legal enforcement	Territorial enforcement authorities can prosecute/enforce independently without notification to system administrator	Territorial enforcement authorities can prosecute/enforce independently without notification to system administrator
8.	**Governing rules**	Policy statements of the company set by the company's attorneys	Set by the democratically elected body, likely in conjunction with or deference to existing legal territorial regimes	The user has full discretion	Basic terms of use set by the system administrator. American Constitution-like in its simplicity and open to interpretation. General moral and legal principles	Basic rules set up for each geographic or professional node based on existing laws. Additionally governed by the community's norms
9.	**Checks and balances**	None, private corporation makes its own rules, users have the option of not participating. Open market competitors might exist	Democratic voting system	None, users has have absolute control over their online destiny. Participation or openness to the peers	A removal decision must be okayed by a pre-set threshold of independent users based on the guidelines defined by the Service Owner	A removal decision must be okayed by a pre-set quorum/ threshold of independent users based on the democratically defined guidelines
10.	**Responsibility to govern**	Depends solely on the dictator	Depends solely on the democratically defined service governing charter and elected governing body	Depends solely on the user	Depends solely on the Service Owner's voluntary delegation of most (but not all) responsibilities to the entire nodal community + the overseer	Depends solely on the involvement in a particular class of the transactions of the entire nodal community or geographically/professionally defined sub-segment quorums of the global community

Contd...

Contd...

1	2	3	4	5	6	7
11.	**Speed of response to threats**	Slow, relies on bureaucracy	Slow, relies on bureaucracy	Instant	Can be very fast, depending on the egregiousness of the violation. Relies on a quorum. Users might act faster if they perceive an injustice	Can be very fast, depending on the egregiousness of the violation. Relies on a quorum. Users might act faster if they perceive an injustice
12.	**Acceptance of anonymity**	Accepted, but the underlying information is always known. Can be subjected to disclosure according to law or even corporate policy	Unknown	Unlikely to accept	Accepted, but can be tracked down by the territorial enforcement authorities if absolutely necessary. To ascertain identity is difficult but not impossible	Accepted, but can be tracked down by the territorial enforcement authorities if absolutely necessary. To ascertain identity is difficult but not impossible
13.	**Liability for defamatory content**	None according to the CDA safe harbor provisions (Zeran v. AOL)	None	Inapplicable	None	None
14.	**Main weaknesses**	• Users interests are completely up to the dictator's discretion • Users have no power • Bad reputation for customer service	• Impossible to establish a set of uniform global Internet rules due to enormous variations in world-wide community standards	• 'Reverse-chilling' effect, overly broad blocking or filtering criteria prevent users from some content • Prevents the interconnection of strangers	Inapplicable	• There must still be an overseeing body to determine the community's terms of use and review challenged removal decisions

Contd...

Contd...

1	2	3	4	5	6	7
14.	**Main weaknesses**		• Potential imbalance of representation due to the digital divide • Difficulties in enforcement of democratic Internet governance rulings by some territorial governments	• Restricting the participation of new users • A bad actor can pretend to be a good actor up until a certain point, as there is no way to ascertain character forever • Changes the basic architecture of the Internet		• Initially unfeasible to implement on an Internet-wide basis; a global service provider would have to comport with each geographic node's norms and laws • Requires safeguards against users that could form an 'angry online mob' that might censor speech in their community by fulfilling the flagging threshold

Endnotes

1 See Telecommunications Act 1996, Pub. LA. No. 104-104, 110 Stat. 56 (1996) *http://www.fcc.gov/telecom.html* (last visited, August 10, 2006).

2 A Declaration of the Independence of Cyberspace *http://homes.eff.org/~barlow/Declaration-Final.html* (last visited, August 10, 2006). Specifically, Barlow's manifesto was in response to the Communications Decency Act, Title V of the Telecommunications Act. See *http://hotwired.lycos.com/wired_online/4.06/declaration/* (last visited, August 10, 2006).

3 See Footnote 5, Pg. 4, ¶4.

4 *http://www.ic3.gov/media/annualreport/2005_IC3Report.pdf* (FBI's Internet Crime Complaint Center cites that from January 1, 2005 to December 31, 2005, complaint submissions increased by 11.6% from the previous year. Dollar loss was pegged at $183.12 million. (Charts for dollar loss available in the above pdf for 2001–2005) (last visited, August 10, 2006).

5 *See* David R Johnson, Susan P Crawford and John G Palfrey, Jr., *The Accountable Internet: Peer Production of Internet Governance*, 9 VA. J.L. & TECH. 9 (2004).

6 *See* John G Palfrey, Jr., *Submission to the Workshop on Internet Governance February 26–27, 2004*, International Telecommunications Union, Geneva, Switzerland.

7 Also known as decentralized action.

8 Clive Thompson, Google's China Problem (and China's Google Problem), *New York Times* Magazine, April 23, 2006.

9 See *http://discover.aol.com/aolfeatures.adp* (last visited, August 10, 2006).

10 The Cardozo Law School's Floersheimer Center for Constitutional Democracy's Occasional Paper #2, January 2005.

11 American Library Association v. United States, 201 F. Supp. 2d, 401, 446.

12 Caspi v. Microsoft Network, L.L.C., 732 A.2d 528, 531, (N.J. 1999).

13 Community standards are the unsaid rules by which any community conducts itself. See ACLU v. Reno, 217 F.3d 162.

14 Britain: Sex Education Under Fire: United Nations Educational, Scientific, and Cultural Organization, *http://www.unesco.org/courier/2000_07/uk/apprend.htm,* (last visited, August 10, 2006).

15 For more information on world-wide content monitoring and filtering see *http://www.opennetinitiative.net/modules.php?op=modload&name=Archive&file=index&req=viewarticle&artid=1* (last visited, August 10, 2006).

16 Internet Filtering in Iran in 2004-2005: A Country Study *http://www.opennetinitiative.net/studies/iran/* (last visited, August 10, 2006).

17 Yahoo! Inc. v. La Ligue Contre Le Racisme, 433 F.3d 1199, 1202 (Prohibition on sale of Nazi Memorabilia in France).

18 'Digital Divide' refers to the gap between those able to benefit from digital technology and those who are not. See International Telecommunications Union: *http://www.itu.int/ITUD/digitaldivide/* (last visited, August 10, 2006).

19 See International Telecommunications Union: Statistics on Worldwide Internet Access *http://www.itu.int/wsis/tunis/newsroom/stats/* (last visited, August 10, 2006).

20 Ian King, Internet Governance: An Analysis of the Need for Change, 19th British and Irish Legal Educational Association (BILETA) Annual Conference, 2004/.

21 La Ligue Contre le Racisme et l'Antisemitisme, *et al.,* Petitioners v. Yahoo! Inc., 433 F.3d 1199, 1221 (2006) US court refused to enforce ruling of French court prohibiting certain content on Yahoo because it violated the first amendment.

22 The Berne Convention *http://www.wipo.int/clea/docs/en/wo/wo001en.html* (last visited, August 10, 2006).

23 Hofmann, Jeanette (2005) "Internet Governance: Eine regulative Idee auf der Suche nach ihrem Gegenstand", in: *Gunnar Folke Schuppert (Hrsg.): Governance-Forschung – Vergewisserung über Stand und Entwicklungslinien, Band 1 der Reihe Schriften zur Governance-Forschung,* Nomos-Verlag: Baden-Baden, S. 277-301. (Hofmann warns that Peer Production self-governance might run up "against the limits of its regulatory capacity".)

24 For example, disallowing content containing the word "breast" will omit results containing "breast cancer" and "chicken breast", neither of which is sexually suggestive.

25 This would especially affect users that were "coming out" of a digital divide situation and who would likely not know anyone online to provide them with the required references.

26 As evidenced by the philosophy behind the Internet Protocol: *http://www.ietf.org/rfc/rfc0791.txt* (last visited, August 10, 2006).

27 eBay Inc. is an example of a trust based (but not reliant) transactional system. For every transaction conducted on eBay, users may opt to leave each other feedback regarding the success of the transaction. Some bad actors were able to effectively circumvent the eBay trust system by spending a few months building up positive feedback for sales and purchases completed successfully, basing this positive feedback on small low priced or fictional transactions. After a few months and a full portfolio of positive feedback, these bad actors have been known to start aggressively selling more expensive items that were either broken or nonexistent.

28 *http://www.usatoday.com/tech/news/2006-01-08-myspace-teens_x.htm* (last visited, August 10, 2006).

29 In a network where all participants are connected to each other, a virus or spam sent to one user would potentially have the ability to affect every interconnected user.

30 A geographic node can be replaced with a professional organization node. For the purposes of this paper, I will only discuss the applicability of a geographic scenario, but the general aspects and ideals would be applicable in both situations. Examples of applicability will be stated as they apply throughout this paper.

31 Or a professional organization.

32 Zeran v. America Online, Inc. 129 F.3d 327 (4th Cir, 1997).

33 See Lawrence Lessig, Code and Other Laws of Cyberspace, 192-193 (1999).

34 Coexisting where the CNBUG participants could flag a post and, in addition, a legal action could be taken where applicable.

35 For example, on Craigslist, the flagging guidelines prohibit posts that contain link referrals, designating them as an example of content that should be flagged under 'spam'. However, if no users flag these posts, they simply remain on the system, the implication being that they are either comport with the local community's normative standards, are inconsequential, or have simply gone unnoticed by those who would otherwise flag them.

36 NYC is considered progressive while the rest of the state is more conservative.

37 Utah is governed with a significant participation of the Mormon Church, whereas liberally inclined Massachusetts is the first US state to legalize gay marriage.

38 *http://www.opennetinitiative.net/studies/singapore/* (last visited, August 10, 2006).

39 Also, conceivably professional associations, international standards bodies and similar closed-membership groups that are governed by by-laws and utilize proprietary enforcement mechanisms can use CNBUG online governance model.

40 Or in a professional organization context, the association memberships' community standards.

41 Netherlands Ministry of Foreign Affairs: A Guideline to Dutch Policy on Drugs *http://www.minbuza.nldefault.asp?CMS_ITEM=6D389503422F4A58867070C835BCF837X1X55968X17* (last visited, August 10, 2006).

42 In a professional association context, a book on the history of evolution posted in a forum for history professors might not be flagged, but the same book posted on a religious elementary school teacher's association Web site might be removed, especially if it were not posted in a critical context.

43 For example, if a user is posting pornographic photos in an inappropriate category, community users might flag this post. If the photo involves minors, law enforcement authorities would not be precluded from involvement, even if such content were already flagged.

44 International Shoe Co. v. Washington, 326 U.S. 310 (1945).

45 Similarly, professional associations usually deploy proprietary regulatory and ethical frameworks enforced by both state regulators and their professional community's standards.

46 See: *http://www.craigslist.org/about/help/reasons.html#wronggeo* (last visited, August 10, 2006).

47 nyc.newyork.NODE (Refer part two of this article).

48 Refer part 2 of this article for a suggested CNBUG implementation.

49 S Srinivasan, Role of Trust in E-Business Success, *Information Management & Computer Security*, Vol. 12, No. 1, 66-72, 2004.

50 Canzaroli, A, Tan, Y H and Thoen, W "The Social And Institutional Context Of Trust In E-Commerce", Proceedings Of Autonomous Agents, 65-66, 1999. Workshop on Deception, Fraud and Trust in Agent Societies, (1999).

51 Nimrod Kozlovski, Designing Accountable Online Policing, *http://islandia.law.yale.edu/isp/digital%20cops/papers/kozlovski_paper.pdf* (last visited, August 10, 2006).

52 Judith Stafford and Kurt Wallnau, Is Third Party Certification Necessary? In Proceedings of the 4th ICSE Workshop on Component-Based Software Engineering, Toronto, Canada, May 2001.

53 Susan Crawford blog The Theory of Everything *http://scrawford.blogware.com/blog/_archives/2004/2/6/18830.html* posted February 6, 2004 (last visited, August 10, 2006).

54 McIntyre v. Ohio Elections Commission,. 514 U.S. 334 (1995) (The Supreme Court applied exacting scrutiny to determine that anonymity in political speech is a specially protected right under the First Amendment).

55 As defined below, on Craigslist there are four different flags that may have triggered a posts removal. The threshold must have been met for but ONE of the four flags. Meeting the required threshold across several flags (i.e., if it is flagged as spam and also prohibited, but there are insufficient flags to satisfy the threshold for one or the other), then the post is not removed. In this case, I expect that CNBUG would encompass the four basic Craigslist flags (miscategorized, prohibited, spam, discussion), as well as some new ones (i.e., Intellectual Property or notify local police).

56 The term 'objective' signifies here that the input values could be determined according to the system's normal usage statistics, rather than by a single person or entity. For example, if there are 100 posts in a particular category determined at a certain time of day, i.e., in a non-volatile

category with 10 new posts daily, the algorithm would compute a threshold value that when triggered (say by 5 flags) would remove a post in that category when the threshold was met. (From a comment on the first draft, courtesy of Prof. Susan Crawford.)

57 An appropriate analyst would determine the actual flagging variables and the algorithm itself could be adjusted if it were found ineffective.

58 Or, if applicable, to a professional association, etc.

59 This issue may not be as prevalent on a professional organization whose rules and regulations are less dependent on geography.

60 Philip Weiss, The Rise of Craigslist and How It's Killing Your Newspaper, *New York Magazine,* January 31, 2006.

61 *http://www.craigslist.org/about/pr/factsheet.html*

62 Philip Weiss, The Rise of Craigslist and How It's Killing Your Newspaper, *New York Magazine,* January 31, 2006.

63 Craigslist gives the option to anonymize an e-mail address, which creates a random address such as anon-22222@craigslist.org to avoid spam.

64 *http://www.craigslist.org/about/pr/factsheet.html*

9

Addressing the Issues of Internet Governance for Development: A Framework for Setting an Agenda for Effective Coordination*

William H Dutton

For the first few decades after the emergence of the Internet, its governance was dominated by few technical expert groups, Internet Engineering Task Force (IETF) and Internet Society (ISOC) and the US department of defense. This period saw the emergence of flexible, decentralized and pluralistic Governance arrangements. The idea that the Internet governance has to address not only technical issues but also several social, political, commercial and governmental issues, has paved the way for the emergence of Multistakeholders model. This paper illustrates that the Internet Governance Forum (IGF) provides a 'Light Touch'

* This statement was prepared as a submission to the first Internet Governance Forum. It originated as a presentation 'Issues on Internet Governance' presented to the Joint ICAIAMCR Symposium on Internet Governance: New Political and Regulatory Frameworks for Global Network Communication, Kurort Rathen, Hotel Rathener, Germany, 15-18 June 2006. The author thanks Malcolm Peltu for his comments and assistance in preparing this submission.

Source: www.people.oii.ox.ac.uk. Oxford Internet Institute, 30 July, 2006.

framework that maintains the coherence of Internet governance with multiple stakeholder without allowing the unwanted fragmentation of the Internet governance mosaic.

Overview

The World Summits on the Information Society (WSIS) in 2003 and 2005, including the establishment by the United Nations of the Working Group on Internet Governance (WGIG) after the first Summit, signalled the growing global significance of the opportunities and threats (e.g., see Dutton 2004) created by the development and use across the world of the Internet and related information and communication technologies (ICTs). The formation of the Internet Governance Forum (IGF), following the WGIG (2005) report, was an important step in creating a flexible procedural structure for identifying, discussing and addressing key issues through a growing multistakeholder policy dialogue. This paper outlines a framework for agenda setting that could help the Forum to ensure these processes identify and attend to the key substantive issues that merit discussion at the Forum. It is anchored on the view that most issues of Internet governance for development are being grappled with by many separate but interdependent actors and agencies at various levels. However, this creates a need to identify issues that are not 'owned', or not well understood, in order to facilitate the creation of bridges between actors and agencies trying to tackle the same or similar issues. It draws on various research initiatives at Oxford University's Oxford Internet Institute (OII), particularly an international forum on Internet governance[1] (see Dutton and Peltu 2005) and a series of seminars reflecting on civil society participation in the WSIS.[2]

Towards a New Era of Multistakeholder Internet Governance

The Transformation of Internet Governance

In the first few decades after the emergence of the Internet in the late 1960s, awareness of this technology and its potential uses and impacts remained mainly within expert groups of ICT developers and a largely academic and research user base. This period saw the emergence of highly flexible, decentralized and pluralistic governance arrangements,[3] albeit dominated by technical expertise. These included the Internet Engineering Task Force (IETF)[4] from 1986 and the Internet Society (ISOC), established in 1992 to provide an institutional home and financial support for the Internet standards process which by then had to accommodate growing commercial interests in this network of networks.

Such governance arrangements reflected the pioneering Internet community's shared commitment to maintaining the founding design principles of end-to-end (e2e) openness, core architectural stability and independence as a shared resource for the benefit of all. This community was small and homogenous enough to allow for decision making that was both consensual and reasonably efficient in translating agreed standards into effective technical enhancements, as well as in solving problems within the operational infrastructure. Participants in these arrangements may not have thought of themselves as being involved in 'governance' activities, as that term is often too narrowly perceived as necessarily implying governmental regulation. However, they were indeed involved in undertaking governance functions. As in any policy formation effort needing to balance the interests of stakeholders with different and sometimes conflicting interests and perceptions, the processes they were using were also inherently 'political' even if their focus was primarily on technological oriented issues. They were political in the sense that they were about determining how different actors interact in shaping who gets what, when and how, in relation to issues addressed in policy making forums.

For instance, a key point of control in the Internet infrastructure is the 'root zone file'. Who exercises control over this file and the highest level Internet 'root servers', and under what terms, matters to many stakeholders in Internet development and use, as this control underpins a number of practical and symbolic issues, such as the allocation of domain names (Mueller 2002). From the outset, the US Government through the Department of Defense was the ultimate policy authority for this file. But during the first technically oriented phase of Internet governance, root server administration tasks were performed routinely by the late Jon Postel, an early Internet pioneer.[5] However, there was a growing concern within the US government and among some other major stakeholders that no individual, however technically trusted, was well positioned to take account of the broad range of governmental, social, commercial and political issues that could be substantively affected by technical Internet governance decisions. This view was a key factor that led to the establishment of a more formal Internet Assigned Numbers Authority (IANA) and then to the establishment in 1998 of the Internet Corporation for Assigned Names and Numbers (ICANN), an internationally organized not-for-profit corporation based on the laws of California that is responsible for Internet Protocol (IP) address space allocation. This evolution of Internet governance structures was not well chronicled and remains highly contentious, the subject of academic and policy debates. Nevertheless, the formation of ICANN signalled a significant step towards a new phase of wider stakeholder participation in Internet governance.

The Emerging New Multistakeholder Model

The availability of the World Wide Web in the 1990s triggered an explosive growth in Internet use across a vast spectrum of individuals, groups, communities, commercial and not-for-profit enterprises, governments and nongovernmental organizations (NGOs). Their everyday activities and strategic decisions could be affected or even transformed by the use (or nonuse) of the Internet and related ICTs (Dutton 2004). However, it has only been in the 21st Century that the Internet's full impact as a global socioeconomic, as well as technical phenomenon, has been realized by a broad range of actors. This has been achieved through the widespread enactment in everyday life of the much forecast convergence of digital technologies and their diverse uses and implications, from User Generated Content (UGC) to a huge range of online multimedia content, mobile consumer devices and an increasing use of embedded sensor networks to monitor the environment and movements of people, vehicles and other entities.

WSIS, and the WGIG and IGF that developed from it, signify a global recognition of the need to pay greater attention to this phenomenon. They also represent milestones in the acknowledgement of the need to take account of a broad multistakeholder model of global governance, including significant civil society participation,[6] when seeking to develop effective and equitable policies to meet the UN's Millennium Development Goals. The decentralized, borderless and increasingly complex technical nature of the Internet means that neither traditional intergovernmental governance processes nor purely technical governance arrangements are likely to be suitable models for the future, as they lack sufficient accountability and are open to capture—real or perceived—by special interests.

A major new challenge for Internet governance posed by the new politics of the multistakeholder model is to try to preserve and strengthen the so far successful insulation of the technology's essential core infrastructure from political and commercial manipulation. At the same time, appropriate processes need to be developed to address the diverse range of substantive issues and stakeholder needs raised by the increasing intertwining of the Internet and its use with wider social, economic and political issues and activities. This is a difficult challenge as it involves pressures from diverse and often conflicting viewpoints and interests, reflecting very different values and cultural and political understandings. For instance, such conflicts include: governments seeking to empower and safeguard or exploit and subjugate their citizens; enterprises wanting to promote locally driven development or dominate and manipulate new markets; users seeking creative benefits or defensive protection from their online connections; and experts striving to maintain the integrity of the architecture or undermine it maliciously.

The Impacts of Realworld political issues in Internet governance is illustrated by a current debate on 'network neutrality', a fundamental Internet design principle aimed at creating a network that provides e2e routing without inspecting or changing the data being carried. In the US, network neutrality has recently become a hotly contested area among telecommunications infrastructure suppliers, Internet Service Providers (ISPs), media content corporations, consumers, regulators and others because some infrastructure suppliers are seeking to gain commercial advantages by creating tiered services that charge differential rates for access to its channels for different types of content (e.g., on demand video). Continuing global and intergovernmental debate over who should 'own' or most influence the Internet root servers, also indicates how apparently technical issues can have much wider social, economic or political significance.

The OII WSIS seminar series also highlighted important issues relating to the politics of civil society representation in multistakeholder forums and policy making, for instance, in terms of clarifying who comprises civil society, how different interests are represented, how conflicts between different interests can be resolved and the degree to which support is given to enable civil society to have a meaningful influence on actual policy outcomes (e.g., see Cammaerts and Carpentier 2005; Padovani and Tuzzi 2005).

Addressing the Diversity of Internet Governance Issues and Stakeholders

As Internet governance processes have moved from being the preserve largely of a technical elite towards a wider ownership of the substantive issues that could be affected by Internet development, availability and use, the politics involved have become more critical, more global and more diverse. This is indicated by the multilayered, complex and generally highly distributed nature of Internet governance. It is useful to understand that the Internet itself is not one technology, but an assembly of many at different levels. Similarly, governance is not one process, but several at different levels and in overlapping arenas addressing specific issues. This means different government models and agencies, involving many different institutional, group and individual stakeholders, will continue to be needed to address different governance issues.

Such diversity poses one of the greatest threats to Internet governance: that the emerging 'Internet governance mosaic' (Dutton and Peltu 2005) will become too complex to coordinate effectively if it fragments into too many different social, cultural, economic, technical, application, and governance specializations. The sound establishment of the IGF's foundations was an important move towards building a 'light touch' framework that could help to understand and maintain a 'big picture' coherence that can avoid an unmanageable fragmentation of the Internet governance mosaic. IGF could develop a particularly important role in setting an agenda that helps to move the focus of Internet governance debate and policy making from the procedural structures of governance to the identification of the substantive issues involved and the key 'owners' of these issues in the realworld arenas where practical outcomes are shaped through interactions between relevant decision-makers.

A key aim in this coordination process would be to ensure substantive issues are not neglected and a balance of interest and effort is maintained across the Internet governance spectrum. Table 1 illustrates a proposed framework for

Table 1: Classification of Internet Governance for Development Issues		
Type	**Key Issues**	**Examples relevant to Development**
I: Internet Centric	Protection and advancement of the Internet's core open architecture and operational infrastructure, including the preservation of its independence from undue influence by particular stakeholders. Smooth evolution of efficient, reliable, secure core Internet architecture and operations. Timely adaptability to continuing and often rapid technological and other changes affecting the Internet.	• Global standards setting to enable equitable access to the Internet and World Wide Web. • Assignment of Internet addresses and routing of data traffic in ways that do not privilege certain countries, enterprises or other stakeholders. • Maintenance of stability of Internet Protocol (IP) to allow innovations (e.g., wireless technologies) that can assist disadvantaged areas and groups.
II: Internet User Centric	How use or misuse of the Internet is regulated and policed within local, regional, national and international levels and jurisdictions in ways that safeguarding users' interests while avoiding the stifling of adaptability to rapid change and user creativity that has propelled the Internet's growth.	• 'Network neutrality' treating all Internet users and uses equitably. • Closing divides in access and user capacities to assist socioeconomic development. • Free and 'open source' software. • Consumer protection for users. • Violations of users' privacy. • Cybercrimes (e.g., online fraud). • Viruses and other 'badware'.
III: Non - Internet Centric	Policy and practice anchored in local and international bodies and jurisdictions not concerned primarily with Internet related issues. The main issues here concern the intersections between wider governance processes and Internet infrastructure development and use. Covers a vast range of socioeconomic issues.	• Closing digital divides other than in Internet access (e.g., relating to wealth, age, gender). • Supporting cultural and linguistic diversity. • Freedom of expression and communication (e.g., degree, or absence, of political or commercial control over content). • Copyright, intellectual property rights (IPR), trademarks.
Developed from Table 1 in Dutton and Peltu (2005: 7)		

classifying Internet government issues, particularly in relation to development. This offers a potentially productive way of categorizing diverse governance issues into more manageable chunks within a big picture that ties them together.

There are many overlaps and much interaction between the three governance types in Table 1 because of the growing intersection between what happens in the Internet's cyberspace and wider policy issues and behaviour in the real world. For instance, unwanted spam e-mail can raise serious concerns in all three types: spam that disables a Website affects the Internetcentric level; Type II issues include the fraudulent solicitation of money through spam; and at the wider Type III level digital divides can be exacerbated because the extra costs and special hightech resources required to deal with and prevent spam are unevenly distributed among different countries, regions and social groups. The names and numbers given to Internet entities may seem to be a clear Type I issue to be managed by ICANN, but the registration of a trade (or service) mark as a domain name with the intention of selling it back to the owner, called 'cybersquatting', has led to governance issues that are also the concern of Type III international organizations, like the World Intellectual Property Organization (WIPO), and national and international legislation and regulations that cover more traditional trademark concerns.

The way this cybersquatting issue was addressed, demonstrates that it is possible to coordinate a coherent response to overcome fragmentation, provided the relevant governance bodies are aware of the problem and are willing to collaborate to achieve a mutually acceptable approach. This solution came through an administrative dispute resolution mechanism, the Uniform Domain Name Dispute Resolution Policy (known as UDRP).[7] Policies for this were developed by WIPO in consultation with relevant stakeholders and agreed by its Member States, but their implementation is dependent on ICANN.

The Interdependence of Internet Governance and Development

Helping to Understand why Internet Governance is Relevant to Development

The concept of Internet governance may be only hazily understood (or misunderstood) by many people, which means large numbers of those who could be affected by such governance decisions are unaware of their relevance until the outcomes of the decisions directly affect their own activities. For instance, although certain civil society organizations were active in the WSIS, many potential participants were absent, including some significant players in the development sphere. A key reason for this seems to be that the absent organizations did not seem to be aware of, or understand why, the Internet or 'information society' should be a priority concern in their own areas of concern.

The WSIS seemed at times to separate artificially, Internet governance from development issues, rather than seeing them as separate but interrelated fields. An important role for a coordinating body like the IGF could be to highlight this interdependence by alerting existing development agencies and affected stakeholders to the Internet governance issues of intrinsic relevance to their development activities, but which may be obscured to them by the opaqueness to nonexperts of some key innovations in the Internet and related digital technologies. This could also involve seeking to establish, where necessary, appropriate new institutions, processes and links where none exist for particular substantive issues.

Broadening the Digital Divides Agenda

An important way of trying to interest more development stakeholders in Internet governance could be to move debates on ICT for development away from their focus on 'the' digital divide in access to ICT infrastructure and systems (e.g., see Dutton *et al* 2003), and a consequent focus on a fund to address global inequities,[8] to a broader view of the many important differential impacts of use that may affect disadvantaged countries, regions and groups. This narrow focus on the access divide has led some policy makers and researchers to announce that 'the digital divide is over', making it seem that there is perhaps little left to do in Internet governance to assist development.

A draft report from the World Bank (2005), for example, suggested that the global digital divide is narrowing at a faster rate than expected, using a statistic such as the 77 percent of the world's population estimated to be under the 'signal footprint' of a mobile provider. However, this identifies only potential users and social research in this field (e.g., Norris 2001; Dutton, Shepherd and di Gennaro 2006) is increasingly showing that there is not just one 'access divide'. Instead, there are actually many divides based on multiple social, economic, cultural, geographic, political and other dimensions. These follow and reinforce similar socioeconomic divides across and within societies, as well as creating new ones, such as across generations. The closing of a divide in physical access can also mask growing and newly opening divides in other aspects affecting the same groups, which explains how a gender gap and a digital divide in the use of technology in paid and unpaid work, leisure, study and employment remain significant, although the physical ICT access gap between genders is narrowing (Liff *et al* 2004).

The kind of Internet governance agenda that has been favoured in developed western countries, which has sometimes focused on market liberalization as the prime solution to 'the' divide in access, also needs to be widened to take account of the specific needs of developing countries and regions. For instance, governments in developing countries are often a major source of ICT knowhow, infrastructure development and capacity building, together with the private sector, universities and NGOs. Such governments also generally view Internet access as a key to many economic and social development areas. It is unrealistic to expect these governments to stand aside from active participation in Internet governance processes, as some would prefer. Given developing countries' financial, political, cultural and other constraints, building a better understanding between them and developed countries could also be valuable in addressing Internetrelated regulations affecting key nonInternet-centric areas, such as freedom of speech, human rights and IPR.

The technological scope at the core of a broad conceptualization of 'digital divides' should also be widened from a focus on the Internet and PCs to include the continuing stream of other ICT innovations (e.g., mobile phones, iPods, UGC) and options for mediated access to ICTs (e.g., via help centres or over-the-counter services). The value that can be gained from applying still-relevant older technologies, often in conjunction with the latest ICTs,[9] should also be supported.

Revealing the Dynamics of Multistakeholder Decision-making

Dutton (2004) has defined an approach that can help to understand the realworld contexts and interactions shaping outcomes from Internet governance processes. This is based on the concept of an 'ecology of games', where a 'game'[10] is defined

Table 2: Selected Games Shaping Internet Governance for Development

Type	Game	Main Players	Goals and Objectives
I: Internet centric	Transnational jurisdictional governance 'turf struggles'	Governments, regional entities, Internet and other governance agencies (e.g., IGF, ICANN, WIPO), experts	Participation in governance bodies to gain or retain, limit or expand control over Internet resources (e.g., the root servers).
	Names and numbers	Individual experts, ICANN, Registries, ISPs, users	Obtain, sell, allocate domain names, etc. for sites, servers, users.
	Standards	Standard setting bodies, experts, governments, users	Establish and propagate Internet standards for stable Internet evolution.
II: Internet user centric	Network neutrality	Telecom infrastructure suppliers, ISPs, content providers, consumers, media businesses, regulators, civil society activists, lawyers, public policy makers.	Negotiate terms of access to Internet content, taking account of different stakeholder views (e.g., on social equity, development, free markets, Internet open e2e design principles).
	Free and open source software (F/OSS)	Activists favouring free software, commercial proprietary software producers and distributors, users.	Promotion of software development and distribution models that prioritize social equity or free market goals.
	Privacy and data protection	Governments, citizens, regulators, private firms, lawyers, journalists, civil liberties activists	Prevent or seek disclosure of personal data depending on negotiated or imposed criteria.

Contd...

Contd...

III: Non-Internet centric.	Digital divides.	Governments, NGOs, local activists, special interest groups, local communities, investors	Close socioeconomic, health and other divides by the effective use of the Internet and related ICTs.
	Copyright, digital rights management.	Legislators and regulators, creative industries and other content providers, telecom suppliers, ISPs, ICT vendors.	Negotiate access and rights terms to balance players' goals (e.g., low cost access for consumers; highest return on assets for content creators and suppliers).
	Freedom of expression.	Political and religious activists, writers, artists, media rights advocates, news media, bloggers, governments, censors.	Individuals, groups, organizations aim to facilitate or constrain the expression and exchange of certain viewpoints.

Adapted from Table 2 in Dutton and Peltu (2005: 910)

an arena of competition and cooperation structured by a set of rules and assumptions about how to act to achieve a particular set of objectives. Internet governance can then be seen to be the outcome of a variety of choices made by many different players involved in separate but interdependent governance games. A few such games related to development are illustrated in Table 2.

The ecology of games concept illustrated in Table 2 indicates that no single set of actors actually seeks to control governance as such, but that each player pursues more focused goals in collaboration or competition with other actors. For example, actual goals could be: 'creating an equitable market for registering and managing Internet names' (Type I); 'enhancing socioeconomic development by promoting equity of Internet access' (Type II); or 'closing wealth divides with the help of Internet use' (Type III). Actors could own all these goals, while at the same time participating in 'Internet names and numbers', 'Internet diffusion' and 'economic development' games.

Conclusion: Focusing on Key Internet Governance Issues

Setting the Agenda

The digital convergence that eventually became a reality in the 21st Century has accelerated pressures to develop a multistakeholder governance model. Nevertheless, many Internet experts have also argued that 'governance' is irrelevant to the Net, although as indicated in this paper, related governance structures and processes have been co-evolving since its inception as its everwidening user base and socioeconomic real world entanglement has grown. Such views may reflect experts' anxieties about losing their traditionally strong influence over what were primarily Type I Internet governance issues. It should be remembered that, although the roots of the Internet go back many decades, we are still in relatively early days of understanding and addressing key issues raised by widespread digital convergence. This is indicated by the uncertainty among some participants at the first WSIS in 2003 about what the Internet actually meant to them, let alone an understanding of the more complex notion of 'Internet governance'.

Given the growing demand for widening multistakeholder participation across an expanding range of diverse Internet governance issues, this paper has argued that the next steps in global and national Internet governance should be to focus on identifying the key substantive issues and their most relevant fora, while developing coordination processes to ensure all issues are addressed in the most appropriate forums for their effective resolution. Just because an issue is important to the future of the Internet doesn't necessarily mean it should be addressed by a body focused on Internet governance as such. But it is important that those stakeholders closest to an issue are engaged in their arena's governance process in ways that take account of relevant Internet dimensions. Those issues for which there is no adequate mechanism to deal with Internet aspects should be brought to the attention of relevant stakeholders who have legitimate jurisdiction over the substantive issues, while new forums or institutions should be created to deal with substantive issues that do not yet have a 'home', such as those tied to emerging new ICTs and the socioeconomic transformations tied to them.

The paper explains why the IGF is in an excellent position to play a pivotal coordinating role in shaping and lightly guiding such an approach. It also outlines a framework for helping to classify Internet governance issues to assist identify and prioritize issues on the global Internet governance agenda that could help to promote development. It has also highlighted the importance of recognizing the inherently political nature of Internet governance processes, which obviously include those involved in the identification of such issues.

The political scientist E E Schattschneider (1960: 2) once compared political conflict to a fight: "Every fight consists of two parts: (1) the few individuals who are actively engaged at the center and (2) the audience that is irresistibly attracted to the scene... The outcome of every conflict is determined by the extent to which the audience becomes involved in it." Contestants with a clear lead in such a conflict might well try to defend the status quo by keeping their own side intact while keeping the spectators in the stands. In contrast, losing contestants can change the odds by dividing their opponents or drawing spectators into the game.[11] Given the importance of agenda setting in the policy process, the IGF could have a major role to play in shaping the future of Internet governance.

Research to Support Issue-based Multistakeholder Internet Governance

The approach recommended in this paper could be supported well by research that offers both practical and conceptual insights relevant in the areas discussed.[12]

The kinds of issue-based policy research most likely to be of value in this context include technical advances in design, empirical studies of actual uses[13] and action research[14] based on a strong scholarly grounding for analysing experimental uses of the Internet. Research on Internet governance itself could support the institutionalization of governance structures and processes. Good empirical data and evidence-based analyses would enable researchers to work with policy makers and practitioners to identify and evaluate the priorities that are most likely to lead to sustainable strategies and institutions to assist in meeting development goals.

Improved understanding, including through targeted research, can also offer effective responses to key concerns of civil society participants in multistakeholder policy and decision making processes (e.g., use of the technology to assist disadvantaged areas and groups by closing socioeconomic divides or promoting information rights.) Academic researchers could play a valuable role in helping to understand the nature and dynamics of the politics of such civil society representation, which is a vital issue for the IGF in its engagements with such representatives. Researchers could also help to articulate "grassroots" user and social requirements to policy makers and product, system and service designers and developers.

(William H Dutton, Director, Oxford Internet Institute, University of Oxford and can be reached at Director@oii.ox.ac.uk).

Endnotes

1 Organized in collaboration with the Berkman Center for Internet and Society at Harvard Law School and sponsored by Afilias, the *Economist,* Nominet UK and the Public Internet Registry.

2 The seminar series (see *www.oii.ox.ac.uk/research/project.cfm?id=30*) was supported by grant RES451260295 from the UK Economic and Social Research Council.

3 Simonelis (2005) details the history of Internet governance bodies. Also, see Mueller (2002).

4 A large international community of network designers, operators, vendors and researchers responsible for the development and stability of the Internet's architecture.

5 For example, in 1984 Postel became a member of one of the founding Internet governance bodies, the Internet Advisory Board. This evolved into the current Internet Architecture Board (IAB).

6 For instance, the (Cardoso 2004: 3) report to the UN SecretaryGeneral on strengthening UN systems concluded: "The rise of civil society is indeed one of the landmark events of our times. Global governance is no longer the sole domain of Governments. The growing participation and influence of nonState actors is enhancing democracy and reshaping multilateralism. Civil society organizations are also the prime movers of some of the most innovative initiatives to deal with emerging global threats".

7 See *http://www.icann.org/dndr/udrp/policy.htm*

8 Within the WSIS, this became known as a voluntary Digital Solidarity Fund (see www.dsffsn. org).

9 For instance, the Kothmale Community Radio and Internet Project (www.kothmale.org) integrates radio and Internet services. This includes allowing listeners to send questions to the radio station. Staff at the station obtain answers from the Internet and broadcast them over the radio.

10 The term 'game' is used here only in this sense and should not be seen as trivializing an arena by suggesting it is like a sporting or entertainment game.

11 This discussion draws from Dutton (1999): 8384.

12 An example of efforts to develop networks of academics involved in research related to Internet governance is the Global Internet Governance Academic Network (GIGANet), proposed at an International Association for Media and Communication Research (IAMCR) conference in June 2006 in Kurort Rathen, Germany (see *www.cipaco.org/article.php3?id_article=835*). The GIGANet Startup Group including Wolfgang Kleinwächter of the Department of Media and Communication Sciences at the University of Aarhus and Peng Hwa Ang of the School of Communication and Information of Nanyang Technological University of Singapore.

13 For example, the World Internet Project covering over 20 countries *(www.worldinternetproject.net)*, including the OII's Oxford Internet Surveys (OxIS) in Britain *(www.oii.ox.ac.uk/research)*.

14 An example of such action research is *StopBadware.org*, an initiative run by the OII and Berkman Center for Internet and Society to provide practical defences against malicious software programs *(www.StopBadware.org)*.

References

Cammaerts, B and Carpentier, N (2005), "The Unbearable Lightness of Full Participation in a Global Context: WSIS and Civil Society Participation", in Servaes, J and Carpentier, N (eds.), *Towards a Sustainable Information Society: Deconstructing WSIS, Bristol:* Intellect, 1749.

Cardoso Report (2004), We the Peoples: Civil Society, the United Nations and Global Governance: Report of the Panel of Eminent Persons on United Nations–Civil Society Relations, Document A/58/817, New York: UN, 11 June. *http://daccessdds.un.org/doc/UNDOC/GEN/N04/376/41/PDF/N0437641.pdf?OpenElement*

Dutton, W H (1999), "Society on the Line: Information Politics in the Digital Age," Oxford: Oxford University Press.

Dutton, W H (2004), "Social Transformation in the Information Society," Paris: UNESCO Publications for the WSIS.

Dutton, W H, and Peltu, M (2005), "The Emerging Internet Governance Mosaic: Connecting the Pieces", OII Forum Discussion Paper, No. 5, Oxford: Oxford Internet Institute, University of Oxford. Available at *www.oii.ox.ac.uk/resources/publications/FD5.pdf*

Dutton, W H, Shepherd A, di Gennaro, C (2006 forthcoming), Digital Divides and Choices Reconfiguring Access: National and Cross *National Patterns of Internet*

"Diffusion and Use", in Anderson, B, Brynin, M, and Raban, Y (eds), *Information and Communications Technologies in Society,* London: Routledge, pp. forthcoming.

Dutton, W H, Gillett, S E, McKnight, L W and Peltu, M (2003), "Broadband Internet: The Power to Reconfigure Access". OII Forum Discussion Paper No. 1., Oxford: Oxford Internet Institute, University of Oxford.

Liff, S, Shepherd, A, Wajcman, J, Rice, R E and Hargittai, E (2004), "An evolving gender digital divide", OII Issue Brief No. 2, Oxford: Oxford Internet Institute, University of Oxford. Available at *www.oii.ox.ac.uk/resources/publications/IB2all.pdf*

Mueller, M L (2002), "Ruling the Root: Internet Governance and the Taming of Cyberspace," Cambridge, MA: The MIT Press.

Norris, P. (2001), "Digital Divide: Civic Engagement, Information Poverty, and the Internet Worldwide," Cambridge: Cambridge University Press.

Padovani, C and Tuzzi, A (2005), "Communication Governance and the Role of Civil Society: Words and Networks in the World Summit on the Information Society: Reflections on Participation and the Changing Scope of Political Action", in Servaes, J and Carpentier, N (eds.), *Towards a Sustainable Information Society: Deconstructing WSIS,* Bristol: Intellect, 5179.

Schattschneider, E E (1960), "The Semi Sovereign People: A Realist's View of Democracy in America" (New York and London: Holt, Rinehart, and Winston).

Simonelis, A (2005), "A Concise Guide to the Major Internet Bodies". Ubiquity 6(5), 16-22 February. Available at *www.acm.org/ubiquity/issues6.html*

World Bank (2005), Financing Information and Communication Infrastructure Needs in the Developing World: Public and Private Roles, Washington, DC: World Bank, Global Information and Communication Technologies Department

WGIG (2005), Working Group on Internet Governance, Report of the Working Group on Internet Governance, Geneva: United Nations. Available at *www.wgig.org*

Section III

Country Perspectives

10

Internet Governance, National Interest and International Relations*

Kenneth Neil Cukier

The Internet is a global resource whose control and allocation is a matter of political power; instead of doing away with geopolitics, the Net creates new areas of national interest and foreign policy concerns. The article explains the Internet governance as 'infrastructure coordination' activity taking care of Root servers, Protocols, IP Numbers, names etc. The author elaborates on the national interests related to the Internet control, with an emphasis on US interests.

Six long words. Three big concepts. One small idea. The title of this essay comprises things not normally associated together. When one considers the Internet and foreign affairs, it is usually viewed in terms of cross-border regulations on content and usage, or the effect of the medium abroad (for example, regarding "soft power"), or the change in the process of diplomacy itself.

---

* This essay is based on a seminar, the author presented at the National Center for Digital Government at Harvard University on March 16, 2004

Source: www.cukier.com, Background paper for the United Nations ICT Task Force Meeting, 24-26 March 2004.

However, there is another dimension, which is the focus of this essay: who controls the network's operation and evolution? This is currently done by ICANN, the Internet Corporation for Assigned Names and Numbers. It was created by the US in 1998 as an international, public/private-sector body to oversee the Internet's domain name system – a task previously managed by the US Defense Dept., which initially funded the Internet.

The one simple idea is this: *The Internet is a global resource whose control and allocation is a matter of political power; instead of doing away with geopolitics, the Net creates new areas of national interest and foreign policy concerns.*

This essay doesn't presume to offer a doctrine for foreign policy in the Internet age. Its more modest goal is to raise a number of empirical matters that governments collectively face regarding the network. Together, they reveal a new and mature way of understanding the medium.

The first part explains Internet governance, or "infrastructural coordination." Part two looks at it from the perspective of national interest, with an emphasis on US interests. Part three notes how these interests map to specific ICANN issues, which are concerns of international relations. The fourth part tries to explain why ICANN matters not just for students of politics and international affairs, but for ordinary individuals, companies and other stakeholders. Finally, the essay concludes by analyzing current tensions concerning the Internet's institutionalization.

I. Internet Governance

It is a regrettably misleading term (since "governance" sometimes presumes it is the sole responsibility of governments). A better term may be "coordination of Internet technical functions" though they may present public policy concerns, too. There are four aspects:

- **Names** (global ones like .com; territorial ones like .iq for Iraq). Who says "who is" a registry, a valuable economic asset that effects free speech? Who says "who" gets a country-code, an important way to establish presence online, and symbolically important?

- **IP numbers** (e.g. "255.255.255.0"). A valuable and finite resource that affects the types and number of devices that can connect seamlessly to the network. When the network was young, huge blocks of numbers were given to US companies and universities, so some benefit from abundance while entities outside the US deal with relative scarcity.
- **Protocols** (TCP/IP, SNMP, etc.). Most communications standards have been set by national and intergovernmental bodies; the Internet's standards exist outside that process, which has historically led to tension with the ITU, among others.
- **Root servers** (1 master, 12 slaves, +30 mirrors). The computers match domains to their authoritative name servers for routing traffic. Currently, three are outside the US (Sweden, UK and Japan); the majority are under US governmental control. Mirror servers have been broadly diffused globally, providing advantages in routing, but meaningless in terms of internationalized political control.

These function sound technical and arcane – and they are. That's one reason why many countries have been late to understand their geopolitical importance. Control over these aspects of the Internet is akin to a central bank's control over a nation's money supply. Names are the real estate of the Internet; numbers are the oxygen or oil of the network; the protocols are the utilities, or the legal system (from which the term intentionally derives); root servers are the central nervous system. Together, the system is important, and its daily operation as well as the influence over the substance of policy and institutional process represents important power in the modern age.

II. National Interests Related to Internet Control

The question of what constitutes a national interest is a long-standing debate among scholars; this essay won't go there. Nor, try to separate vital from secondary interests; that's for another time. Instead, it is meant for identification, not prioritization.

A few interests, along with where they fit in with the ICANN-related functions, include:

- Access to numbering resources (IP address space).
- Stability and robustness of network (root servers and protocols).
- Access to improved media resources (domain names and content).
- Greater economic efficiency via new technology (protocol development).

These interests aren't universal; in fact, in some cases they may conflict with interests of certain nations, for instance:

- An authoritarian regime would prefer a closed medium to control information flows.
- Greater technical efficiency may jeopardize the revenue of existing state-run firms.

But the interests correspond to objectives the Internet can support and fuel:

- Economic development.
- Openness, transparency, accountability.
- Free expression and information sharing.
- Continuing technical innovation.
- Global political, economic and social stability.

Of course there is nothing about the Internet that inherently supports these goals – it must be shepherded in the right way. But the Internet, as a more open medium compared to all other communications technologies, can potentially further these goals by dint of its end-to-end design principle. This provides for its decentralization, lower cost, and openness.

III. How Internet Governance Interests Dovetail with Foreign Affairs

There are pragmatic concerns facing Internet governance and nation-states, that have escalated to the level of international relations. They include:

- National sovereignty over information infrastructure
- Control over shared information resources

- Influence over policy process and substance
- Access to content and its restriction

Each of these areas contain practical policy concerns, and merit closer consideration.

National Sovereignty Over Information Infrastructure

- *ccTLDs: Who is a country?* – ICANN and its predecessor organization, has always sought to avoid the issue of what is a state, yet is inherently unable to skirt it. For instance, in 2003, Chinese authorities raised the issue with US and ICANN officials of why .tw existed since it seemed to legitimize the island as an independent nation, which China regards as a province. Though China stopped short of asking its removal (there are a number of non-national territories in the ISO 3166 list, including .hk for Hong Kong), the incident is indicative of the offline politics that can easily enter domain name policy discussions. Secondly, in March 2000, ICANN established .ps to represent the Palestinian Authority, another example of how politics is implicit in Internet addressing.
- *ccTLDs: Who controls the domain?* – There is a policy ambiguity over who has ultimate authority over county-codes. In 2003, Singapore's governmental country-code registry withdrew its application for a trademark on its two-letter domain, .sg, after ICANN informed it that the country didn't actually have rights to the domain; instead, ICANN controlled it. Rather than force the issue, the government acquiesced. The incident exposes the ambiguity of whether countries have sovereignty of their country-codes, and why ICANN asserts it ultimately does, when the US government's 1998 statement of policy (White Paper) that established ICANN's principles indicated the contrary. At the UN World Summit on the Information Society in Dec. 2003 in Geneva, Zimbabwe's President Robert Mugabe emphatically called this an example of neo-colonialism.

Control over Shared Information Resources

- *International domain names* – IDNs are a nascent technology that permits domain names in languages other than that don't use the Roman alphabet characters; it opens up Internet addressing to all the world's scripts. However, unlike country-codes where there is normally one acknowledged entity that represents the nation, major languages often transcend one specific country, such as Arabic or Chinese. China initially claimed sovereignty over the language for the domain name system; it has since relinquished the stance. But the question of who decides what entity is legitimate to steward and set policies over a script is uncertain. Because the values and traditions of the speakers vary widely across cultures that share a language, the entity designated to register names can affect the degree of free speech or privacy online.

- *Internet protocol numbers* – The addresses represent important economic value and their access is vital for widespread deployment of Internet-enabled devices. Japan's consumer electronics industry is dependent on access to IP addresses; in 2001, the country's minister of industry travelled 40 hours roundtrip for a three-hour visit to an ICANN board meeting in California, to make that point. China relies on access to IP addresses due to its huge population; for that reason it specifically obtained an unprecedented two seats on executive council of APNIC, the regional Asia-Pacific IP number registry, so it has greater influence over the allocation process. Lastly, global mobile phone companies or handset makers will depend on access to IP numbers. These allocation concerns will remain despite an upcoming enhancement called IPv6, which increases the number of addresses exponentially.
- *Root servers* – The constellation of 12 secondary root servers, capped at that number due to technical limitations, are managed by both private and public entities that are only loosely affiliated with ICANN, for historical reasons. Many countries have requested to operate a root server, including France and China. Global deployment is important for better regional traffic routing and quality of service, for network resiliency, for symbolism of internationalized Internet control and national prestige. It could potentially prevent any one entity from having a preponderance of control to unilaterally affect the addressing content that the rest of the Internet adheres to for universal interoperability. The use of mirror servers have led to better regional traffic routing, but confers no political control, and lacks the symbolic power that control infers.

Influence over Policy Process and Substance

- *Process* – The central intergovernmental debate at ICANN is over the role of the state versus private stakeholders, such as industry, technologists or civil society. ICANN's Governmental Advisory Committee has no formal policy-making powers, which some member states feel is inappropriate. ICANN itself is a creation of the US government and lacks the formal legitimacy that international treaties confer. Moreover, the GAC exhibits classic politicization of offline disputes, such as when China walked out of a meeting in Melbourne in March 2001 when it saw "Taiwan" name cards for the island's representatives, rather than the traditional diplomatic word-play "Chinese Taipei."
- *Policy* – ICANN has set policy in a few areas, either by action or non-action, that impact national law. For instance, one of the first acts the organization took was to establish a uniform dispute resolution procedure (UDRP) for generic, global domain names. This was a method of enforcing trademark rights globally, by adopting the procedure developed by WIPO. Secondly, ICANN has not changed the public nature of the WHOIS database for global domains, which makes openly available the name, address and phone number of registrants. It has been roundly criticized for violating norms of privacy. The reason it remains public is due to the influence of intellectual property holders who insist on having an easy way to contact Website owners in cases of infringing content. These two examples underscore how the substance of ICANN decisions, by action or inaction, affect national policy matters and apply globally.

Access to Content and its Restriction

- *Protocol* – The way the technical code of the Internet works makes identifying, tracing and monitoring traffic difficult. There is also an inherent trade-off between security that protects the integrity and confidentiality of communications needed for e-commerce with the potential for surveillance capability needed by law enforcement. In 1999, the US Department of Justice sought to develop wiretap capabilities directly into the protocol of the Internet, via the standards body IETF, which is affiliated with ICANN. The initiative was rebuffed by the technical engineers, but underscores an area where national interests coincide with how the Internet operates, for that matter for international relations.

These areas are of course not exhaustive. And the examples used are often just ones that stand for a number of similar incidents. Lastly, one of the most important aspects of the Internet relative to governments is network security, but this analysis has not included it as a point because, so far, there has not been a political dispute in that regard.

IV. Why ICANN Matters

ICANN's actions affect how people use the Internet on a daily level. It does so because of its control over names, numbers, protocols and the root server system that holds it together. However, due to the idiosyncratic ways that the Internet evolved (informally, often non-governmentally, inherently internationally, etc.) its institutional structure remains largely outside the realm of classic national and intergovernmental control. Any entity that strives to "govern the Internet" in terms of the quasi-technical related functions will possess significant power, but also confront contentious issues.

Names

- The power to decide the words that everyone in the world will use to communicate, identify content and interact online. This responsibility over the upper-most hierarchical terms is crucial for helping users navigate and give semantic meaning to the online world.
- That lets the institution delegate an enormous economic and political asset to an entity, to operate the domain registry.
- The delegation permits it to influence the policies that the registry must follow concerning the appropriate use of words for domain names, which directly impacts freedom of speech and democratic dissent. It also determines the degree to which trademark holders are protected.
- Oversight of registry operations and as a result, the WHO IS database, gives it control over the degree to which privacy and anonymity exist at the most primal aspect of Internet communications – online identity, and entry-point of access.

- Authority over the system lets it regulate the companies that sell domains, to ensure fair competition, consumer protection, and to a certain degree, the prices users pay.
- This power effects the visibility of individuals and companies on the Internet.

Numbers

- The control of IP number assignments effects the way the Internet evolves in terms of its growth, cost, future services and openness to technical innovation.
- Power to determine address allocations impacts the number of devices that can connect directly to the Internet, which affects how many people or machines are online.
- The policies determine the cost of IP addresses (one-time or annually-recurring fee), and effects the price that consumer and businesses pay to go online, as well as the economic model of businesses that rely on the deployment of network infrastructure.
- Power to control access to IP numbers impacts the types of services users are offered, by affecting a company's ability to bring onto the network millions of devices or objects via embedded addresses.
- Oversight of allocations if implemented, can be used as a mechanism to achieve non-technical, policy goals, such as, positively identifying users and their precise geographic location, for activities like surveillance, taxation, etc.
- Controlling address availability impacts the openness of the Internet as a medium for technical innovation, by ensuring widespread address distribution so that devices can connect directly to other devices without the need for intermediaries that could act as a choke-point for network control. (Such control could entail prohibiting applications like Internet telephony or peer-to-peer file sharing, etc.).
- Power over the network's openness assures the degree of user independence relative to the Internet service provider, that enables competition and usually lowers costs.

- The ability to preserve network openness affects democratic values of free expression; control of IP addresses could otherwise provide power over who may participate online.

Protocols

- Control over the development of new protocols effects the degree of technical innovation that can happen online, and what users are able to do.
- New protocols can be a means to remedy problems with the current design and operation of the network, such as devising service quality systems.
- That power over can translate into control over code development to achieve mainstream policy-related objectives, such as privacy, censorship, surveillance, etc.
- This control could also be used to prohibit certain activities such as content restrictions, or hobbling functional capabilities of the network, like file-sharing.

Root Server System

- Oversight authority ensures the stability and smooth functioning of the critical infrastructure of the Internet, so that traffic is routed efficiently and accurately, leading to quality of service for users and confidence in the network for new and sophisticated uses.
- Geographic distribution of root servers provides more efficient traffic routing (of address queries), which lowers cost and increases quality of network performance.
- This decentralized distribution, if coupled with control of the server, can risk a fragmented addressing system, if the entity decides to change any of the content in the zone file (adding or deleting a name, or changing the authoritative name server address).
- Contrary-wise, decentralized distribution can act as an insurance policy to assure that no single actor holds so much control that it can unilaterally change the zone file in a way that other root operators have an incentive to unwillingly follow to prevent fragmenting the addressing system.

- Control of a root server could be used for surveillance (albeit extremely inefficient) of Internet traffic connections (though not content).

Final Thoughts: Institutions and Governance

This analysis points to a paradox of Internet governance. It might be framed as the paradox of power and plausibility: the more horrific the scenarios of how Internet governance can be potentially abused, the less likely it will actually happen.

This should provide some relief. It injects a dose of reasonability and proportion to the debate, since it isn't always big, abstract principles and hypothetical scenarios one considers, but practical questions of how to implement concrete policies in the real world.

Still, there are some fundamental tensions regarding the institutionalization of Internet governance. It is essential to balance:

- the need for openness with specialized expertise;
- representation with the naturally unequal influence of diverse stakeholders (and ability to continually add new ones);
- the application of the rule of law with the risk of politicization;
- established processes with flexible implementation for new circumstances;
- stability with experimentation to preserve continued innovation.

If there is an underlying conflict that drives the debate, it may be the question: "What is the Internet?" It is not a metaphysical concern, for the answer one gives effects whether one regulates/controls/manages/coordinates/oversees/ignores the medium.

Questions about what constitutes the Internet include:

- Global public resource or common private good?
- Innovation at the core or at the edge?
- Commercialization of infrastructure or at higher layers?

Ultimately, we can hope there's more Internet governance or less of it; we can strive to centralize or decentralize the processes – and it seems appropriate to initiate a global discussion with ever-increasing numbers of stakeholders on these matters. But that is, provided we are willing to do the harder work of agreeing on answers.

Conclusion

After having examined the specifics of Internet governance, it may be useful to return to the bigger picture – and the "one small idea" with which I began this essay. If a hands-off approach or watching (and, hopefully, learning) from the sidelines was an acceptable policy for governments in the 1990s, it clearly isn't an option anymore. The Internet has become too important for governments to remain passive observers to its development, and the issues, this essay has sought to argue, has become an urgent matter of national interest, power, security and sovereignty. And thus, a matter of foreign policy.

As such, there are two extreme directions in which governments may go:

- Deviating in some way from the ICANN-sanctioned naming and numbering system.
- Becoming excessively engaged, seduced by ICANN's true or perceived power.

On the former, why one ought to care if a country decides to drop out of the ICANN addressing system is strait-forward: the value of a network decreases for all parties if less users participate, albeit the effects are felt disproportionately more by the smaller group. For the US, this disadvantage is borne economically in increased transaction costs of routing traffic and e-mail, as well compliance with multiple technical standards. Most importantly, it sets back Western foreign policy interests for an Internet that can export the values of transparency, free expression and economic development.

However, from a practical standpoint, the key challenge facing ICANN isn't a country dropping out, but countries being so enamoured with ICANN that the Internet gets smothered in their embrace. Like the curse of Othello, the risk isn't that of not loving enough, but too much. That governments try to become so involved that they harm the Internet's openness, is a real risk.

As an observer of Internet governance for almost a decade, I take a moderate view. I don't think the issues surrounding Internet governance are so drastic that extreme positions are likely to seriously emerge for long. Instead, I believe that the world can settle these matters as it does in so many other realms – with difficulty, with discomfort, gradually and never perfectly. But eventually, well enough.

(Kenneth Neil Cukier, Research Fellow, National Center for Digital Government John F. Kennedy School of Government, Harvard University and can be reached at kn@cukier.com).

11

Internet Governance Priorities and Practices: India

Dieter Zinnbauer

The report highlights some of the most important findings and insights regarding Internet Governance in India. It emphasizes the persistent importance of basic infrastructure issues such as access, affordability and speed of Internet in India, and also issues related to local content and local language software, which are pressing concerns for the Internet community in India.

Background: Internet Governance and ORDIG

Why Care About Internet Governance?

Internet use in the Asia-Pacific region has grown in leaps and bounds over the last decade. Between 2000 and 2003 alone the Internet population in the region grew by an annual average of 38 percent to 250 million users, making the Asia-Pacific region the world's largest Internet community. Estimates put this number today at over 300 million and predict further strong growth. These impressive numbers notwithstanding, overall penetration rates are still very low

This article is originally published by UNDP Asia-Pacific Development Information Programme and is available in full text at http://www.apdip.net/news/ordigcountryreport.

in most countries. Many remain excluded from the benefits of the information society and much remains to be done to make new information and communication technologies (ICTs), in particular the Internet, work for inclusive human development.

In response to these challenges UNDP's Asia-Pacific Development Information Programme (UNDP-APDIP) has established an Open Regional Dialogue on Internet Governance (ORDIG), an initiative to take stock of the status quo in Internet Governance in the Asia-Pacific and provide a forum for all stakeholders in the region to share their priority needs and concerns; identify emerging best policy practices; and develop a stronger, more inclusive representation in the international policy arena.

Following the definition adopted by the UN Working Group on Internet Governance (WGIG), Internet governance in this context refers to *"the development and application by Governments, the private sector and civil society, in their respective roles, of shared principles, norms, rules, decision-making procedures, and programmes that shape the evolution and use of the Internet."*[1]

ORDIG and India

Over the last year, ORDIG has carried out a wide variety of consultative and research activities across the region, creating a wealth of information on Internet governance views and practices of different stakeholder groups in more than 37 Asia-Pacific countries. Activities include a multilingual online survey with more than 1,200 respondents from across the region, more than ten presentations and consultations at various sub-regional conferences, and a three-week online discussion forum with almost 200 participants. The Internet community in India has responded with great enthusiasm to these initiatives and a sizeable number of policy makers, Internet entrepreneurs, infrastructure providers, as well as users from India have actively participated in ORDIG's activities.[2]

This report draws on the extensive body of knowledge compiled through all these activities and summarizes the most important findings and insights with particular relevance to India. It is hoped that this will contribute to a better understanding of the Internet governance priorities and challenges for India and stimulate a multistakeholder dialogue at the domestic level on how to best move forward. This report is not an exhaustive analysis of the Internet policies in place, but rather a country-specific analysis of ORDIG's work. It builds on and should be read in close conjunction with other ORDIG outputs, including the Internet Governance Primer, Survey and Forum Reports and, especially, the Input Paper to WGIG and the UN World Summit on the Information Society (WSIS), whose structure and categorization of Internet governance topics are followed by this report. Reference is also made to the final report and related materials produced by WGIG, which provides the framework for agreeing on concrete steps for Internet governance reform during the upcoming second part of WSIS in Tunis in November 2005.[3]

Internet Country Profile

The following basic ICT indicators below provide a general backdrop for discussion on Internet governance in India. In order to place India's Internet coordinates in a regional context, comparative data is also provided for four other major reference countries in the Asia-Pacific: China, Indonesia, Pakistan and Thailand.

Figure 1: Basic Internet Parameters

Country	Internet users (2003)	Internet users per 100 population (2003)	Computers (2003)	Computers per 100 population (2003)	Internet host computers (2003)	Internet host computers per 100 population (2003)
China	79,500,000	6.32	35,500,000	2.76	16,0421	0.01
India	8,080,000	1.75	7,500,000	0.72	86,871	0.01
Indonesia	18,481,000	3.76	2,519,000	1.19	62,036	0.03
Pakistan	1,500,000	1.03	600,000	0.42	15,124	0.01
Thailand	6,972,000	11.05	2,461,000	3.98	103,700	0.16
AP Average		7.22		4.83		0.60
AP Industrialized Country Average		49.49		40.67		10.74

Source: ITU, 2004[4]

Figure 2: Competition Situation

Country	Local phone services	Domestic long distance	Intl. long distance	XDSL	Data	VSAT	Leased lines	Fixed Wireless Broadband	Internet services
China(1)	P	P	P		P	C	P		
India(2)	C	C	M		C	C			C
Indonesia(1)	P	P	P	C	C	C	C	C	C
Pakistan(1)	C	C	C	C	C	C	C	C	C
Thailand (1)	P	P	M	P	P	C	C	P	C

Key: M=Monopoly; D=Duopoly; P=Partial competition; C=Full competition

(1)=2004 data; (2)=pre-2004 data

Source: ITU, World Telecommunication Regulatory Database

Internet Policy Priorities in India: Overview of ORDIG Survey Results

156 individuals from all stakeholder groups in India participated in the UNDP-APDIP online survey on Internet governance priorities in the Asia-Pacific region. For maximum outreach, the survey was made available online in a low-graphic, easy-to-complete format and promoted through various local partners to reach different stakeholder groups.[5]

Survey takers were invited to register their views on 26 Internet governance issues and provide some general information about themselves and their Internet use. Detailed results for all questions are presented in Annex III.

In general, respondents from India exhibit considerable optimism about the benefits and potential of the Internet, but are slightly more sceptical than their colleagues in other countries, especially with regard to the role of the Internet in combating poverty. More than 95 percent of Indian respondents believe that the Internet should be available for everyone and that its benefits will further grow in the future. But only half of the Indian survey takers think that the Internet also helps to combat poverty, as compared to a significantly larger share of 61 percent in other Asia-Pacific countries.

This guarded optimism is also reflected in the survey responses to 22 specific topics in Internet governance, many of which are met with a considerable degree of dissatisfaction by the Indian Internet community.

Figure 3: Internet Governance Priorities for India (ranked by Level of Dissatisfaction with Management of status quo)

Rank in AP region	Rank In India	Issue	% Dissatisfied	% Satisfied	% No view
1	1	Cyber crime, online fraud	90.8	7.8	1.3
2	2	Virus attacks	89.6	9.7	0.6
3	3	Spam	89	11	0
4	4	Illegal content	80.3	16.4	3.3
14	5	Availability of local content	68.6	20.9	10.5
6	6	Availability and cost of Internet	62.8	35.3	1.9
8	7	Wireless Internet: spectrum and access	62.0	18.7	19.3
5	8	Privacy online	61.9	32.9	5.2
13	9	Availability of local language software	60.8	27.5	11.8
9	10	Online access to government information	59.6	38.5	1.9
7	11	Reliability and speed of Internet	58.3	41.7	0.0
16	12	Network interconnection/backbone access	53.3	34.2	12.5
12	13	Internet telephony (VoIP)	45.1	30.7	24.2
11	14	Fair access to / protection of intellectual property	42.7	36.7	20.7
10	15	E-commerce payment systems	42.5	46.4	11.1
15	16	ISP market conditions	41.7	31.8	26.5
17	17	Secure server/encryption	33.8	34.4	31.8
19	18	Domain names with non-Roman character sets (IDN)	32.7	15.6	51.7
20	19	Domain name management	30.0	41.3	28.7
18	20	Access to technical standards and their adaptability	29.3	45.3	25.3
21	21	IP address allocation/management	27.3	36.0	36.7
22	22	Own skills for using Internet	3.8	94.9	1.3

The Internet Policy Challenges in Detail

This analysis follows the framework that the UNDP-APDIP input paper to WGIG and WSIS has adopted for organizing Internet policy issues.[6] According to this framework, all Internet policy topics mentioned above can be grouped under one or two of the following categories:

- the *infrastructure dimension,* which covers issues of physical network characteristics and roll-out such as Internet availability, reliability, speed, costs, network interconnection, Internet market conditions, and emerging technologies such as wireless and Internet telephony (VoIP);
- the *logical dimension,* which comprises data routing and software development topics such as domain name and Internet Protocol (IP) address management, internationalized domain names and software standards;
- the *content dimension,* with topics ranging from availability of government information and local content to adverse issues such as illegal content, virus attacks, spam and online fraud; and
- the *social and development dimension,* which covers topics related to the empowering and development-oriented use of the Internet such as online privacy, individual ICT skills, and availability of e-commerce payment systems, as well as issues of online cultural diversity as related to software and content in local languages.

The Infrastructure Dimension: Persistent and New Challenges for Access, Affordability and New Technologies

Percentage of respondents that are modestly unsatisfied, unsatisfied or very unsatisfied with the current status with regard to availability and cost, reliability and speed, network interconnection and backbone access, wireless, market condition and internet telephony (see Figure 4).

General Situation

The roll-out and expansion of Internet infrastructures has continued apace, most strongly in the Asia-Pacific region. According to industry data, Internet capacity in 2004, measured in bandwidth, grew rapidly by 77 percent across Asia, the highest growth rate of all regions.[7] Nevertheless, Internet penetration rates in

Figure 4: ORDIG Survey Results: Infrastructure Topics

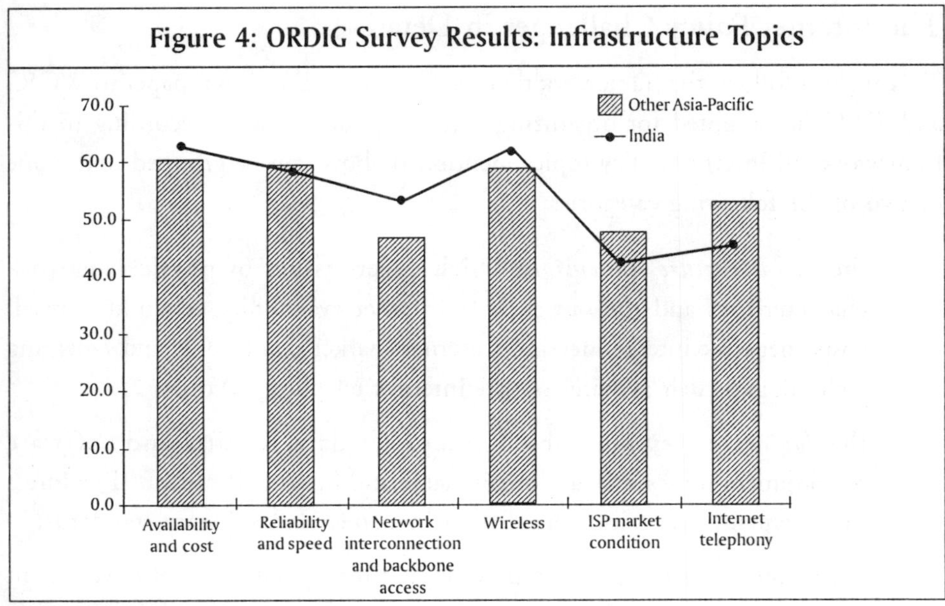

most countries in the region remain very low and struggle with a particularly significant gulf between urban and rural penetration rates. As Figure 4 shows, around 60 percent of the respondents from India express their discontent with the availability, costs, reliability and speed of the Internet, as well as with the status quo on IP telephony and wireless Internet. Other statistics underscore these fundamental challenges. Although cheaper than the four other reference

Figure 5: Internet Access Costs

	Total monthly costs for 20 hours of Internet access (subscription plus metered costs in USD for August 2003)	As percentage of Gross National Income per Capita
China	10.14	13
India	**8.74**	**21.9**
Indonesia	22.26	37.6
Pakistan	15.61	45.7
Thailand	6.98	4.2
AP Average	—	39.7
AP Industrialized Country Average	—	1.0

Source: ITU, 2004[8]

countries, the Internet is expensive relative to purchasing power. As Figure 5 shows, purchasing an individual dial-up subscription to the Internet would consume over 20 percent of per capita income in India, which is well beyond the means of the majority of households in the country.

What factors drive these costs? Availability of and costs for international backbone access are a first factor to consider. As Figure 6 shows, transit prices for Internet traffic in Asia have fallen sharply over the last year, but continue to be twice as high as European or US prices.

STM-1 IP Transit Price Declines by Region, Second Quarter of 2003 (Q2 2003) to Second Quarter of 2004 (Q2 2004)

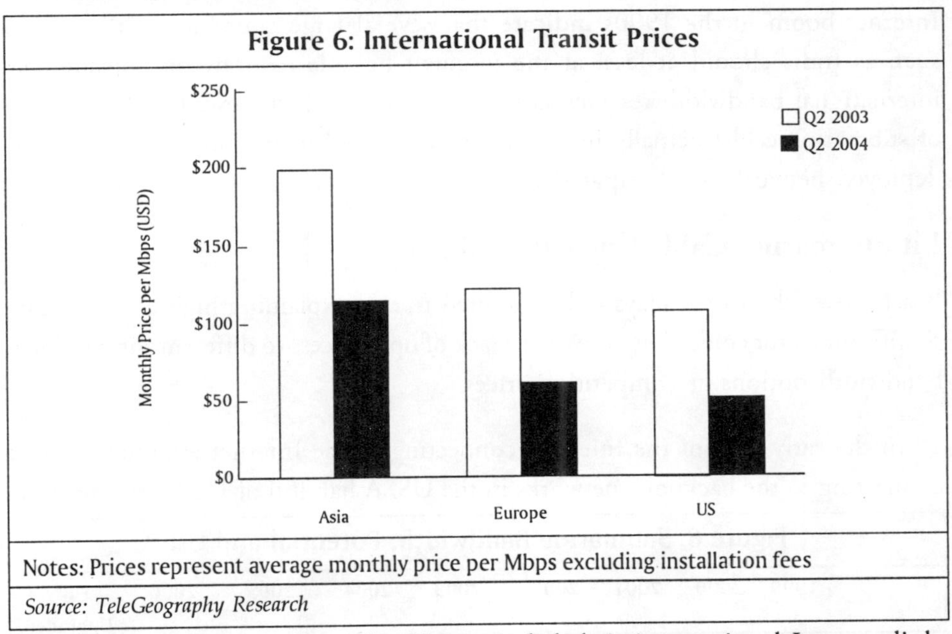

Likewise, countries have considerably expanded their international Internet links but relative to population size the deployed bandwidth is still limited as Figure 7 indicates.

Is absolute scarcity in international bandwidth causing these high charges and limited deployment? Is this situation attributable to physical infrastructure bottlenecks? Maybe this is the case for some landlocked and remote island country. However, the massive overinvestment and infrastructure build-out during the

Figure 7: International Bandwidth

	International bandwidth	
	Total (Mbps) 2003	Bits per inhabitant 2003
China	27,216	21.7
India	**3,000**	**2.8**
Indonesia	573	2.7
Pakistan	567	3.8
Thailand	1,437	22.8
AP Average	--	55.0
AP Industrialized Country Average	–	285.3

Source: ITU, 2004[9]

Internet boom in the 1990s indicate that several large countries in the region such as India should at least at the moment be able to draw on considerable international bandwidth reserves as Figure 8 shows, which describes the capacity of submarine cables actually in use (lit) as compared to the full potential of the deployed networks (fully upgraded):

Lit Submarine Cable Capacity (Gbps)

If a bandwidth crunch plays only a limited role in explaining high costs, a more significant factor could therefore be the lack of open access to different international bandwidth options at competitive prices.

In the early days of the Internet, connecting to the Internet essentially meant connecting to the backbone networks in the US. A handful of US-based operators

Figure 8: Submarine Bandwidth, Potential and Use

	1999	2000	2001	2002	2003	2004	2005	2006	Fully Upgraded
Trans-Atlantic	163	533	1,843.00	2,022.40	2,337.90	2,337.90	2,641.90	2,982.70	12,297.90
Trans-Pacific	42.9	182.9	262.9	1,042.90	1,042.90	1,042.90	1,230.90	1,456.50	6,502.90
Intra-Asia	**25**	**40**	**560**	**560**	**560**	**560**	**670**	**802**	**15,810.00**
U.S.-Latin America	13.1	213.1	293.1	303.1	513.1	518.1	637.7	749.2	5,165.60
Europe-Africa-Asia	21.1	31.1	31.1	41.1	61.1	61.1	73.1	87.5	251.1

PriMetrica, Inc. 2004
Source: TeleGeography Research

that owned these major backbones were widely believed to be able to dictate interconnection terms to foreign Internet service providers (ISPs), with the latter ending up subsidizing the entire international link. Since then, this situation has been ameliorated somewhat. The boom and bust cycle in the Internet infrastructure market together with innovation in long-haul data transmission technologies have expanded choice of suppliers, as well as transformed ownership structures of international links with more non-US players, including Asian ones entering the market for international bandwidth.[10]

However, high access charges for international bandwidth persist, indicating a more general competition problem that appears at least partly related to domestic regulations. Many countries in the Asia-Pacific continue to impose restrictions on domestic ISPs with regard to owning or purchasing international bandwidth. As survey data from the International Telecommunication Union (ITU) suggests, in none of the four reference countries (China, Indonesia, Pakistan and Thailand) can ISPs other than the incumbents and their affiliates, own or lease their own international data gateways. This dramatically reduces the dynamics of a domestic market for international bandwidth.

In contrast, India has made considerable progress in establishing more open policies.[11] ISPs can obtain licenses for international gateways. For operating international satellite links alone 24 such licenses are in use in 2004, thereby expanding to the international link the dynamics of the domestic ISP market in India,[12] which boasts almost 400 licensed ISPs, 200 of which are active.

These vibrant markets notwithstanding, the choice of smaller ISPs in purchasing upstream connectivity can be limited by a lack of interconnection arrangements in the region, both at domestic or sub-regional level. Figure 9 indicates that the Asia-Pacific region as a whole suffers from a very low number of Internet exchange points (IXPs). The relative backwardness of the Asia-Pacific becomes even more apparent, when factoring in population sizes, which would relegate the region to the last place in terms of per capita density of IXPs.

Perceived shortcomings with the status quo for interconnection arrangements are particularly widespread in India. Over 53 percent of the respondents reporting to be unhappy about the current situation as compared to an average of 46 percent

Figure 9: Number of Internet Exchanges per Region

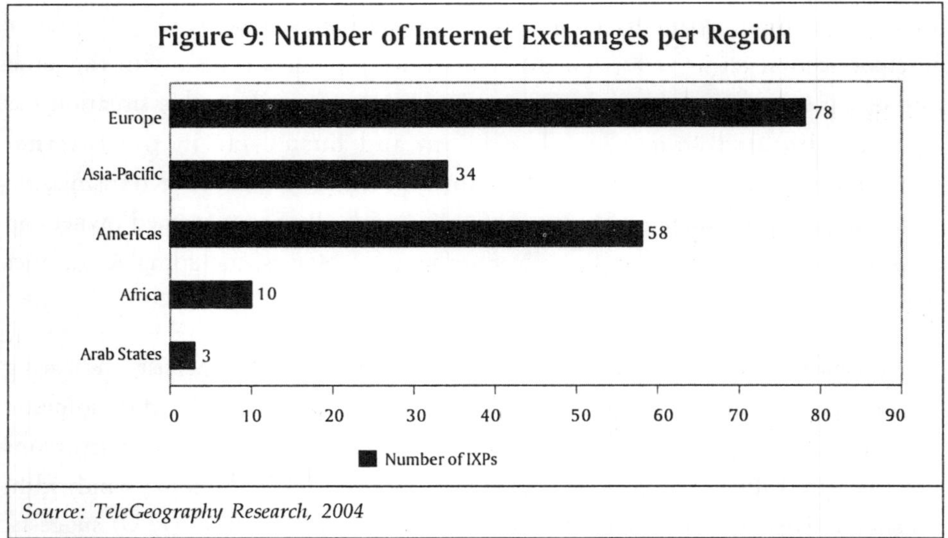

Source: TeleGeography Research, 2004

in other countries of the region indicate that problems with interconnection at the domestic level are an important concern.

In sum, the ORDIG survey indicates that considerable challenges persist to expand Internet connectivity in India. Dissatisfaction with Internet affordability, availability and speed remains real and widespread, despite the progress made in creating a competitive policy environment. New technologies might hold the key for reducing the costs of Internet connectivity further. Getting the accompanying policy framework right is essential to unlock this potential.

Governance Issues for Emerging Internet Technologies

The ORDIG survey has specifically solicited opinions about two topics, wireless Internet and Internet telephony. For both of these topics, dissatisfaction with the status quo in India roughly mirrors the responses from the region as a whole. Slightly more Indian respondents (62 percent) are voicing their dissatisfaction about the current policies for wireless Internet, while governance of IP telephony is viewed less negative than in other Asia-Pacific countries with 45 percent of Indian respondents stating to be unhappy with the status quo as compared to 52 percent elsewhere in the region. As a response to what still amounts to significant levels of discontent, UNDP-APDIP has commissioned a number of follow-up research papers to shed more light on the challenges in this area.

As Samudra E Haque points out in his paper for UNDP-APDIP, wireless Internet technologies hold enormous potential to make Internet connectivity more available and affordable.[13] Wireless technologies are less vulnerable to natural disasters and sabotage. They can be deployed more flexibly and rapidly with less hassle of negotiating the right of way for physical networks, and they typically incur lower last mile costs to reach the end-subscriber. These advantages weigh heavily in countries such as India where expanding connectivity in rural areas is a major challenge. Haque estimates that the use of wireless technologies to transmit data over distances between 1 and 60 kilometres could cut costs for equipment and infrastructure in half as compared to conventional wire-based infrastructures.

Furthermore, new methods for transmitting and receiving digital data enable a significantly larger number of operators to share the same spectrum without disruptive interference, thus removing a regulatory rationale for licensing in the face of spectrum scarcity and congestion. With the regulatory landscape for wireless technologies still in the making, a key policy challenge is to retain low barriers to market entry and spectrum access, in order to allow technical innovation and the experimentation with innovative business models. The multistakeholder WGIG arrives at the same conclusion:

"Policy and regulatory incentives and more open access policies are also needed, if private investment and community networks are to be effective in expanding ICT access to high cost (predominantly rural) and low income populations to address the so-called "bottom of the pyramid" populations."[14]

The enormous success of Wi-Fi technologies, which have flourished in countries that grant open, unlicensed access to spectrum, impressively underscores the advantages of such a light-touch approach to governing the wireless Internet infrastructure. Although it is only one of many wireless Internet technologies, the treatment of Wi-Fi appears to set the standard for emerging governance models for other new wireless services such as the longer range Wi-max. In contrast to China and Pakistan, India has taken encouraging first steps to create an enabling environment for new wireless technologies by de-licensing access to the Wi-fi spectrum as Figure 10 shows.[15]

In addition, the Indian regulatory authority is proposing to lower access barriers to other spectrum bands and to encourage the use of converged Wifi-GSM

Figure 10: Regulating Treatment of Wi-fi in the 2.4 GHz Band

Country	Unlicensed	Licensed	Prohibited
China		✓ "Network Access License"	
India	✓		
Indonesia	✓		
Pakistan		"site approval" required	
Thailand	✓ Unlicensed for secondary usage		

Source: Open Spectrum International, 2005

handsets, initiatives that, if approved by the Ministry of Communications, could dramatically leverage the benefits of the new wireless technologies and establish India as one of the policy pioneers in this area.

The emergence of Internet telephony, the use of Internet infrastructures for the partial or full routing of voice calls often referred to as voice over Internet protocol (VoIP) is another new regulatory challenge at the intersection of Internet and conventional telecommunications policies. VoIP has the potential to offer local and long-distance telephone services that are cheaper than conventional phone calls, thus exerting a competitive pressure on telecommunication services that are in many countries dominated by a handful of incumbent operators.

Moreover, VoIP strengthens the demand for Internet applications, helps recoup infrastructure investment costs and opens opportunities for new future business model, including community-based telephone services.

As Figure 11 indicates, Internet telephony is the most dynamic growth sector for international voice communication.

Research for UNDP-APDIP by Onno W Purbo suggests, that Internet telephony markets are fairly well developed in India, as well as in the other four reference countries when measured by the existence of exchange markets where providers offer and purchase services for terminating VoIP calls or routing VoIP traffic.[16]

Figure 11: Growth in Voice Traffic – Different Categories

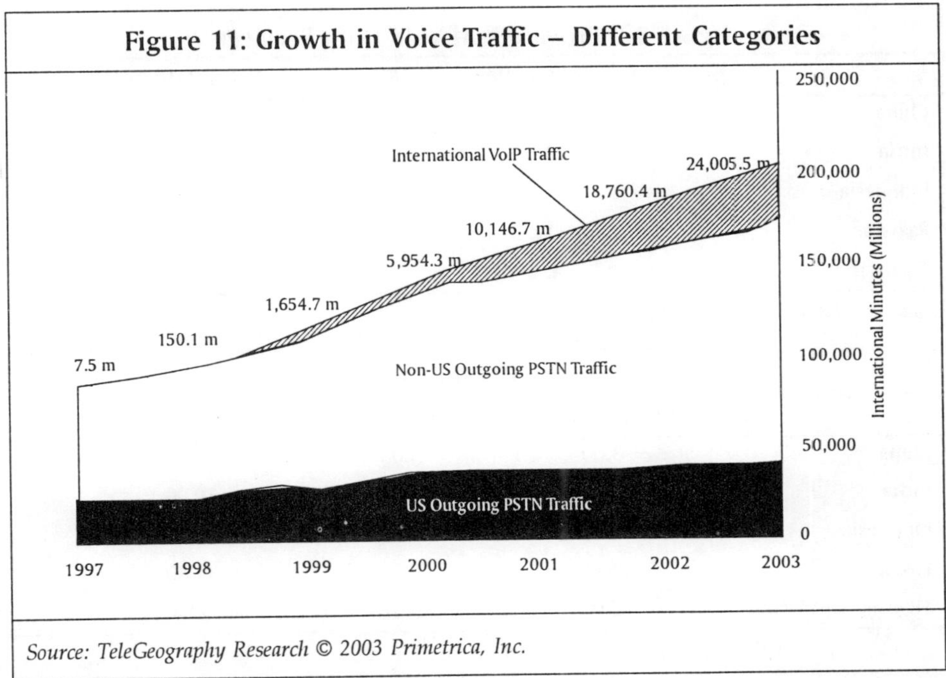

Source: TeleGeography Research © 2003 Primetrica, Inc.

To some extent, this dynamic VoIP development is aided by India's large population size, which makes the aggregation of VoIP traffic more cost-effective and helps negotiate more advantageous transit or termination rates with international providers. Nevertheless, population size and number of providers is not a guarantee for low rates, as estimates by Onno W Purbo confirm:

Typical PC to phone rate for Asia-Pacific countries (calling Asia-Pacific countries via Internet phone services)

To some extent differential rates reflect different costs for accessing and purchasing Internet data transmission, the underlying infrastructure on which VoIP builds. But the regulatory environment also plays an important role as it shapes the barriers to market entry and competition in the VoIP market itself. Clear, transparent and non-discriminatory licensing in Singapore, for example, has helped to bring about the lowest VoIP rates in the region with average PC to phone rates of $ 2.47 per minute. India has adopted a licensing regime for VoIP in 2002 and as of December 2003 118 ISP have been granted a license for this service.

Figure 12: Providers of VoIP Data Services

	Call Termination	VoIP Providers List
China	11	10
India	**21**	**36**
Indonesia	1	7
Pakistan	11	11
Thailand	4	9

Source: UNDP-APDIP research

Figure 13: VoIP Rates

	Minimum (cent$)	Average (cent$)	Maximum (cent$)
China	3.00	3.00	3.00
India		**15.60**	**19.00**
Indonesia	5.60	14.30	22.10
Pakistan	26.00	32.50	33.80
Thailand	7.02	9.62	9.88

Source: UNDP-APDIP research

Regulators could help to maximize the synergies between VoIP and conventional PSTN telephone infrastructures by supporting the so-called ENUM numbering system that integrates both networks more seamlessly and enables VoIP participants to be reached via normal phone numbers. However, no country in the Asia-Pacific has taken this step so far.

The Logical Dimension: Local Language Software as Top Concern

Percentage of respondents that are modestly unsatisfied, unsatisfied or very unsatisfied with the current status with regard to:

Compared to infrastructure or content issues, governance of the logical layer receives better marks from Indian respondents to the ORDIG survey. Less than 40 percent of the respondents are dissatisfied with the status of domain name management, internationalized domain names, IP address management and standards. However, the survey results do not support the claim that the status quo for these issues is viewed as flawless, since a sizeable group of almost one-third of the respondents still record their discontent with domain name management

Figure 14: ORDIG Survey Results: Logical Layer Topics

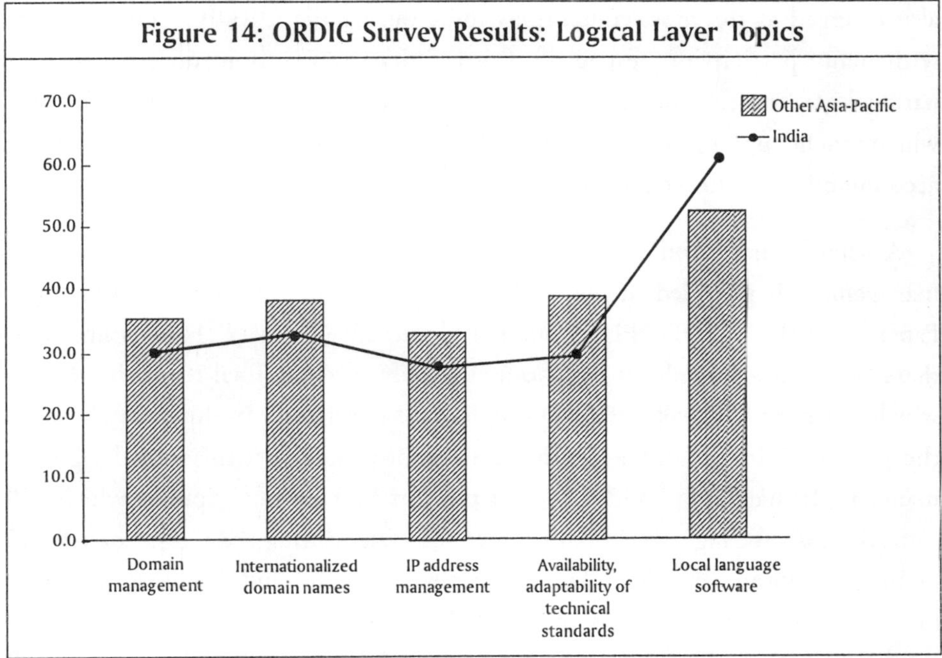

and internationalized domain names, while a quarter registers concerns about IP address management and technical standards issues.

The only significant exception to all this is the topic of the availability of local language software. Here, the degree of dissatisfaction among respondents from India is striking, with more than 60 percent indicating that they are not happy with the status quo.

The global management of IP addresses and domain names has not emerged as a top priority for survey takers from India. However, since these topics are among the most visible and contentious Internet governance problems they deserve to be briefly addressed.

Currently, the management of Internet names and numbers is overseen by ICANN, a multistakeholder, not-for-profit entity, contractually endorsed by the US Government and registered in California, while regional Internet registries coordinate the disbursement of IP addresses at the regional level. The question of whether this organizational set-up is appropriate for the tasks at hand is one of the most vexing issues in the international Internet governance debate and has also emerged as the most contentious topic during the ORDIG Online Forum with many participants, especially from China, demanding more control for national governments and a fairer allocation system. The issue is an intricate one, which touches upon principles of national sovereignty, stakeholder self-governance, accountability, inclusiveness and fairness.

A detailed discussion of the various competing claims pertinent to IP address management is provided in the ORDIG Forum Summary[17], the ORDIG Input Paper[18] and the UNDP-APDIP Internet Governance Primer.[19] How contentious these issues have turned out to be can also be seen in the final report by WGIG which was meant to make a reform proposal for governance in this area. However, the group could not agree on the most appropriate institutional design for managing IP names and addresses, but presents four possible options which will form the basis for high-level discussion of the issues during the second part WSIS in Tunis in November 2005.[20] This country report cannot indulge in an exhaustive presentation of all the issues involved, but aims to provide some additional information to facilitate the debate. Figure 15 presents details on current IP address allocation patterns in the five reference countries.

The transition to a new generation of IP address system (IPv6) is currently under way. IPv6 uses different numbering conventions that make a direct comparison between the size of IPv4 versus IPv6 difficult. However, where IPv4 in theory provides addresses for 2^32 individual devices connected to the Internet, IPv6 provides addresses to at least 2^48 networks which themselves can consist of a large number of individual devices.

Even when assuming that each of these networks deployed under IPv6 would only consist of one individual device, IPv6 would support about 65,000 times the number devices of IPv4. The deployment of IPv6 is in its very early stages. Figure 16 presents some information on the current deployment status. In a simple thought experiment Figure 16 also calculates the number of networks per country and per future population size in 2015, if IPv6 were to be allocated to render the same relative shares of available IP address space that each country currently holds for IPv4.

Figure 15: IPv4 Allocations, June 2005					
	IPv4 Total	Per Internet Host	Per Internet User	Per Computer	Per Person
China	63,013,376	393	0.79	1.78	0.0487
India	**4,921,600**	**57**	**0.61**	**0.66**	**0.0047**
Indonesia	1,053,696	17	0.06	0.42	0.0049
Pakistan	324,608	21	0.22	0.54	0.0022
Thailand	2,127,104	21	0.31	0.86	0.0342

Source: Own calculations based on data by APNIC, ITU, UNDP-HDRO

It should be borne in mind that nothing in the current policy or technical environment would suggest that such a conservative distribution key is desirable, plausible or even stable for the IPv4 environment. At the moment, the fastest growing destination for IPv4 allocations in the Asia-Pacific is China while new allocations for the Asia-Pacific region as a whole are larger than for any other world region.[21]

Given all this, the calculation of hypothetical IPv6 contingents is only done for illustrative purposes, in order to get a better sense of the size of the new address space and its capacity to support future network growth.

All parties will have to make a considerable effort to arrive at a consensual solution for IP and domain name issues and WGIG outlines the principles that should govern this continuing debate:

Figure 16: IPv6			
	IPv6 total, June 2005 (networks)	IPv6 hypothetical	IPv6 hypothetical per person in 2015
China	925,696	4,129,644,609,536	2,945
India	**393,216**	**322,541,977,600**	**259**
Indonesia	327,680	69,055,021,056	276
Pakistan	65,536	21,273,509,888	104
Thailand	335,872	139,401,887,744	2,003

Source: Own calculations based on data by APNIC, UNDP-HDRO

"In general, the existing system has functioned well for more than two decades. Adjustments, where needed, both for technical/operational and for political reasons, must be done so as not to interfere or disrupt the operational qualities of the system in terms of stability and security, and must be done in a way that assists, and does not hinder, further development of the Internet."[22]

The Content Dimension: Overwhelming Concern with Cyber Crime, Virus Attacks, Spam

Percentage of respondents that are modestly unsatisfied, unsatisfied or very unsatisfied with the current status with regard to: availability of Government information, local content, fair access to protection of intellectual property, virus attacks, spam, cyber crime etc. (see Figure 17).

On content-related governance issues, survey respondents from India confirm virus cyber crime, spam and virus attacks as the three issues that are considered the most important Internet governance priorities across the region with around 90 percent regarding the development of solutions to these three problems as important.

Network security statistics underscore these concerns and report rising frequency and sophistication of cyber crime, spam and virus attacks. Here are some exemplary numbers reported by a major globally operating Internet security provider:

- in mid-July 2004, antifraud filters were blocking 9 million phishing (emails with deceiving claims to gain access to sensitive information or defraud the recipient). By the end of December this number had increased to a weekly average of over 33 million messages being blocked per week;
- in the same period, the vendor documented 1,403 new software vulnerabilities, an increase of 13 percent over the previous reporting period; and
- during the same period monitored organizations received 13.6 attacks per day, up from 10.6 in the preceding six months. [23]

Research into network security issues in the Asia-Pacific region by Salman Ansari for UNDP-APDIP confirm these trends and document the increasing

Figure 17: ORDIG Survey Results: Content Related Topics

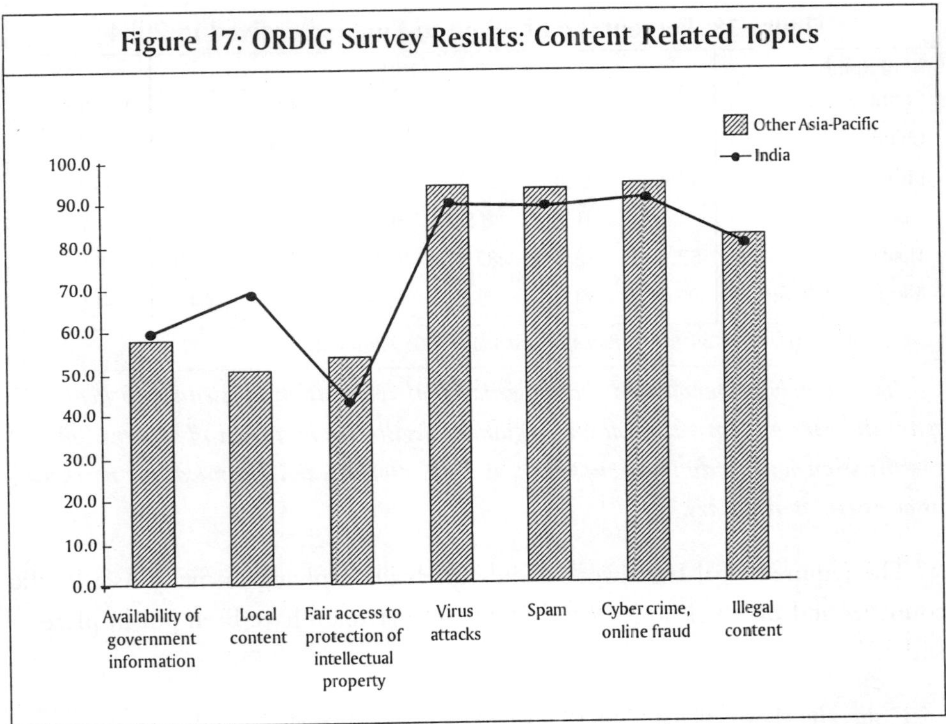

sophistication and damage of attacks that more and more include pivotal Internet infrastructure services on their target lists.[24]

While India currently does not rank high as an originator of virus attacks or spam mail, the problem is on the rise. Indian users are increasingly victims of spam as research by Suresh Ramasubramanian for UNDP-APDIP shows:[25]

Both Ansari and Ramasubramanian identify a comprehensive set of policy shortcomings and remedies to address these issues, including enhanced awareness and user education about network safety problems, improved rapid response and information sharing for infrastructure providers, and appropriate legal provisions. All this suggests that combating cyber crime, spam and virus attacks require a concerted effort by all stakeholders, the technology community, the Internet industry, government and end-users alike.

WGIG emphasizes this point in its background report on the spam issue:

Figure 18: Percentage of Spam in Emails Received in 2004

% of Spam	Month						
Country	Jan	Mar	May	Jul	Sep	Nov	Average
China	0.0	8.0	51.5	47.6	48.9	67.5	47.8
India	**14.4**	**13.0**	**31.4**	**25.9**	**38.5**	**39.2**	**34.4**
Indonesia		0.0	8.8	9.1	9.0	13.6	9.4
Thailand	52.9	58.4	87.2	79.0	74.2	72.0	68.9
Average AP Region	37.0	24.6	33.2	43.9	45.5	64.4	44.6

Source: Messagelabs, as quoted in Ramasubramanian, 2005 (abridged)

"It is widely acknowledged that international cooperation is essential to deal with spam in terms of both technical and regulatory/legislative matters and cooperation and coordination with industry groups such as ISPs, mobile carriers and direct marketing associations is necessary."[26]

The required legal framework is only gradually evolving in many Asia-Pacific countries and by 2004 no legal provisions against spam have been put in place in India.[27]

Concerns about illegal content also feature prominently in replies to the survey from India with 80 percent of the respondents expressing their dissatisfaction with the status quo of this issue, while the availability of local content also emerges as a major concern with 68 percent of Indian respondents registering complaints.

The Social and Development Dimension Percentage of respondents that are modestly unsatisfied, unsatisfied or very unsatisfied with the current status with regard to: privacy, local language software, local content, International domain names etc., can be had from the survey results (see Figure 19).

As the survey results indicate, topics such as the availability of local content or local language software, often subsumed under the theme of online cultural diversity, are major issues in India, a country with more than 400 living languages, many of which rely on non-Roman character sets. This poses additional challenges for domain names and general software compatibility.[28]

The survey results are likely to be an underestimation of the level of dissatisfaction on these issues because the very communities who are most

Figure 19: ORDIG Survey Results: Social and Development Layer Topics

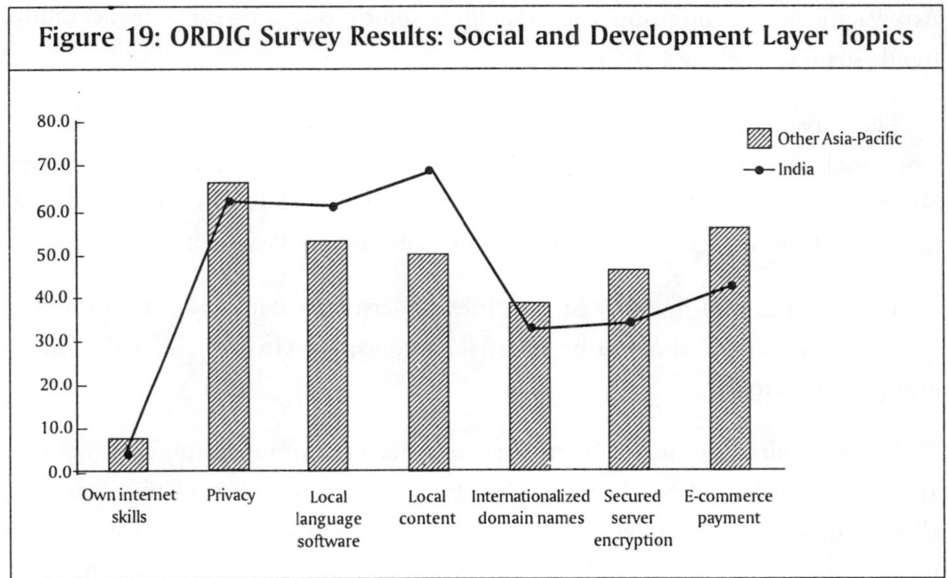

marginalized in the online environment are also unlikely to be adequately represented in the ORDIG online survey in the first place.[29]

Besides issues of cultural diversity, privacy is also a widespread concern. The protection of privacy in the online environment is found wanting by more than 60 percent of the respondents from India. WGIG underscores the importance of the privacy issues:

"Privacy, a fundamental human right according to Article 12 of the Universal Declaration of Human Rights, becomes even more important over the Internet, where the intrinsic nature of the Internet makes it possible to effectively track an individual in cyberspace and use information about him/her illegally or without authorization. Threats to personal privacy increase the mistrust towards the Internet."[30]

Concluding Remarks

As this country report shows, Internet governance covers a wide range of different issues and is perceived as far from perfect. Survey takers, as well as forum and conference participants from India have registered their concerns about a large number of different topics. They agree with their peers in other countries in the

Asia-Pacific on the top priority of developing solutions against cyber crime, online fraud, spam and virus attacks.

The survey results emphasize the persistent importance of basic infrastructure issues such as access, affordability and speed of the Internet in the country. Survey takers from India also attach a greater weight to issues of local content and local language software than their colleagues in many other Asia-Pacific countries.

This breadth and diversity of priorities underscores that action is required at many fronts and, in order to be effective, a concerted effort by all stakeholders groups is required.

Many important topics in Internet governance have an international dimension and are currently addressed in patch-work manner by a variety of different fora, all with their own principles for operation and participation. All this conspires to make effective participation by stakeholders from developing countries a challenging endeavour, thereby placing capacity building, enhanced transparency and openness of international governance entities at the centre of a long-term strategy for inclusive and equitable Internet governance.

The final report of WGIG recognizes these challenges. It consensually recommends the "creation of a new space for dialogue for all stakeholders on an equal footing", thereby setting the stage for moving productively forward with the Internet governance agenda during WSIS, a process all countries in the Asia-Pacific region should follow closely and actively contribute to.

Given the breadth and complexity of all Internet governance topics covered, this country report cannot claim to deliver a comprehensive analysis by any standard. But it hopes to provide a richer picture on the Internet governance challenges that lie ahead for India and to offer some stimulating food for thought for a national, multi-stakeholder dialogue on these issues, as an important step towards Internet policies that maximize the benefits of the information revolution for everyone in the country.

(Dieter Zinnbauer is a Internet Policy Advisor, UNDP-APDIP, Kuala Lumpur, Malaysia.)

Endnotes

1 WGIG Report: *http://www.wgig.org/docs/WGIGREPORT.pdf*

2 For details see Annex I.

3 All related materials are available at *http://www.wgig.org*

4 ITU (2004): Asia-Pacific Telecommunication Indicators 2004, Geneva: ITU.

5 For details on the composition of Indian response to the survey see Annex II.

6 *http://igov.apdip.net/ORDIG_Paper.pdf*

7 Global Internet Geography (2005) Executive Summary: *http://www.telegeography.com*

8 ITU (2004): Asia-Pacific Telecommunication Indicators 2004, Geneva: ITU.

9 Ibid.

10 For some background on past and ongoing policy initiatives in this area, see the WGIG Issue Paper on International Internet Connections: *http://www.wgig.org/docs/WP-Peering.pdf*

11 Data on international gateway for 2004 from ITU World Telecommunication Regulatory Database, data on ISP licenses from APT Yearbook 2004, Bangkok: APT.

12 Additional information on India from APT Yearbook 2004, Bangkok: APT, and Malik, P (2005) Regulation and Investment: Case Study of the Indian Telecommunications Industry, in: Mahan, A K and Melody, W H (eds.): *Stimulating Investment in Network Development: Roles for Regulators, Regulateonline.Org.*

13 Samudra E. Haque (2005): Internet Governance for Emerging Technologies: Wireless, UNDP-APDIP Research Paper.

14 WSIS Task Force Report on Financing Mechanisms: *http://www.itu.int/wsis/tffm/index.html*

15 For details see *http://www.volweb.cz/horvitz/os-info/india.html*

16 Onno W Purbo (2005): Internet Governance for Emerging Technologies: VoIP and Convergence, UNDP-APDIP Research Paper.

17 *http://igov.apdip.net/undp-apdip%20forum%20summary.pdf*

18 *http://igov.apdip.net/ORDIG_Paper.pdf*

19 Forthcoming, will be available at *http://igov.apdip.net*

20 WGIG Report: *http://www.wgig.org/docs/WGIGREPORT.pdf*

21 Issue 12 of Apster, APNIC's quarterly newsletter, December 2004.

22 WGIG: Background Report, *http://www.wgig.org/docs/BackgroundReport.doc*

23 Symantec Internet Security Threat Report , Volume II, published March 2005.

24 Salman Ansari (2005): Network Stability and Security, UNDP-APDIP Research Paper.

25 Ramasubramanian (2005): Spam Issues in the Asia-Pacific Region, UNDP-APDIP Research Paper.

26 WGIG: Background Report, *http://www.wgig.org/docs/BackgroundReport.doc*

27 See ITU World Telecommunication Regulatory Database and Ansari, 2005.

28 See *http://www.ethnologue.com*

29 See Danny Butt (2005): Cultural Diversity in Cyberspace: Minority Content, UNDP-APDIP Research Paper; Norbert Klein (2005): Cultural Diversity in Cyberspace: Software Customization, UNDP-APDIP Research Paper.

30 WGIG: Background Report, *http://www.wgig.org/docs/BackgroundReport.doc*

Annex I: Input from India to ORDIG

Internet policy makers, researchers, users and entrepreneurs from India were very active contributors of views and information in a host of outreach and consultation activities carried out by UNDP-APDIP, including:

- a three week online discussion forum (13 January-17 February 2005) on Internet governance priorities in the Asia-Pacific region with more than 180 participants from 27 countries, including 17 participants from India;
- regional and sub-regional consultations and presentations on Internet policies sponsored by UNDP-APDIP at more than ten ICT policy, technology and civil society conferences. Representatives from India participated in the Asian Civil Society Forum (Thailand, November 2004), APRICOT (Japan, February 2005), UNESCAP sub-regional WSIS Meeting for South and Southwest Asia (Nepal, March 2005), UNDP-APDIP ORDIG Advisory Panel Meeting (Thailand, March 2005), UNESCAP High-Level Asia-Pacific Preparatory Conference for WSIS (Iran, May 2005); and
- a major regional survey on Internet governance issues in the region with a total of more than 1,200 respondents. The survey was conducted from 8 February to 7 March, 2005. Participation from India was very strong with 156 respondents, 12.6 percent of the total number of replies received from the region.

Annex II: Composition of Survey Respondents: India

Breakdown by affiliation of respondents from India

	Responses	Percentage of total
Government	36	23.1
Academia	25	16.0
Private industry	37	23.7
Civil society	18	11.5
International/regional organization	11	7.1
Student	21	13.5
Other	8	5.1

Breakdown by principal interest in Internet as reported by respondents from India

	Responses	Percentage of total
Internet research and development	29	18.7
Internet infrastructure provider	17	11.0
Internet policy-making / regulator	10	6.5
Internet user	92	59.4
E-commerce participant	7	4.5

Breakdown by principal place for Internet access for respondents from India

	Responses	Percentage of total
Home	30	19.2
Work/place of study	120	76.9
Library/Internet Café	6	3.8
Other	0	0.0

Annex III: Detailed Survey Results: India

In percent of all responses (N=156) received from India.

Question: "What do you think about the following statements?

Issue	-3 strongly disagree	-2 disagree	-1 somewhat disagree	1 somewhat agree	2 agree	3 strongly	no view agree
1. At present the Internet does not provide any significant benefits for most people	32.1	19.9	5.1	15.4	18.6	9.0	0.0
2. The Internet helps to combat poverty	10.3	20.5	12.8	25.6	18.6	5.1	7.1
3. The Internet is an essential tool for all people and should be available and affordable for everyone	1.3	1.3	0.6	7.1	21.3	67.7	0.6
4. Over the next few years (3-5) the benefits that the Internet provides will grow significantly	0.6	1.9	0.6	9.7	29.7	56.1	1.3

Contd...

Contd...

Question: "How satisfied are you with the current status of Internet-related issues?

Issue	-3 very unsatisfied	-2 unsatisfied	-1 modestly unsatisfied	1 modestly satisfied	2 satisfied	3 very satisfied	no view
5. Availability and cost of the Internet	15.4	38.5	9.0	23.1	10.9	1.3	1.9
6. Reliability and speed of the Internet	14.7	23.1	20.5	23.1	17.3	1.3	0.0
7. Your own skills for using the Internet effectively	0.0	2.6	1.3	13.5	42.3	39.1	1.3
8. Online access to government information / services	14.1	23.1	22.4	24.4	12.2	1.9	1.9
9. Protection of personal information and privacy online	15.5	25.2	21.3	20.0	11.0	1.9	5.2
10. Availability of e-commerce payment systems	7.8	25.5	9.2	30.1	14.4	2.0	11.1
11. Availability of the software that you use in your local language	21.6	24.8	14.4	15.0	9.8	2.6	11.8
12. Availability of useful content on the Internet in your local language	27.5	30.7	10.5	11.8	6.5	2.6	10.5
13. Network interconnection and backbone access	10.5	22.4	20.4	12.5	20.4	1.3	12.5
14. Wireless Internet, spectrum and access	25.3	21.3	15.3	8.7	10.0	0.0	19.3
15. Domain name management	6.0	8.7	15.3	19.3	19.3	2.7	28.7

Contd...

Contd...

16. Domain names with non-Roman character sets	10.2	12.9	9.5	8.2	6.8	0.7 5	1.7
17. IP address allocation and management	4.7	9.3	13.3	14.0	20.0	2.0	36.7
18. Secure server administration, digital signatures, encryption	5.3	13.2	15.2	16.6	16.6	1.3	31.8
19. Access to technical standards and their adaptability	5.3	12.7	11.3	16.7	25.3	3.3	25.3
20. Fair access to and protection of intellectual property	7.3	20.0	15.3	18.0	14.0	4.7	20.7
21. ISP market conditions	7.3	19.2	15.2	19.9	11.3	0.7	26.5
22. Internet telephony (VoIP)	11.1	22.9	11.1	20.3	9.8	0.7	24.2

Question: "How important do you consider the development of solutions to the following problems"

←→

Issue	**-3 very important**	**-2 unimportant**	**-1 somewhat unimportant**	**1 somewhat important**	**2 important**	**3 very important**	**no view**
23. Virus attacks	9.1	0.6	0.0	7.1	11.0	71.4	0.6
24. Spam, unsolicited commercial email	7.1	1.9	1.9	4.5	15.6	68.8	0.0
25. Online fraud, cyber crime	4.6	1.3	2.0	5.9	9.8	75.2	1.3
26. Illegal content	9.2	3.9	3.3	12.5	15.1	52.6	3.3

12

Internet Governance: Towards the Modernisation of Policy Making Process in Turkey*

Yaman Akdeniz

Given the global, decentralized and borderless nature of the Internet, it is not possible for individual governments (national governments) to regulate effectively or address problem satisfactorily. This paper highlights the need for national governments to act proactively and fine-tune their policies and procedures to effectively address Internet related issues. The author identifies various possible modes and models appropriate for Internet Governance in Turkey.

Executive Summary

The global, decentralised and borderless nature of the Internet means that it is not possible for the individual governments to regulate effectively and satisfactorily to address Internet related problems and issues. This means that

* This policy paper has been supported by the Open Society Institute – with the contribution of the International Policy Fellowships and Information Policy Fellowship Programmes of OSI-Budapest. OSI International Policy Fellowship Project (March 2003-April 2004): Civil Society Participation to the policy making process of the Turkish Government in relation to the development of an Information Society in Turkey.

the nature of government regulation, thinking, and policy making need also to adopt to the changes that are the result of improvement in technology and in global communications.

At the same time the role of the governments are still crucially important and pivotal but there needs to be more emphasis on such concepts as "risk analysis", "co-operation", "co-ordination", "consultation", "co-regulation", and "self-regulation". Rather than rushing into legislating, governments need to assess carefully the "risks" associated with Internet usage. This also needs to be done by a policy process which is open, transparent, and inclusive of the views of all interested parties. Consideration of alternatives to state legislation will also need to be part of the government agenda for developing Internet related policies.

It is the purpose of this policy paper to address these issues and make recommendations for Good Internet Governance in Turkey. The report recommends to the Turkish Government that they should:

- Modernise the Turkish policy making process in the short-term
- Provide an open and transparent policy making process
- Conduct risk analysis prior to regulation and consider the alternatives to state legislation
- Ensure that policymaking in this field is undertaken by policymakers who are well informed about the unique nature of the Internet and have direct experience with its use
- Ensure that such policies are developed with substantial input and comment from all interested parties including the Internet industry, the academia, non-governmental organisations and Internet users.
- Respect fundamental human rights enshrined in the Universal Declaration of Human Rights, the International Covenant on Civil and Political Rights, and the European Convention on Human Rights.
- Enable access to government information including legislative, judicial and executive branch information through the Internet. Public authorities should comply with the requirements of the Right to Information Act 2003 which came into force on 24 April, 2004.

- Ensure access by Turkish citizens to the Internet and enable full participation in the global information society. In particular, access to the Internet by schools, libraries and other public institutions should be viewed as a policy goal, subsidised as necessary.
- Ensure that the eEurope+ 2003 Turkey plan (as part of the European Commission's eEurope+ 2003 Plan) is fully implemented in the short-term.
- Ensure that the recently launched E-Transformation Turkey project's Short Term Action Plan is compatible with the normative and process conditions explained in this report. Ensure that Turkish policy is in line with EU policy
- Monitor systematically international legal and policy initiatives
- Ensure systematic representation and participation of Turkey within the international forums that develop Internet related policies (including but not exclusively at the Council of Europe, United Nations, the OECD, and the European Union level)

Part I – Introduction

Aims and Objectives

This policy paper entitled *Internet Governance: Towards the modernisation of policy making process in Turkey* aims to identify the various possible modes and models appropriate for Internet governance in Turkey. The paper will argue that the modernisation of the Turkish policy making process in the short-term is needed for good Internet governance. Only an open, transparent and co-operative policy making process which includes all stakeholders within the policy process can achieve the best results towards the creation of an Information Society inTurkey.

Therefore, apart from the option of government regulating and legislating (including advantages and disadvantages of government regulation), alternatives to state legislation such as self-regulation and co-regulation and the role of other stakeholders such as the industry, the NGOs working in this field, and the society as a whole will also be highlighted in this policy paper.

Impact of the Internet on Nation-State Policy Making

The policy paper takes as its theme Internet governance and how new communications technologies such as the Internet affects nation-state policy making including in Turkey and how nation-states foster policies related to the Internet. Obviously, there may be different approaches to the growth of the Internet in different societies and the impact of the Internet on different nation-states may have different results.

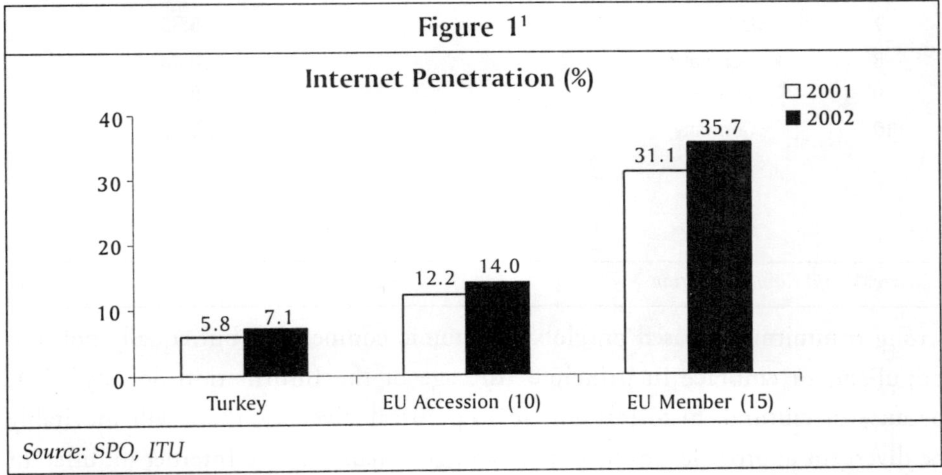

Figure 1[1]

Source: SPO, ITU

Different nation-states present a different level of economic development, respect for rights, trans-nationality, technological sophistication, and e-readiness.

While Turkey maybe considered at a developing stage with respect to the Internet, other states may be far more sophisticated with regards to Internet access, use, and penetration. Inevitably, this will be reflected upon the policy making process and the development of policies and in most cases the level of policy making process and nation-state approaches to Internet governance will be in different stages with different priorities.

The discourse of governance is especially relevant to analysis of the Internet within Western Europe, not only because of the inherent nature of the technology but also because of the political and social nature of Western Europe. Of course there will be challenges and difficulties in recognising the legitimate socio-cultural differences and approaches to Internet and its governance by nation-states. At Member State level within the European Union, there is no doubt that there is a

Figure 2[2]: e-readliness Index

Rank	Country	Point
1	Finland	5.92
2	USA	5.79
3	Singapore	5.74
4	Sweden	5.58
5	Iceland	5.51
6	Canada	5.44
7	UK	5.35
8	Denmark	5.33
9	Taiwan	5.31
10	Germany	5.29
...	...	...
...	...	...
50	TURKEY	3.57

Source: World Economic Forum

strong commitment, based on global economic competition but equally political populism, to embrace in principle "the age of the Information Society". Yet, because of cultural, historical and socio-political diversity, there will inevitably be divergent approaches to the growth and governance of the Internet in different European societies. For example, while the German government has political fears and sensitivities about the use of the Internet by Neo-Nazis, the United Kingdom takes a more relaxed attitude to the dangers of racism but conversely has a long cultural tradition of repression towards the availability of sexually explicit material. It is then for the European Union to try to reflect these differences. However, in an ideal world, "states within Western Europe should especially avoid pandering to the lowest common denominator, where the least tolerant [such as in respect of racist expression in France[3] and in Germany[4]] can set the pace."[5] Normative conditions such as the international human rights standards that nation-states adhere to can help to prevent the least tolerant states setting the standards.

Multi-layered Approach?

The development of new communications technologies such as the Internet and its global and decentralised nature will undoubtedly affect any state including

Turkey. At the same time, as mentioned above, different societies have different concerns about the Internet and their Internet policy, and the Internet governance is a reflection of the nature of the state of development, and cultural, historic and political background of that society.

A multi-layered approach to Internet governance (see Figure 3 below) is therefore, unavoidable and, will be adopted throughout this policy research paper in the light of not only national developments but also in the light of supranational (e.g., European Union), and international (Council of Europe, United Nations, OECD, G8) developments which will have an impact upon the development of policies at the national level.

A multi-layered model would mean that different players at different levels may be involved in the governance of different matters. While the Internet provides a great challenge for governance, the fragmented levels of governance may or may not include all the levels offered in Figure 3.

Figure 3: Internet Governance

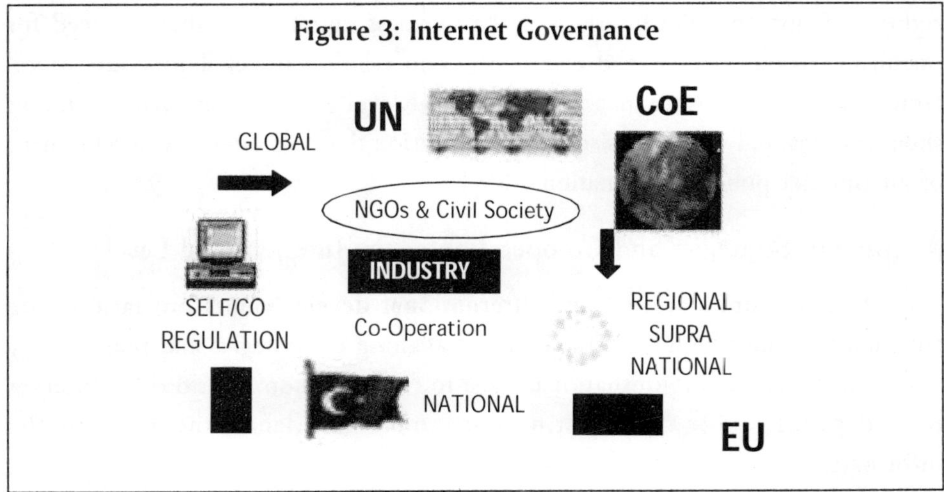

At the same time multi-layered governance must function with both public and private governing bodies in both national, supranational, and international level. The level of involvement and modes and models of governance will depend upon the "problem" or the subject matter of the policy issue to be governed. While self-regulatory models maybe more appropriate for the development of e-commerce both at the national and international levels of governance, the same may not be true for governing criminal matters on the Internet, though there is a strong emphasis on self and co-regulation even in that field, especially at the European Union level.

As a multi-layered governance system is inevitable and can be a useful tool for regulating complex networks, there is an important emphasis on "co-operation" between various nation-states and governing supranational and international bodies. Such co-operation for the establishment of a global information society should be subject to normative substantive and process conditions. At a national level, it is now widely accepted that "government cannot simply regulate to achieve its aims in this new global electronic environment."[6] Although there has been much emphasis for a partnership between the government and the industry "to get the right balance" to build confidence and to protect consumers in the information age, that balance should reflect and respect the rights of the individual Internet users, an issue often undermined and not considered by the regulators and by the industry. To achieve such a balance which takes into account individual rights and not only the interests of the business community, there is need for openness, accountability, and transparency in relation to regulatory initiatives[7] aimed at Internet governance at the national level. Civil society representation should be ensured within this sort of co-operation that leads into the development of an Internet policy at the national level.

Aligning of Strategies and Co-operation at the International Level

The effect of supranational and international developments on nation-state governance cannot be underestimated and aligning of strategies and policies may also be necessary at an international stage to find common solutions for Internet related problems or for boosting consumer confidence and trust in the information age.

It has been the intention of the Turkish government to align its strategies and regulatory system with the EU following its recognition as a candidate country to EU membership in December 1999. So the current regulatory differences that are the result of the membership/non-membership to the European Union may be less significant, the closer Turkey gets to the European Union. An eventual membership to the EU will force Turkey or any other EU candidate state to align its policies including those related to the Internet to EU policy. Furthermore, there will inevitably be future aligning of policies with the international organisations of which Turkey is a member such as the Council of Europe. An important policy development at the Council of Europe level has been provided with the drafting of the Cyber Crime Convention in 2001. The development of such policy on the international stage will undoubtedly have an impact upon the future of law and policy at the national level.

The Role of the Civil Society

> *"If a popular voice requires detachment from government, then indeed in governance concerned with global human rights, there is a popular voice. It emanates from non-governmental organisations"*[8]

The role to be played by the civil society within the Internet policy making process is significant as the civil society representatives and NGOs working in this field can act as watchdogs for the activities of official bodies and can ensure that the policy initiatives respect fundamental principles of human rights. The important role of the civil society and the NGOs within the international legal system can be defined as follows:

> *"They have some effect on international law-making in certain areas by adding additional expertise and making procedures more transparent, and a stronger effect with regard to supervision and fact-finding as to the implementation of international norms, most visibly in the area of human rights."*[9]

Generally, "NGOs have become an integral part of inter-governmental deliberations on human rights and have had an equally prominent role in some national legislatures and bureaucracies"[10] This seems to be the case also in relation to Internet policy making process and civil society movement has been crucial for raising awareness of human rights issues and bringing a more open, transparent, and democratic process to the policy making process. However, in most cases, the rights of the individuals are not represented while greater emphasis is given to the development of e-commerce and to the financial interests of the Internet industry, and to the interests and needs of the law enforcement agencies.

But government co-operation with the Internet industry and law enforcement agencies should also extend to NGOs and public interest groups while policies are fostered.

Normative Substantive and Process Conditions

Normative conditions such as the international human rights standards and the process conditions can help to set certain criteria for good governance of the Internet if these conditions and values are incorporated into proposals and policy initiatives at the national, supranational, and international levels of Internet governance. Governance can only be legitimised by taking due account of these values.

The European Convention on Human Rights (articles 8 and 10) and other international human rights instruments such as the Universal Declaration of Human Rights, (articles 12, and 19); the International Covenant on Civil and Political Rights, (articles 17, and 19); and the more recent European Union Charter of Fundamental Rights, (articles 7, 8, and 11) enshrine the rights to freedom of expression, access to information, and right to privacy of communications. These core documents explicitly protect freedom of expression and privacy without regard to borders, a phrase especially pertinent to the global Internet.

Although the Turkish Constitution offers protection for both freedom of expression and privacy of communications, these provisions have strict restrictions both in the Constitution and in law.[11] Turkish law and court judgments are also subject to the European Convention on Human Rights and are bound by the judgments of the European Court of Human Rights and there are more than 20 judgments of the European Court of Human Rights involving Turkey and article 10 of the ECHR.[12] It is expected and hoped that the government will review current legislation delineating freedom of expression in the light of the ECHR, especially with regard to the letter and spirit of articles 10, 17 and 18, as well as the related decisions of the European Court of Human Rights.[13] Effective implementation of such measures is also important, as well as training in this field.

The same applies to privacy of communications and despite the existence of constitutional protection to privacy of communications, the right to privacy and to private communications remains rather problematic in Turkey. In practice, Turkey has been a country of "tele-ears"[14] and all forms of communications have been tapped and intercepted through-out the Turkish history, ever since communication technologies have been created.[15] Laws such as the 4442 *Sayı lı Çı kar Amaçlı Suç Örgütleriyle Mücadele Kanunu* and the related regulations[16] intend to regulate and control such unaccountable interception of communications taking place and it remains to be seen whether the practice in Turkey will comply with the requirements of article 8, ECHR and the jurisprudence of the Strasbourg court.[17]

At the same time there is currently no protection of personal data (through data protection laws or through any other regulatory means) in Turkey.[18] This issue deserves the highest consideration from the Turkish regulators. The protection of personal data is essential for not only the development of e-commerce and for establishing confidence and trust with online consumers, and users, but also for ensuring that national laws are consistent with Pan-European laws. Although there has been several attempts at legislation in this field in Turkey, no considerable progress have been made in this field until mid 2003. Currently a draft legislation entitled *Kişisel Verilerin Korunması Kanunu Taslaşı* based upon both the 1981 CoEConvention and the 1995 EU Directive is being considered at the Ministry of Justice. It is expected that this draft law will be considered by the Parliament during 2004.

A more positive development is the enactment of the Right to Information Act 2003, *Bilgi Edinme Hakki Kanunu* (No: 4982) in October 2003[19] which came into force on 24 April, 2004. A freedom of information law in Turkey would help to achieve an open and transparent regulatory process and would promote openness and good practice within government departments. Following the enactment of the new law in Turkey, a Right to Information Assessment (Review) Council will be established to deal with appeals on rejected freedom of information requests. However, the government should avoid the three year delay witnessed in setting up the Turkish Competition Authority following the enactment of the Competition Law.

The information and documents pertaining the state secrets, the economical interests of the state, the state intelligence, the administrative investigation, and the judicial investigation and prosecution are out of the scope of this law. Limitations also apply for the privacy of the individuals, privacy of communications, trade secrets, intellectual property (works of art and science), institutions' internal regulations, and institutions' internal opinions, information notes and recommendations.[20] Although the enactment of the Right to Information Act is a very important first step towards openness, transparency, and democratisation in Turkey, it remains to be seen how transparent the government will be in Turkey. If the implementation is slow, the Act may never be fully functional.

EU Acquis and Recent Political Developments

In the last few years, Turkey has completed comprehensive constitutional and legislative reforms that reinforce and safeguard fundamental rights and freedoms, democracy, the rule of law, and the protection of and respect for minorities, as set out in the Turkish National Programme for the Adoption of the European Union Acquis of 24 March, 2001.[21]

Several international conventions relating to the political criteria have been signed or ratified, among which Additional Protocol No.6 to the ECHR Concerning the Abolishing of the Death Penalty, the UN Convention on the Elimination of All Forms of Racial Discrimination, the UN Covenant on Civil and Political Rights, the UN Covenant on Economic, Social and Cultural Rights, the ILO Convention Concerning the Prohibition and Immediate Action for the Elimination of Worst Forms of Child Labour (No. 182), and the UN Convention on Prevention of All Types of Discrimination Against Women and its Optional Protocol, can be cited.[22] The signing of the International Covenant on Civil and Political Rights in August 2000 is directly related to the normative conditions that are set out in this policy paper. Moreover, the Human Rights Advisory Board, which constitutes an effective platform for dialogue between state and civil society in the area of human rights, has become operational.[23] This is in addition to the establishment of the EU Harmonisation Commission within the Turkish Grand National Assembly which aims to increase the efficiency of the process of legislative harmonisation with the EU. According to the official National Programme for the Adoption of the Acquis document:

> *"The Government has opted to harmonise various laws in order to fulfil the political criteria,the prerequisite to the opening of accession negotiations, through —harmonisation legislationpackages" to accelerate the process. The Government*

is determined, in principle, that the impact of all concluded reforms will be observed simultaneously, in letter and spirit, by June2004."[24]

Despite all these positive developments, a recent resolution by the European Parliament stated that

"Turkey does not yet meet the Copenhagen political criteria and whereas a clear framework for guaranteeing political, civil, economic, social and cultural rights has still not been established, and more far-reaching efforts than reparation and amendments are needed to enhance the coherence between legal provisions and practice, which will underline the radical and fundamental character of Turkey's progress towards membership"[25]

But at the same time, above mentioned recent developments are welcomed by the European Parliament "with regard to making reforms that are revolutionary for Turkey, not only in order to meet the Copenhagen political criteria, in keeping with Turkish authorities' oft-stated commitment to democracy and Europe, but also to advance the economic, social and political conditions of the Turkish people." But it was pointed out by the European Parliament resolution that

"such reforms can only be judged on the basis of their actual implementation in terms of day-to-day practice at all levels of the judicial and security system and of both the civilian andmilitary administration, and that they must have the support of society."

Process Conditions

In many democratic states and as well within the policy making processes of supranational and international organisations such as at the European Union certain process standards are developed and adopted to achieve better regulation. One good example of this is the UK Cabinet Office Regulatory Impact Unit's Better Regulation Guide, and the Principles of Good Regulation, published in October 2000.[26] The intention of the UK government was to get the balance right between "providing citizens with proper protection and ensuring that the impact on those being regulated is not such as to be counter productive."[27] The intention of developing the principles of good regulation was to offer a template for "judging and improving the quality of regulation".[28] These principles have also been incorporated into the UK Government's Guide to Regulatory Impact Assessment.[29] According to the Better Regulation Task Force

> *"Whilst recognising that there are differences about the levels of intervention, allgovernments should seek to ensure that regulations are necessary, fair, effective, affordable and enjoy a broad degree of public confidence."*[30]

The principles of good regulation have been set out to achieve this sort of balance, and these are transparency, accountability, proportionality, consistency, and targeting. In addition to these principles of good regulation, government regulators should also be aware of the five principles (openness, participation, accountability, effectiveness and coherence) that underpin good governance within the European Governance, A White Paper document published by the European Commission.[31] Each principle is important for establishing more democratic governance. They underpin democracy and the rule of law in the Member States of the European Union, but in theory they apply to all levels of government/ governance—global, European, national, regional and local.

Each principle is important by itself. But they cannot be achieved through separate actions. Policies can not be effective unless they are prepared, implemented and enforced in a more inclusive way. These important principles should be applied to all forms of regulatory initiatives at the national level of Internet governance. An open and transparent policy making would generally lead into easy to understand regulation and legislation with clear aims and objectives. Furthermore, under the principles of good regulation, any regulatory action should be proportionate, and the effects of proposed regulatory action on citizens should be identified and a right balance between risks and cost should be analysed. Knee-jerk reactions to public and media pressures should be resisted and informed decisions should only be taken following extensive consultation with all interested parties.

Proportionality is also tied to the standards set out in the European Convention on Human Rights. Consistency is another principle which means that proposed regulation or legislation should be consistent with existent regulation and should be predictable apart from being targeted. Consistency should also take into account supranational developments within the European Union. This would mean that regulation should focus on the problems and reduce side-effects to a minimum and "seek to reconcile contradictory policy objectives".[32]

These process standards and principles (as well as the above mentioned normative standards) should not only be applied to state regulation but also to alternatives to state legislation such as self-regulation and co-regulation. Without due respect for such standards, the policy making process will never be democratic.

Towards a Better Policy Making Process in Turkey

It is important to identify policy objectives which can be achieved through state regulation in Turkey such as to protect and enhance the rights and liberty of citizens and to promote a safe and peaceful society. At the same time it is also important to consider ways of achieving policy objectives "without recourse to state legislation" as many of the same policy objectives that may be considered by governments, regulators, or by quasi-regulatory bodies could also be achieved with "little or no state legislation" (see generally Figure 4). Alternatives to state legislation may be more flexible, cheaper and more effective."[33] Government, industry, and civil society partnership for developing co-regulatory and self-regulatory[34] solutions could also be useful especially in relation to dealing with technical matters or in relation to problems that are multinational in nature such as those created by the Internet. This also applies to the Short-Term Action Plan of the E-Transformation Turkey Project. For example, too much reliance on state regulation may slow down the transformation into an information society. That is why the alternatives to state regulation, with an emphasis on co-operation with the industry and the civil society and NGOs is required.

Regulatory impact assessment ("RIA") exercises[35] should also be adopted in Turkey as part of the modernisation of the policy making process.[36] Such an exercise is crucially important where regulation concerns the development of an information society, e-government, and all aspects of Internet governance in Turkey. Such an exercise would help analysing the risks in terms of a specific problem and the best model of regulation if a regulatory approach is needed to address the problem. Normative and process conditions should be taken into account and the industry and the civil society should be consulted prior to finalising a governmental policy.

Figure 4: Towards a Better Policy Making Process in Turkey

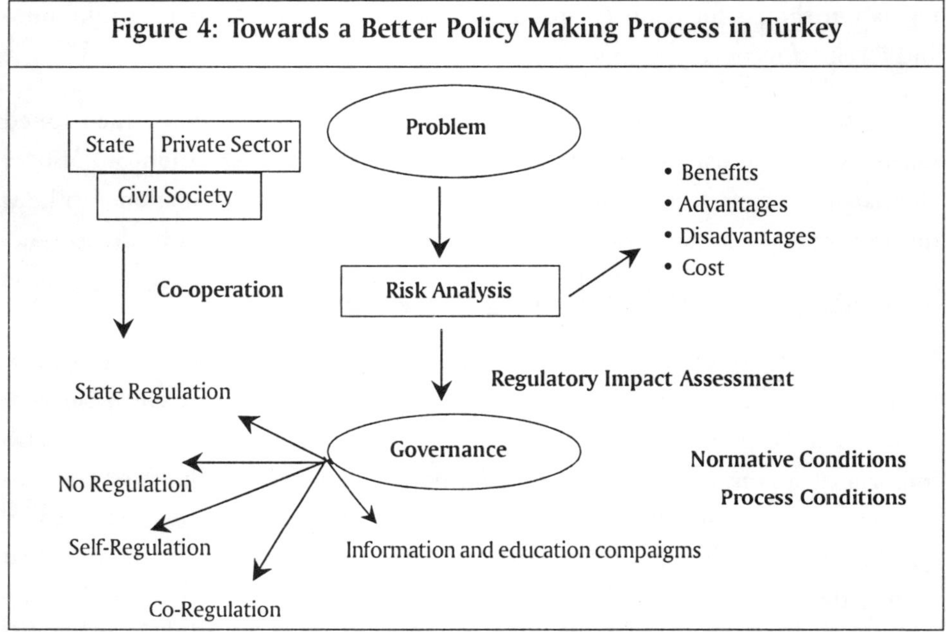

Regulatory Models and Alternatives to State Regulation

Although state legislation is still a strong option and maybe preferred in most instances, problems associated with the Internet may require the careful consideration of alternatives to state regulation. While the enactment of a law on digital signatures may bring legal clarity and certainty, the same may not necessarily be true for content regulation, and cyber-crimes. Due to the global and decentralised nature of the Internet, government regulation may not always be the best option[37]to tackle global problems, and jurisdictional issues should be taken into account while policies are developed at the national level.

Depending upon their application the alternatives to state legislation could sometimes be complimentary and could be seen as an additional tool apart from being an alternative to state regulation. For example, although the best way of tackling the problem of privacy of communications and processing of personal data is by means of introducing a law on data protection, this may not be effective alone to tackle the problem.

Self-regulatory and co-regulatory schemes may be required to backup such a massive piece of legislation, and the government, the industry, and the civil society may be required to work together to effectively introduce the concept and culture of "data protection" and "privacy" in Turkey. The same principles apply for example, in the case of "freedom of information" and the development of a culture of openness and transparency within the regulatory process in Turkey. Laws and rules alone will not be enough to achieve such important state goals.

Regulation is often designed to reduce risk, but alternative methods can be less costly, more flexible and more effective than prescriptive government legislation. These include the option "to do nothing", self-regulation, co-regulation, and information and education campaigns as detailed in the policy research paper *Internet Governance in Turkey.*

The Development of Internet Governance in Turkey

As far as Internet governance is concerned, this will undoubtedly be affected by the decentralised nature of the Internet. So, "effective" rule-making will not be confined to a single nation-state due to the global nature of the medium itself, as well as the influence and impact of supranational, and international developments and agreements in this field as a result of the nature of the medium itself. The result is that the emergence of Internet governance entails a more diverse and fragmented regulatory network with no presumption that these are anchored primarily in the nation-states. This is also in line with post-modern theories in which "the trajectory of social development is taking us away from the institutions of modernity towards a new and distinct type of social order".[38]

Compared to Western Europe, the development of Internet law and policy has been slow inTurkey, and only became the discourse of debate in the past few years. The government had certainly different priorities and Internet governance has not been a top priority within the government agenda, and Turkey's transition to a "knowledge society" has been slow with major concerns about the development of the infrastructure for Information Society services, and access in Turkey.[39]

On the other hand, membership to the European Union in the future will have a major impact upon the governance of the Internet in Turkey. The future membership could shape the Turkish policy. In fact the EU impact is already witnessed on the Turkish policy as Turkey is included as of June 2001 within the *eEurope+* Action Plan programme of the European Commission[40] as a candidate country which mirrors the priority objectives and targets of eEurope programme for the EU member states.[41]The overall aim of the European Commission is to make the whole of Europe "the most competitive and dynamic knowledge-based economy in the world".[42] For this purpose,

> *"positive action on the basis of a strong, political commitment is needed to ensure that the EU Candidate Countries use the full potential offered by the Information Society and avoid a further digital divide with the EU."*[43]

The targets, including acceleration of the putting in place of the basic building blocks for the Information Society, provision of a cheaper, faster, secure Internet, investing in people and skills, and the stimulation of the use of the Internet (including the acceleration of e-commerce), will have to be met by the candidate countries by the year 2003.[44] If these targets are met, Turkey, then in theory could start implementing some of the more specific EU policies such as those provided within the Electronic Commerce Directive.[45]

Furthermore, in general terms Turkey is already making progress towards EU membership and its national programme *for the Adoption of the Acquis*[46] *include* the preparation of a legal infrastructure for

> *"data security and the use of data by taking into consideration technological developments and the development of electronic commerce, and for allowing public access via the internet to information produced by the public and private sector, bearing in mind the need to protect personal data and national data security."*[47]

Although there is no deadline set up for achieving these goals, the document outlining the national programme suggests that this will be achieved in the medium term.[48]

Following the parliamentary elections of November 2002, the Turkish political landscape has undergone significant changes resulting with a single majority government. AKP—the Justice and Development Party established the E-Transformation Turkey Project in early 2003. The project aims to ensure the transition to an information society in Turkey.

Developing a Working Mechanism in Turkey

The global, decentralised and borderless nature of the Internet means that it is not possible for the individual governments to regulate effectively and satisfactorily to address Internet related problems and issues. This means that the nature of government regulation, thinking, and policy making need also to adopt to the changes that are the result of improvement in technology and especially in global communications. The role of the governments are still crucially important and pivotal but there needs to be more emphasis on such concepts as "risk analysis", "co-operation", "co-ordination", "consultation", "co-regulation", and "self-regulation". Rather than rushing into legislating, governments need to assess carefully the "risks" associated with Internet usage. This also needs to be done by a policy process which is open, transparent, and inclusive of the views of all stakeholders and interested parties. As discussed above, alternatives to state legislation will also need to be part of the government agenda for developing Internet related policies.

E-Transformation Turkey Project

E-Transformation Turkey Project was established with a Prime Minister's Circular 2003/12, dated 27 February, 2003. With this circular, the responsible institution

Figure 5: Developing a Working Mechanism?

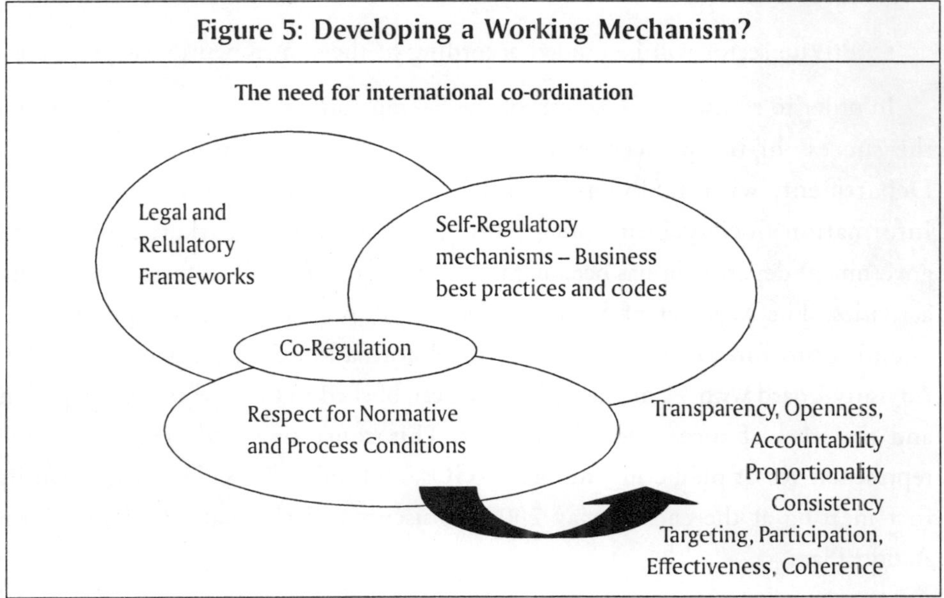

for the E-Transformation Turkey project is identified as the State Planning Organisation ("SPO"), which is affiliated to the Prime Ministry. Apart from the Prime Ministry, all public institutions, and NGOs are identified as affiliated organisations for this project. The E-Transformation Turkey project has the following aims and objectives:

- Policies, laws, and regulations regarding ICT will be re-examined and changed and adapted if necessary, with respect to the EU acquis; eEurope+ Action Plan, initiated for the candidate countries.
- Mechanisms that facilitate the participation of citizens to decision-making process in the public domain via using ICT will be developed.
- Transparency and accountability for public management will be enhanced.
- Good governance principles will be put in place in government services through increased usage of ICT.
- ICT diffusion will be promoted.
- Public IT projects will be co-ordinated, monitored, evaluated and consolidated if necessary in order to avoid duplicating or overlapping investments.
- Private sector will be guided according to the above-mentioned principles.

In order to realise the objectives of the E-Transformation Project and to ensure the success of the project, a new co-ordination unit, Information Society Department, within SPO is established.[49] With the establishment of the Information Society Department, for the first time in Turkey, a dedicated government department has been named as the co-ordinator of information society activities. The Minister of State, the Deputy Prime Minister was appointed as e-minister to foresee the activities of the Information Society Department. An Advisory Board with 41 members has been established to increase the participation and the level of success for the project. This consulting body consists of the representatives of public institutions, NGOs, and universities. The Board had its first meeting at the end of May 2003 to discuss and elaborate the Short-Term Action Plan.

Apart from assuming the responsibility of the E-Transformation Turkey project, the Information Society Department is also responsible for the overall co-ordination of the European Commission's eEurope initiative which includes Turkey within the eEurope+branch. There is a strong emphasis on eEurope 2005's goals and harmonisation of Turkish legislation to EU acquis to fulfil the objectives of the e-Transformation Turkey Project.[50] In a system of governance, in which supranational and international agencies and regulatory bodies are already significant and are growing in scope, and have an impact upon the way policies are shaped, nation states remain as agencies of representation,[51] though their continued role should not be underestimated. European Union initiatives are obviously having an impact upon candidate countries even before they become full members. In this case, it could be argued that the impact of the eEurope+ project on Turkey has been positive in dealing with social, economic, and technical aspects of information society.

Short Term Action Plan (STAP) – Vision and Goals

The initial focal point in the E-Transformation Turkey project is the Short Term Action Plan ("STAP"), which covers 2003-2004, for implementing specific tasks. There are currently 73 action items under eight headings within the STAP and the plan was developed during the course of 2003. STAP came into effect with a Prime Minister's Circular 2003/48 published in the Turkish Official Gazette, No: 25306, on 04 December, 2003.

Actions aiming to establish inter operable and secure online information services have the first priority in STAP. Moreover, actions in STAP are in line with actions of the government' soverall Urgent Action Plan that covers restructuring of public management, increasing efficiency in public services, and the introduction of citizen-oriented services. As mentioned above, eEurope 2005's goals and harmonisation of Turkish legislation to EU acquis has been taken into account while STAP was developed. During the preparation of STAP, priorities of eEurope 2005, such as broad band, security, eInclusion, eBusiness and eGovernment are all taken into account, and each of them has been covered with several actions.

An "Information Society Strategy" will be established during 2004 under the STAP. It is expected that the Strategy will encompass every part of society and will maximise national benefits. This strategy according to STAP will enlighten Turkey's transformation from labour-intensive society to information society, and from traditional production-consumption economy to knowledge economy. The changes in production, consumption and use of global information technologies may also force the nation-states into democratic changes.[52]

The impact of the E-Transformation Turkey Project and the Short Term Action Plan remains to be seen. The government favoured a co-regulatory approach while formulating the E-Transformation Turkey Project and that is to be welcomed, as it includes representatives of all stakeholders including civil society within this initiative. However, it should also be ensured that the Short Term Action Plan is compatible with the normative and process conditions mentioned in this policy paper and explained in detail in the policy research paper entitled *Internet Governance in Turkey.*

Recommendations for Good Internet Regulation in Turkey

The Turkish Government should

- Modernise the Turkish policy making process in the short-term.
- Provide an open and transparent policy making process.
- Conduct risk analysis prior to regulation and consider the alternatives to state legislation.
- Ensure that policy making in this field is undertaken by policy makers who are wellinformed about the unique nature of the Internet and have direct experience with its use.
- Ensure that such policies are developed with substantial input and comment from all interested parties including the Internet industry, the academia, non-governmental organisations, and Internet users.
- Respect fundamental human rights enshrined in the Universal Declaration of Human Rights, the International Covenant on Civil and Political Rights, and the European Convention on Human Rights. Enable access to government information including legislative, judicial and executive branch

information through the Internet. Public authorities should comply with the requirements of the Right to Information Act 2003 which came into force on 24 April, 2004.

- Ensure that the legislative and administrative reforms concerning associations, and foundations are implemented effectively to support the development of the civil society and its participation in the Turkish democratic life.
- Ensure access by Turkish citizens to the Internet and enable full participation in the global information society. In particular, access to the Internet by schools, libraries and other public institutions should be viewed as a policy goal, subsidised as necessary.
- Ensure that the eEurope+ 2003 Turkey plan (as part of the European Commission's eEurope+ 2003 Plan) is fully implemented in the short-term.
- Ensure that the recently launched E-Transformation Turkey project's Short Term ActionPlan is compatible with the normative and process conditions explained in this report.
- Ensure that Turkish policy is in line with EU policy monitor systematically international legal and policy initiatives
- Ensure systematic representation and participation of Turkey within the international forums that develop Internet related policies (including but not exclusively at the Council of Europe, United Nations, the OECD, and the European Union level).

While such a principled approach is incorporated to the government thinking, high priority should be given to respect normative and process conditions, and to raise trust and confidence as a pre-requisite to entry to the information age. But the modernisation of the Turkish policy making process in the short-term remains as a high priority to be able to achieve the overall state goal of developing an information society in Turkey.

(Dr. Yaman Akdeniz, is Lecturer in CyberLaw, University of Leeds, UK. He is Director, Cyber-Rights & Cyber-Liberties (UK), and a 2003 Fellow of the International Policy and Information Policy Fellowship programmes of the Open Society Institute. He can be contacted at lawya@cyber-rights.org).

Endnotes

1 See the Information Society Department pages of the State Planning Organisation at<http://*www.btdb.gov.tr*>.

2 Turkey is ranked at number 56 within The Networked Readiness Index 2003-2004 prepared by the World Economic Forum, at *<http://www.weforum.org/pdf/Gcr/GITR_2003_2004/Rankings.pdf>*.

3 League Against Racism and Antisemitism (LICRA), French Union of Jewish Students, v Yahoo! Inc. (USA), Yahoo France, Tribunal de Grande Instance de Paris (The County Court of Paris), Interim Court Order, 20 November, 2000; Akdeniz, Y, Case Review of the Yahoo! Case, [2001] Electronic Business Law Reports, 1(3) 110-120.

4 Criminal case of Somm, Felix Bruno, File No: 8340 Ds 465 JS 173158/95, Local Court (Amtsgericht) Munich. An English version of the case is available at *<http://www.cyber-rights.org/isps/somm-dec.htm>*.

5 Walker, C, & Akdeniz, Y, "The governance of the Internet in Europe with special reference to illegal and harmful content," [1998] *Criminal Law Review,* December Special Edition: Crime, Criminal Justice and the Internet, 5-19, at 14.

6 Per Tony Blair, foreward to the Cabinet Office Report, e-commerce@its.best.uk, September 1999.

7 See the Cabinet Office Regulatory Impact Unit's Better Regulation Guide, and the Principles of Good Regulation at *<http://www.cabinet-office.gov.uk/regulation/taskforce/2000/PrinciplesLeaflet.pdf>*. Note also the CR&CL Response to Better Regulation Task Force Review of E-Commerce, 12 October, 2000, at*<http://www.cyber-rights.org/reports/brtf.htm>*, and the Task Force's report, Regulating Cyberspace: Better Regulation for E-Commerce, 14 December, 2000.

8 Gordenker, L, "NGOs: The People's Voice in International Governance?" A presentation made at a UNPublic Forum on Human Rights and NGOs ,18 September 1996, UNU, Tokyo, Japan, at *<http://www.soc.titech.ac.jp/ngo/lecture14.html>*. See further Weiss, T G, and Gordenker, L, NGOs, the UN and Global Governance, (Boulder, CO, Lynne Rienner, 1996).

9 See Malanczuk, P, Akehurt's Modern Introduction to International Law, London: Routledge, 1997, seventh edition, at 97. See also H Thoolen & B Verstappen, Human Rights Missions: A Study of the Fact-Finding Practice of Non-Governmental Organisations, 1986. T V Boven, "The Role of Non-Governmental Organisations in International Human Rights Standard-Setting: A Prerequisite of Democracy" (1989) CWILJ20, 207-225.

10 Gordenker, L, "NGOs: The People's Voice in International Governance?"

11 See articles 20, 22, and 26 of the Turkish Constitution. Note the recent changes within the Turkish Constitution in relation to article 26. *Türkiye Cumhuriyeti Anayasas ı n ı n Baz ı Maddelerinin De ğ i tirilmesiHakk ı nda Kanun,* No: 4709, Kabul Tarihi: 3.10.2001, T.C. Resmi Gazete, No: 24556 (Mukerrer) 15 October, 2001. Note also the Supreme Board of Radio and Television (RTUK) Bill (No 4676).

12 Among others see: *Erdo ğ du and Ince judgment* of 8 July 1999, Reports 1999, *Sürek and Özdemir judgment* of 8 July 1999, Reports 1999, Okçuoglu judgment of 8 July 1999, Reports.

13 Republic of Turkey, National Programme for the Adoption of the Acquis, Official Gazette, 24 July 2003 No.25178 bis, at <*http://www.abgs.gov.tr/NPAA/up.htm*>.

14 "Susurluk wiretapping," *Turkish Daily News,* May 18, 1999; "Bugging scandal creates rift at police department, Ecevit unconvinced by explanations," *Turkish Daily News,* 09 June, 1999.

15 For a history of interception of communications see Bildirici, Faruk, *Gizli Kulaklar Ulkesi* (The Country of Hidden Ears), Istanbul: Iletisim, 1999. See further Coskun, Enis, *Kuresel Gozalti: Elektronik Gizli Dinlemeve Goruntuleme,* Ankara: Umit Yayincilik, 2000.

16 4442 *Sayı lı Çı kar Amaçlı Suç Örgütleriyle Mücadele Kanunun uygulanmas ı na iliskin* yönetmelik (26 Ocak,2001 tarihli ve 242999 say ı l ı Resmi Gazete).

17 See further TBMM Insan Haklarini Inceleme Komisyonu'nun 7 Haziran 2001 15inci toplantisinda telefondinleme ve bu yolla elde edilen kayit ve bilgilerin medyada yer almasi üzerine gündeme getirilen usulsüztelefon dinleme konusunu arastirmak amaciyla 14 Haziran 2001 tarihinde kurulan alt komisyon raporu(Haziran 2002).

18 The Turkish Ministry of Justice has been working on draft legislation on the Protection of Personal Data during 1998. The new proposals will follow the Council of Europe's 1981 Convention and the European Union Directive. The new proposals cover the collection and processing of data by both public and private bodies. However, the April 1999 elections and a change of Government in Ankara delayed the enactment of this legislation. The new proposals discussed within the May 1998 E-Commerce Laws Working Party Report emphasise both the importance of facilitating the collection and processing of personal data

and the protection of personal data of individuals in the information age. Turkish Republic Foreign Trade Office, E-Commerce Laws Working Party Report, 8 May, 1998.

19 See generally *<http://www.bilgilenmehakki.org>* which was set up by the author together with Mrs. AvniyeTansug and Miss Sevil Albayrak.

20 Moreover, there will be further legislation to clarify the meaning of "state secrecy" and "trade secrets". Infact, the Ministry of Justice published two draft bills on these issues *(Devlet Sı rları Kanunu Tasarı sı , andTicari Sı rlar Kanunu Tasarı sı)* in February 2004. It is expected that these draft bills will be considered bythe Parliament later in 2004. See generally *<http://www.bilgilenmehakki.org/>*.

21 See generally Republic ofTurkey, National Programme for the Adoption of the Acquis, Official Gazette, 24 July 2003 No. 25178 bis, at *<http://www.abgs.gov.tr/NPAA/up.htm>*.

22 Ibid.

23 Republic ofTurkey, National Programme for the Adoption of the Acquis, Official Gazette, 24 July 2003 No.25178 bis, at *<http://www.abgs.gov.tr/NPAA/up.htm>*.

24 Republic ofTurkey, National Programme for the Adoption of the Acquis, Official Gazette, 24 July 2003 No.25178 bis, at *<http://www.abgs.gov.tr/NPAA/up.htm>*.

25 European Parliament resolution on the 2003 regular report of the Commission on Turkey's progress towards accession (COM(2003) 676 - SEC(2003)1212 - C5-0535/2003 – 2003/2204(INI)); Progress towards accession byTurkey, P5_TA-PROV(2004)0274, A5-0204/2004.

26 For a good example of this see the UK Cabinet Office Regulatory Impact Unit's Better Regulation Guide, and the Principles of Good Regulation, October 2000, at *<http://www.cabinet-office.gov.uk/regulation/taskforce/2000/PrinciplesLeaflet.pdf>*.

27 Ibid., per Christopher Haskins, Chairman, Better Regulation Task Force.

28 Ibid.

29 The Cabinet Office Regulatory Impact Unit, Good Policy Making: A Guide to Regulatory Impact Assessment, at *<http://www.cabinet-office.gov.uk/regulation/2000/riaguide/default.htm>*. Note that the Regulatory Impact Unit web page is at *<http://www.cabinet-office.gov.uk/regulation/index.htm>*.

30 Principles of Good Regulation at *<http://www.cabinet-office.gov.uk/regulation/taskforce/2000/PrinciplesLeaflet.pdf>*.

31 European Commission, European Governance, A White Paper, Brussels, 25.7.2001, COM(2001) 428 final.

32 Principles of Good Regulation, page 7.

33 Better Regulation Task Force report, Alternatives to State Regulation, July 2000.

34 Note the Better Regulation Task Force interim report on Self-Regulation, October 1999.

35 The purpose of the RIA is usually to explain the objectives of the proposal, the risks to be addressed and the options for delivering such objectives. It should make transparent the expected costs and benefits of the options for the different bodies involved, such as other parts of Government and small businesses, and how compliance with regulatory options would be secured and enforced. See Cabinet Office, Regulatory Impact Unit, Better Policy Making: A Guide to Regulatory Impact Assessment, January 2003, at*<http://www.cabinet-office.gov.uk/regulation/docs/ria/pdf/ria-guidance.pdf>*.

36 See further, the Research Paper.

37 Better Regulation Task Force report, *Alternatives to State Regulation,* July 2000, at *<http://www.cabinet-office.gov.uk/regulation/TaskForce/2000/StateRegulation.pdf>*.

38 See Giddens, A, *The Consequences of Modernity,* Cambridge: Polity Press, 1990, 46.

39 See generally Republic of Turkey Ministry of Transportation (TUENA), Turkish National Information Infrastructure Masterplan, Final Report, Ankara: TUENA, October 1999, at *<http://www.tuena.tubitak.gov.tr/pdf/tuenafinalreport.pdf>*. See further the Turkish Industrialists and Businessmen's Association report, Information Society and eTurkey Towards European Union, T/2001-07/304, Istanbul: TUSIAD, 2001. This report is available through *<http://www.tusiad.org.tr/>* and the author has contributed to the preparation of this report. See further Approaches to eEurope+ initiative in Turkey at*<http://www.bilten.metu.edu.tr/eEurope+/>*.

40 See eEurope+ 2000: A co-operative Effort to implement the Information Society in Europe, Action Plan, prepared by the Candidate Countries with the assistance of the European Commission, June 2001. See generally *<http://europa.eu.int/information_society/international/candidate_countries/index_en.htm>*. Note also the press release, Commission welcomes eEurope+ initiative of EU Candidate Countries, Brussels, 16 June 2001, at *<http://europa.eu.int/comm/gothenburg_council/eeurope_en.htm>*.

41 eEurope 2002 – An Information society for all – Draft Action Plan prepared by the European Commission for the European Council in Feira 19-20 June 2000, COM/2000/0330 final; Communication from the Commission to the Council and the European Parliament – eEurope 2002: Impact and Priorities Acommunication to the Spring European Council in Stockholm, 23-24 March 2001, COM/2001/0140 final.

42 eEurope+ 2000: A co-operative Effort to implement the Information Society in Europe, Action Plan, p 2.

43 Ibid, p 1.

44 Ibid, p 3.

45 Directive 2000/31/EC of the European Parliament and of the Council of 8 June 2000 on certain legal aspects of information society services, in particular electronic commerce, in the Internal Market, *Official Journal ofthe European Communities,* vol 43, OJ L 178 17 July 2000 p.1.

46 Republic ofTurkey Prime Ministry, The Secretariat General for EU Affairs, Turkish National Programme for the Adoption of the Acquis (NPAA), Ankara, 19 March, 2001, p 387. See generally*<http://www.abgs.gov.tr>*.

47 Ibid, para 4.20, Telecommunications, p 387.

48 Ibid.

49 See generally *<http://www.bilgitoplumu.gov.tr>*.

50 See generally eEurope+ 2003: Interim Report - Turkey, June 2003; Contribution ofTurkey to eEurope+2003: Progress Report, January 2004; eEurope+ 2003: Progress Report, February, 2004, at *<http://www.emcis2004.hu/>*.

51 Hirst, P, & Thompson, G, "Globalization and the Future of the Nation State," (1995) *Economy and Society,* 24 (3), 408 - 442, 431.

52 "Telecommunications played as much of a role as pickaxes and shovels in bringing down the Berlin Wall and the barbed wire of the Iron Curtain." See McGowan, W, "The part as Prologue: The Impact of International Telecommunications," in Hugh Chaloner ed., *Telecom 91 Global Review,* London: Kline Publishing, 1991, 56.

13

Voices from Asia-Pacific: Internet Governance for Sustainable Human Development*

Akash Kapur and Christine Apikul

The article is a summary of UNDP report on the Internet government and sustainable human development - for Asia-Pacific (A-P) region. It starts with a brief on who makes decision in the cyber space and their implications for sustainable human development. Further, it also presents the six key recommendations and priorities produced by the Open Regional Dialogue on Internet Governance (ORDIG) for Internet Governance in the Asia-Pacific region

Summary

Internet governance was one of the two issues on which governments were unable to reach agreement during the first phase of the World Summit on the Information Society (WSIS) in December 2003.

* This article is based on UNDP report on the Internet Government and Sustainable Human Development.

As the Summit plans for its second meeting in November 2005 to make decisions on appropriate actions for Internet governance, it is timely to look at the perspectives and priorities of stakeholders in the Asia-Pacific region.

The Open Regional Dialogue on Internet Governance (ORDIG) was initiated in October 2004 by UNDP-APDIP, in collaboration with other organizations[1] to ensure that the voices from Asia-Pacific are heard in these discussions. The initiative focused on raising awareness, building capacity, facilitating participation and promoting the representation of Asia-Pacific countries in the Internet governance debate. This note presents Asia-Pacific perspectives and priorities on Internet governance.

ORDIG offers six working principles to set the stage for Internet governance discussions in the Asia-Pacific region. These principles extend beyond the technical aspects of Internet protocol (IP) numbering and domain name registration, and recognize the need for a broad, holistic and human development approach that balances global solutions with diverse local interests.

Based on these principles, ORDIG conducted a series of research involving multiple and wide-ranging stakeholders, to produce six key recommendations and priorities for Internet governance in the Asia-Pacific region. They include the need for: subsidiarity; governments to have a role; multi-stakeholder participation; preserving cultural diversity; capacity building; and supplementing law with other tools.

Other emerging priorities and concerns consist of: access costs; voice over Internet protocol; wireless networks; root servers; country-code top-level domains; internationalized domain names; IP address management; technical standards; content pollution (e.g., spam, spyware, viruses); and the related issue of cybercrime (e.g., online fraud, pornography, terrorism).

Introduction

At the start of 2005, there were an estimated 750 million Internet users[2] worldwide and this figure is expected to continue growing at exponential rates, particularly in the Asia-Pacific region – home to over half of the world population. In fact, the Asia-Pacific region contributes a larger share of users (about one-third) than North America and Europe.

Inevitably, such numbers will have a profound impact on the structure and use of the Internet. In turn, these impacts will have transformative effect on commerce and culture around the world. Rapid growth in the use of the Internet raises questions on whether we need Internet governance and if so, in what form. Who will make these decisions and what are the processes for making these decisions?

Internet governance was one of the two issues (the other being related to financing mechanisms) on which governments were unable to reach agreement during the first phase of the World Summit on the Information Society (WSIS) in December 2003.

This led to the establishment of a United Nations Working Group on Internet Governance (WGIG) to develop a working definition of Internet governance; identify public policy issues; define roles and responsibilities; and develop proposals for action at the second WSIS meeting in Tunis 2005.

What is Internet Governance and Why is it Important?

The concept and scope of Internet governance has been the subject of intense debate. Recently, WGIG came up with a working definition of Internet governance:

> *Internet governance is the development and application by Governments, the private sector and civil society, in their respective roles, of shared principles, norms, rules, decision-making procedures, and programmes that shape the evolution and use of the Internet.*

It refers to all policies and interventions that influence the structure, operation and use of the Internet. These policies and interventions are linked to development objectives in many ways. The choice of technical Internet standards determines how easy it is to adapt Internet technologies to local needs, such as multi-lingual capabilities. Likewise, the rules for the global Internet naming and addressing system determine who has access to critical infrastructure components that ensure global connectivity.

Policy decisions in this area influence a wide array of the Internet's practical characteristics including costs for access and content, speed, reliability and privacy of network services. In a nutshell, Internet governance critically determines how widely and how fairly the opportunities of the information society can spread and thus, what benefits the Internet holds in store for all users.

Who is Making the Decisions in Cyberspace: Implications for Sustainable Human Development

WGIG's working definition on Internet governance emphasizes the role of governments, the private sector and civil society in the mechanisms of Internet governance.

Making the Internet work for sustainable human development requires policies and interventions that are responsive to the specific needs of all countries. It requires a strong voice from different stakeholders and their constructive engagement in the policy-making processes related to Internet governance.

This is a huge challenge, especially for developing countries because presently, Internet governance comprises a range of different rule-making bodies and systems. The Internet Corporation for Assigned Names and Numbers (ICANN), for example, manages the domain name system and is under the control of the US government. Helping to set technical standards are the International Telecommunication Union, an international organization; the private-sector-led Internet Engineering Task Force; and the more academic W3C.

They vary dramatically in their structures and operating models, in their degree of openness and transparency and thus, in their accountability, inclusiveness, democratic legitimacy and responsiveness to developmental concerns.

Developing countries are further challenged by the global nature of the Internet that puts many areas of Internet governance beyond the direct control of any individual country and into the realm of global cooperation. Furthermore, participation in far-away fora is often costly and complicated for stakeholders from developing countries.

Timing also poses a problem. The most fundamental rules for Internet governance are already well established or under long-term negotiation and newcomers to the Internet have had little opportunity to generate awareness across all stakeholder groups, mobilize the required policy expertise and coordinate strategies for effective engagement.

In sum, the march of Internet governance continues and threatens to leave behind developing countries that are forfeiting opportunities for an inclusive information society. ORDIG is a timely response to these concerns. Over the last ten months, ORDIG has gathered and analyzed perspectives and priorities through an extensive multi-stakeholder and participatory process that has involved more than 3,000 people in the Asia-Pacific region.

ORDIG's activities include a regional online discussion forum featuring more than 180 participants; a multi-lingual survey on Internet governance that collected 1,243 responses from 37 countries; a series of sub-regional consultations; and a variety of research on governance and other topics.[3]

An Input Paper[4] and Policy Brief [5] of ORDIG's outcomes were presented and endorsed by WGIG at its Fourth Meeting in Geneva on 14-17 June 2005.

The next section summarizes the working principles and recommendations highlighted in ORDIG's Policy Brief.

Where are We Now: Setting Principles and Identifying Issues

ORDIG offers *six working principles* that together establish some parameters and context for discussions of Internet governance in Asia-Pacific. Three working principles are derived from WGIG's own definitions,[6] presented in its preliminary report in February 2005:

1. The terms "governance" and "govern" mean more than "government activities."
2. The enabling dimension includes organized and cooperative activities between different stakeholders.
3. Internet governance encompasses a wider range of conditions and mechanisms than Internet protocol (IP) numbering and domain name administration.

In addition, ORDIG proposes the following three working principles for Internet governance in the Asia-Pacific region:

4. **Broad, holistic and oriented towards human development:** As recognized by the WSIS process, the Internet has an essential role to play in meeting the objectives set forth in the Millennium Development Goals (MDGs), and the outcomes of its governance therefore extend beyond merely the technical domain.

5. **Balancing global and local interests:** Governance mechanisms and processes should recognize the Internet as a unified and coordinated global platform, and should foster international cooperation and coordination. In addition, Internet governance should recognize (and, when possible, reconcile) the genuine conflicts that sometimes exist between the need for global solutions and the desire to safeguard national interests.

6. **Maintain stability and interoperability:** The Internet is an essential service and a critical infrastructure in the region, and it should be governed in a manner that reflects its operating realities and exigencies. Any proposed evolutions or changes that arise through the process of governance should therefore take into account the need to maintain the stability and continued interoperability of the network. Based on these six principles, activities have been implemented and research findings analyzed to produce six key recommendations and priorities for Internet governance in the Asia-Pacific region.

   1. *Subsidiarity:* The Internet is a distributed network and Internet governance should similarly be distributed with its mechanisms and decision-making located as close as possible to the issues or problems that are being addressed. While some issues require global or regional coordination, many others, notably internationalized domain names (IDNs), country-code top-level domains (ccTLDs), and localized content and software, demand local input, and are best designed with the participation of those most directly affected. It is therefore vital to design mechanisms and structures that include representation from the national level, as well as from grassroots and other local communities.

2. *Governments have a role:* National governments have a vital facilitating and enabling role to play in Internet governance. Governments can set up an efficient market environment, establish and monitor broad competition principles, and ensure that the benefits of the network are equitably maximized. A liberal market environment, nurtured by the government is often important in lowering access costs and encouraging innovation. Governments should also encourage the development of comprehensive national ICT agendas to optimize resources and ensure coordinated participation in national and international governance processes.
3. *Multi-Stakeholder participation is required:* Internet governance is a broad-ranging process that affects, and frequently requires collaboration between, a variety of stakeholders. Governance mechanisms should therefore include all stakeholders from government, the private sector and civil society in the processes of decision-making and implementation.
4. *Preserve cultural diversity:* Bodies responsible for international Internet governance functions should reflect the priorities of all affected cultures in their operations. They should ensure an effective voice for all cultures in the deliberations and decision-making processes of these bodies. Such representation will facilitate the development of local content in local languages, help implement IDNs, and ensure that cybercrime is confronted in an effective and culturally appropriate manner.
5. *Enhance participation with capacity building:* Multi-stakeholder participation is most meaningful when supplemented by capacity and awareness building measures. Governance topics (e.g., standards) are frequently complex and require technical knowledge and other forms of expertise. In order to participate in a substantial way, stakeholders need information, knowledge, resources, and the opportunity to participate.
6. *Supplement law with other tools:* Law and regulation are not the only tools available for Internet governance. On a variety of issues (e.g., cybercrime, content pollution and localized software) these traditional tools should be supplemented by a variety of innovative mechanisms, including codes of conduct, self-regulatory mechanisms, and international, multi-stakeholder collaboratives.

In addition, technology itself can play an enabling role in achieving governance goals. Free and open source software, in particular, can help increase participation and network stability, and facilitate the development of local content and localized software.

In addition to the six key recommendations, ORDIG also addresses specific Asia-Pacific concerns and priorities organized around four dimensions – infrastructure; logical, content; and social and developmental. The infrastructure dimension covers the issues of access costs, voice over Internet protocol (VOIP) and wireless networks. Priorities are to:

Access Costs

- Ensure a robust competitive environment with limited barriers to entry and strong protections against monopolistic behaviour.
- Liberalize access to international bandwidth, promote diversity in domestic infrastructure, ease Internet service provider (ISP) licensing restrictions, and encourage "peering" between ISPs.
- Actively seek and develop international fora to solve the problem of high international settlement charges.
- Consider aid and other financial mechanisms to help developing countries develop infrastructure capacity.

VOIP

- Legalize VOIP services and promote a "light touch" approach to any regulation.
- Implement Quality of Service laws, allocate number resources, and provide access to emergency services.

Wireless

- Adopt spectrum management regimes that embrace unlicensed spectrum.
- Promote the use of wireless as a technology to bridge the digital divide and provide social benefits.

The logical dimension sits atop the infrastructure dimension; it is the interface between the hardware (infrastructure) and application (content). It consists of the code and logical switches that make infrastructure work. In this sense, the logical dimension can be considered the "brains" of the network. Here the issues covered include root servers, ccTLDs, IDNs, IP address management and technical standards. Priorities are to:

Root Servers

- Enhance international participation to address concerns over sovereignty.
- Ensure that any steps taken maintain one and only one authoritative root.

ccTLDs

- Promote local control and authority over ccTLDs.
- Take steps to ensure a coordinated local approach that includes all stakeholders.

IDNs

- Ensure a multi-stakeholder and participatory process to build on progress with technical standards.
- Promote greater coordination between language and cultural groups to ensure smooth implementation.
- Begin implementation of IDNs even if technical standards have not yet been perfected.

IP Address Management

- Develop fair and equitable mechanisms for IP version 6 (or IPv6) allocations.
- Reconcile perceived need for national allocations with desire to avoid central-planning type approaches.
- Ensure that increased government involvement does not result in censorship, inhibit innovation, or prevent the deployment of new services.

Technical Standards

- Increase participation in national and international standards-creating organizations.

- Supplement participation with capacity building, including education, awareness raising and resource support.
- Ensure availability of standard specifications.
- Consider the use of Free and Open Source Software to promote open standards.

The content dimension is the one most directly experienced by Internet users. It contains the applications and services through which users communicate, seek information and perform e-commerce transactions. Here the issues covered include content pollution (e.g., spam, spyware, viruses) and the related issue of cybercrime (e.g., online fraud, pornography, terrorism). Priorities are to:

Content Pollution

- Supplement legal measures with technology, user education, and other mechanisms.
- Ensure that legal measures do not diminish the openness of the network or lead to censorship.
- Develop global solutions to solve what is a global problem.

Cybercrime

- Ensure that legal steps do not infringe on civil liberties.
- Promote multi-stakeholder collaboratives and other mechanisms, including codes of conduct and self-regulation.
- Ensure that definitions of criminality are culturally and regionally sensitive and specific.

The social and developmental dimension focuses on cultural diversity and participation, supplemented with capacity building. The priorities are to:

Cultural Diversity

- Carefully consider the impact of technical governance on cultural diversity.
- Enhance localized software and localized content, and consider financial or other support mechanisms.

- Promote the use of Free and Open Source Software to facilitate local content and software.
- Protect indigenous intellectual property rights.

Participation

- Take all steps to promote multi-stakeholder participation in decision-making processes.
- Supplement formal participation with capacity building to ensure that participation is meaningful and substantive.
- Make special efforts to enhance participation by developing nations.

According to the regional survey (see Table), issues relating to Internet use such as cybercrime, spam, viruses, illegal content, and piracy are the areas generating the most dissatisfaction. These are the highest priorities for existing Internet users in the Asia-Pacific region. However, it should be remembered that some issues such as multilingualism or access costs may impact those who are not yet connected, so all of the above recommendations should be considered simultaneously.

What are the Next Steps?

Many of these issues and recommendations have been incorporated in WGIG's final report to WSIS.[7] Both ORDIG and WGIG take a multi-stakeholder and participation-driven framework for effective Internet governance.

WGIG's final report proposes the creation of a new multi-stakeholder forum to deal with all matters related to Internet governance. The report also outlines four organizational models for Internet governance. It is important to note that the framework is likely to evolve over time. The upcoming WSIS in Tunis represents not the conclusion of a process, but rather a milestone on an ongoing discussion that will change over time.

As the discussion continues, it is essential that Internet governance remain as open and inclusive as possible, encompassing the views and priorities of all stakeholders, regions, and communities of the world.

Asia-Pacific Concerns and Priorities (Ranked by Level of Dissatisfaction)

Rank	Issue	% Dissatisfied	% Satisfied
1.	Cybercrime	94	5
2.	Virus	93	6
3.	Spam	93	7
4.	Illegal Content	82	16
5.	Privacy	66	31
6.	Availability/Cost	61	38
7.	Reliability/Speed	59	40
8.	Wireless	59	25
9.	Availability of Public Info	58	39
10.	E-Commerce Payment	53	37
11.	Local Language Software	53	37
12.	IPR	52	42
13.	Local Content	52	42
14.	Internet Telephony	51	30
15.	Network Interconnection	47	39
16.	ISP Market Conditions	46	34
17.	Secure Server/Encryption	44	33
18.	Technical Standards	37	39
19.	IDNs	37	23
20.	DNS Management	35	44
21.	IP Address	32	40

ORDIG is committed to ensuring a voice for the Asia-Pacific region in the continuing discussion. Planned activities include awareness raising and capacity building initiatives at national levels, and the development of an Internet Governance Primer and toolkit. ORDIG will also continue to build on its Asia-Pacific Internet governance portal *<http://www.igov.apdip.net>* as an important forum for information dissemination and sharing.

(Akash Kapur is a Consultant with APDIP. Christine Apikul is also associated with UNDP-APDIP and she can be reached at Christine@apdip.net)

Endnotes

1 These organizations include the United Nations Economic and Social Commission for Asia and the Pacific (UNESCAP), the International Development Research Centre (IDRC), and the Asia Pacific Network Information Centre (APNIC).

2 Gelbstein, E & Kurbalija, J, 2005, Internet Governance: Issues, actors and divides, Geneva: DiploFoundation & Kuala Lumpur: Global Knowledge Partnership. *http://www.diplomacy.edu/isl/ig/*

3 ORDIG's outcome and activities are fully described in the Input Paper. UNDP-APDIP, 2005, Voices from Asia-Pacific: Internet governance priorities and recommendations – An ORDIG Input Paper for the UN Working Group on Internet Governance and the World Summit on the Information Society. *http://igov.apdip.net/ORDIG_Paper.pdf*

4 ibid.

5 UNDP-APDIP, 2005, Voices from Asia-Pacific: Internet governance priorities and recommendations – ORDIG Policy Brief and Executive Summary for the UN Working Group on Internet Governance and the World Summit on the Information Society. *http://igov.apdip.net/ORDIG_Policy_Brief.pdf*

6 Towards a Working Definition of Internet Governance. *http://www.wgig.org/Definitions.html*

7 WGIG, 2005, *Report of the Working Group on Internet Governance.*

Additional Readings

UNDP-APDIP, 2005, Internet Governance Priorities for Asia-Pacific: Summary analysis of a regional survey. *http://igov.apdip.net/ORDIG.Survey.Report.pdf*

UNDP-APDIP, 2005, Open Regional Dialogue on Internet Governance: Summary report of the online forum on Internet governance priorities for the Asia-Pacific region. *http://igov.apdip.net/undp-apdip%20forum%20summary.pdf*

UNDP-APDIP Collection of Resources on Internet Governance *http://www.apdip.net/resources/governance/igov/*

Asia-Pacific Internet Governance Portal *http://igov.apdip.net*

International Telecommunication Union Internet Governance Resources *http://www.itu.int/osg/spu/intgov/index.phtml*

Peake, A, 2005, "Internet Governance: Urgent issues for Asia Pacific" in Chin, S.Y. (ed.) Digital Review of Asia Pacific 2005/2006, Penang: Southbound, pp.15-29. *http://www.digital-review.org*

United Nations Information and Communication Technologies Task Force Global Forum on Internet Governance *http://www.unicttaskforce.org/sixthmeeting/*

United Nations Working Group on Internet Governance *http://www.wgig.org*

World Summit on the Information Society *http://www.itu.int/wsis*

Index